A Smile From
KATIE HATTAN &
Other Natural Wonders

A Smile From
KATIE HATTAN &
Other Natural Wonders

LEON HALE

with drawings by Barbara Whitehead

Shearer Publishing Company · *Bryan*

For my sister Maifred,
without whose loving help
I would never have written
a line.

Dustjacket photograph by BLAIR PITTMAN
Design by WHITEHEAD & WHITEHEAD

First Published in 1982 by
SHEARER PUBLISHING
3208 Turtle Grove • Bryan, Texas

ISBN 0-94067-207-3   LCC NO. 82-060563

*Manufactured
in the United States of America*

FIRST EDITION

FOREWORD

A few minutes before I sat down to begin this foreword, on June 15, 1982, I checked by telephone on Katie Hattan. On this day she is living still at Spanish Camp, Texas, in her 104th year. She will likely be surprised to find her name in the title of this book. She may wonder why it is there. Well, it's there because one day she smiled at me.

The pieces to follow are selected from my column in the *Houston Post*. After their selection, I searched back through the stack for a phrase that I could lift from one of the columns and use in the book's title. I kept returning to the Katie Hattan piece.

Here is a little woman who has lived more than a century in a highly imperfect world. Her parents were slaves. She didn't miss slavery far herself. She has known pain, of body and spirit. She finds now a great deal in the world that doesn't please her. Still, she can produce on that tiny face as brilliant a smile as I've ever experienced. Since I saw it, I have used that smile for selfish purposes. It has come to be, for me, the symbol of encouragement, a reason to be optimistic, to look on this life despite its imperfections as something to celebrate, to smile about.

For twenty-five years now I have traveled my state, writing on whatever I found that seemed worth recording. Katie Hattan's smile is on my list of Texas natural wonders. I wish I could reproduce it for you here. The greatest natural wonder I have experienced, however, is something different and highly personal. For a quarter of a century, I have been privileged to do, for a living, pretty much what I believe I would have done if I'd been rich and never had to work. That is, roam the countryside, visiting with the folks, hearing their tales. Looking at sunrises on the Gulf shore. At sunsets that painted mountains in the Big Bend. Sitting under trees, thinking about the world. Tapping out a few hundred words a day on what I thought about. I never took that for granted. It still seems wonderful that a guy would get to do that and be paid for it.

A good many of these thoughts are included in the columns collected in this book, which was a long time coming. The reason it was, I was hard-headed about it, and a little lazy. For almost twenty years people have been saying to me, "When are you going to put all your columns in a book?" Well, of course there is no way all the columns would go into one book even if they deserved to go there, which many of them do not. I have just now calculated that since the column began in 1956, I have written approximately 3,750,000 words. The word is the unit of measurement most often used in the writing business. Numbers of words. A manuscript of 100,000 words will make a book of respectable size. So if all the columns were included, we would have a set of twenty-one books of 100,000 words each. Obviously, what needed to be done was to pick out some of the better pieces and throw the others away.

"Gather up a couple of hundred of them then," people would say, "and stick them in a book. It'd be easy. They're already written." Yes, but I was able to see that to pick out a couple of hundred columns, I would need to read through 3,750,000 words of my own stuff, to see which ones were worth being in a book. I am a slow reader. It would take me seventeen forevers to read that much. So I kept putting it off, and putting it off, and instead of getting better the problem got worse. Because every day there would be several hundred more words to deal with.

Then one day Bill Shearer said to me, "You don't have to read all that stuff yourself. Let somebody else do it." I said no. It was my own stuff and nobody else could read it and choose what I would want to keep for a book and what I would want to pitch out. "Well, let's try it anyhow," Shearer said. "If you don't like the selection, we can change it."

Shearer became the publisher of this book. He hired an editor, Margaret Ingram, to do all that reading and selection. We decided to pick from the last ten years of columns. So Margaret had to read only 2,500 pieces. Something like 1,250,000 words. To pick 155 columns for the book.

I was doubtful. I suspected Margaret would fling out every piece I ever did that I was fond of, and keep all the ones I hated. There are many of the latter in the files. In fact, some of the early ones I can no longer read if my stomach is the least bit off balance. After she had been working a few weeks, I dropped by Margaret's office. I told her I came by to say hello. The truth was, I wanted to see what she was weeding out, so I could make her put it all back in.

Well, I was astonished. I still am. I wish I may never again see a sunrise if she wasn't doing it just exactly the way I would have done it myself. This hurt my feelings a little. I've always had a mighty possessive attitude toward the column. I felt it was all mine and nobody else could make sound decisions about it. When we were through, I think Margaret and I had had a mild argument over only two of the pieces. She won the first dispute. She let me win the second.

Now then, if you're a regular customer of the column in the *Post* and if you have favorite stories you remember, I hope they're in the book somewhere. If they're not just wait awhile. We may do this again, with different stuff, now that I've learned I don't have to do all the work myself.

You won't find in this volume any of the recurring characters of the column. What I mean, none of the fortune-teller stories are here, even though they run once a month in the paper. The My Friend Mel columns, with one or two exceptions, are not here either, or the Dear Aunt Emma letters or the Dear Boss letters. Somehow they just didn't fit in the book. Margaret set them all aside and I agreed. "Maybe we can do a separate book on them, later," she said. I'm not sure about that.

A column that *is* included is the one about the flounder dog. That yarn got more response from the customers than any other I've written in twenty-five years. It's not really one of my great favorites, but with a lot of the customers it was. It was written by Arp Harper of Houston. He sent it to me, and I just polished it up and put it in the paper. I think the next-most-response came from the Chamber of Commerce Bull column. It's here, you may be certain, and at least it's all mine and not any of Harper's.

One way a columnist judges what the customers like is by requests for clippings. People sometimes write or call and ask for a clipping of certain pieces. Because they've lost the paper and they want to send a piece to kinfolks in Kansas. The all-time grand champion most-requests-for-clippings title goes to a silly little yarn about a snake in a hanging basket. It was sent to me by one of the customers, and I don't even know who it was. It's the kind of thing that many people like to carry in their purse or billfold. At social gatherings they'll pass the clipping around, hoping to elevate the level of merriment. The snake yarn is not in the book. So I am going to put it in this foreword. Because I know blamed well that when the book comes out the phone will ring and the very first critic will say, "How come you didn't put the snake story in?"

So here I am putting it in. It's about a fellow who'd been in the hospital. A friend asked him why he'd been in the hospital and he told why. His wife had a creeping charley plant in a hanging basket. A freeze was forecast, so she brought the basket in the house. Coiled up in the basket was a green snake. Wife didn't see it until it warmed up and came out of the basket and slithered across the carpet. She screamed. Her husband was taking a shower. He came running in naked to see what the scream was about. Wife said snake, snake. Where? he asked. Under the sofa, she said. He got down on his hands and knees to look under the sofa for the snake. Family dog came along and cold-nosed him from the rear. He thought it was the snake and fainted. Wife thought he'd had a heart attack and called an ambulance. Ambulance guys came and loaded the husband on a stretcher. Snake came crawling out from under the sofa. Ambulance guys saw it and dropped the stretcher and broke the husband's leg and that's why he was in the hospital. There, it is done.

I anticipate a couple of other questions. One is about the old home town I refer to frequently without naming it. Sometimes the customers wonder what town it is. The reason I don't name it, it's not always the same town. Before I left home I lived in nine different West Texas towns with my family. So I lump them together and call them one home town. They were all alike anyhow, and I can't remember what happened in which place.

Something else, these pieces have not been re-written or updated. If a column was done in 1974 and somebody's age was given as thirty-six, for the purposes of this book he's still thirty-six. We haven't changed things to make him forty-three. If a building mentioned in a 1972 column burned in 1978, in the book it's still standing. Except for minor editing to improve the flow, the pieces run as they appeared in the paper.

Something that makes this a happy sort of book is that it doesn't matter how you read it. You can start in the middle if you want to. You can read it back to front. You can read the rear half before the front half. You can skip around. Doesn't make much difference.

The material in the body of the book does not belong to me or to the publisher. It is the property of the *Houston Post*, which holds the copyright. I have already been paid to write the columns for the paper. So my thanks go to the *Post* for permission to publish them again. My thanks also to the many parties who had a part in the columns and the production of this book. And thanks especially to Katie Hattan for smiling.

LEON HALE

1

"Anyhow,
that's why everybody
at San Leon was talking
about Chester's
Dog."

A good many of the strangers who come into Epsie Potter's grocery store at Rayburn don't want to buy anything. They come to ask directions on how to find somebody's house. Mrs. Potter will stop what she's doing and walk to the front door and show them which road to take.

"This is a general information bureau," she said, when I stopped there to visit, to catch up on my country store sitting. I consider hanging around country stores to be important. Maybe you'd like to try it yourself. Sometimes the world becomes a foreign place to me, and I get to feeling out of it, as the kids say. I can spend a while in a country store and it's a little like going home, back to my beginning where I understood everything.

I'd never stopped at Rayburn before. It's a small place maybe twelve miles east of Cleveland on State 105, in Liberty County. Mrs. Potter's store, a frame building with gas pumps out front, is the community's center. Harvey Potter, her husband, has a concrete business a short way on east, near the Trinity River at the Gravel Pits. When people around Rayburn say Gravel Pits, you can tell they mean for it to have capital letters. Most of the paychecks Mrs. Potter cashes come from the Gravel Pits.

Only one customer was in the store when I got there. She was Janice Kelley. Her husband, Andy, "follows construction work." She'd come in to drink a soda pop and wait for the mail carrier. The day before she'd given the carrier a package to mail and didn't have enough cash to pay the postage. "I'd forgotten how much the rates have gone up," she said. "Little one-pound package cost eighty cents to mail." She stood by the window and watched, so she could catch the carrier and pay what she owed.

Customers came and went one at a time. Suddenly Mrs. Potter jumped up and said quickly, "My beans, my beans," and rushed to the back of the store by the meat counter and turned down a pot of beans cooking there on a small stove.

"They may be scorched a little but that won't hurt 'em," she said. I told her I was raised on beans. "So was I," she said, "and I haven't gone back on my raising." I asked her what she was going to have with the beans for supper, and she said cornbread.

"Most exciting thing ever happens around Rayburn is when I burn a pot of beans," she laughed.

A tall girl—I say a girl, I suppose she might be twenty-five—came in with one of the Gravel Pit paychecks. "I want to pay some on my bill," she said.

"How much you want to pay?" Mrs. Potter asked.

"Twenty-five dollars."

Mrs. Potter got out her charge book. "Is that all you can pay?"

"Yessum. My husband quit at the Gravel Pits, and he didn't make nothin' last week."

"All right," Mrs. Potter said. She cashed the check and took $25 out and gave the girl the change. The girl said, "I'll pay cash for what I get today." I watched while she got two loaves of bread, peanut butter, baking powder, nutmeg, four little cans of peach nectar, a bottle of green shampoo, and several other items I missed.

While Mrs. Potter was checking the girl's groceries a tall man in a cowboy hat entered. He stood just inside the door and pushed his hat back. So he hadn't come to buy anything. When Mrs. Potter glanced up he said, "I'm lookin' for a man named Roberts?"— with a question mark on the end of his sentence that way.

"Which one?" Mrs. Potter asked.

"That's just my trouble, I don't know. The family's got a boy in the service, and home on furlough."

"That'll be Dewey. H. D. Roberts. That first house yonder, just across the road." The man pulled his hat down and said thank you ma'am and left.

Then the mail carrier came and Janice Kelly gave him what she owed and went home. The tall girl paid cash for her groceries, $4.30. We watched her cross State 105 and tiptoe over a cattle guard and gradually grow smaller, carrying her grocery sack down Palmer Lake Road. I asked Mrs. Potter how far the girl had to walk. She said not far.

The other afternoon I came through Glen Flora and stopped in at Scheller's Place, just to rest up from the road and see who was present, and Gus Cervenka was sitting in there braying like a mule.

I wish there was a way to take a sound and put it in the paper, the way these radio folks can record rackets and noises and uproars and send them out over the air. If I could do that in the paper, I would give you the privilege of hearing Gus do his bray, as he is the best at it I ever heard, and in fact I will put him up against any actual mule you can name.

Gus is naturally proud that he is able to do this thing that nobody else can do, or at least not anywhere near as well as he can, and he will do it on request at any time. You will find little taverns and filling stations and grocery stores scattered all over this state that have regular customers with special talents that way. The folks who operate such businesses are happy to have this talent on hand, as it provides entertainment for the patrons.

Just like there in Scheller's the other afternoon, some important people had come in to visit with Pud Joines, who runs the place. I don't know who they were, but they were important because they were dressed up and had a long car, and had come all the way from El Campo, which is fifteen miles south. All right, when sort of a lull came in their visit, Pud called out to Gus, "Gus? Show 'em how you can bray like a mule." And here he went, letting it fly. And I mean, it just made you want to get up and go look for a *mule,* it was so real. It gives Gus standing there around Glen Flora, and respect, that he can go like a mule so well.

In other places you will find citizens known and respected because they can crow like roosters, or do bulls bellering in the distance, or maybe they can stand up and copy Mel Tillis when he stutters. Things like that. You think it doesn't make a difference in their lives, that they can do that? Shoot.

All right, look at Coy Moore, back in the old home town. He could do cat fights. Could he *ever* do cat fights! Old Coy could make you *see* a cat fight, when there wasn't a cat inside of a mile. He'd cup his hands up here around his mouth some way, and make four noises come out at once. He'd spew, and spit, and yowl, and rowl, and you could pretty near see the fur fly, and there wasn't a thing to it except old Coy making noises. People would just be confounded by it. They'd say, "I *swan* I don't see how Coy Moore does them cat fights like he does."

Well, he practiced, is how he could do it. And it paid off for him, too. Why, wouldn't anybody in town heat grease for a fish fry or water for a stew without first they invited old Coy Moore, to come do his cat fights.

While I was at Scheller's, Pete Nelson and his wife came in. They're from on down at Wharton. So far as I know Pete hasn't got any special talent that he's known for, unless it's being able to count a large flock of birds and tell you exactly how many are in it.

This time of year you hear a lot of talk about great flocks of geese and ducks on the coastal prairie, and it's customary to try to establish how many birds are in those bunches. Pete said he'd just seen a flock that had 7 million in it. No, he didn't get to count every one of them. Said he counted only 4 million and estimated the rest.

"That ain't nothin'," Gus Cervenka said. "Yesterday I seen a bunch didn't have *none* in it." That one drove me off. As I was pulling away, Gus let loose another explosion of brays from inside. And you could see the folks there in downtown Glen Flora turning and looking around, trying to locate where that mule was.

Going through Madisonville, I stopped to say hello to Ross Madole, who is a city secretary, and we got to talking about twelve o'clock whistles. Ross said Madisonville doesn't have a whistle that blows at noon, or five o'clock, or eight o'clock. Not that it needs one. Most small towns no longer have such whistles. But I thought Madisonville is the kind of place that still might. It reminds me in a lot of ways of the town I did most of my growing up in. In our old town, the very breath and heartbeat of the people seemed regulated by steam whistles that blew at key hours, and the last time I was there at least one was still being blown.

But the public whistle has been fading from the Texas scene for more than twenty years. Ross Madole said he doesn't believe Madisonville has had a whistle since its cotton gin days, before everybody quit farming and went to running cattle. Ross grew up a few miles west of town, in times when "every country community had its own school and church and store and gin," and even if you were way down in a creek bottom picking cotton, you could always hear at least one gin whistle blow at dinner time.

The whistle I remember best was blown off the steam line at the power plant, back in my old home town. That plant wasn't really in town but out on the river, three-four miles from the courthouse. But its whistle had a good deep steamboat quality, and I used to imagine the sound of it covered our entire county. I want to say it blew at six, not five. On long summer days we'd be way off in the mesquite somewhere, miles from home, and when we heard that power plant whistle we stopped whatever we were doing, no matter how interesting or at what stage it was, and headed in. Because when we left we were told, "When you hear the six o'clock whistle, you trot home."

There was one period in the life of that little town when everybody who could get up a head of steam was blowing whistles, including two tailor shops and a steam laundry. We had seven o'clock whistles and eight o'clock whistles and twelve o'clocks and five o'clocks and six o'clocks. So if you were late getting somewhere, you always had the excuse that you heard the six o'clock whistle and thought it was the five. A few Texas towns still have such whistles. Some use the fire siren.

The passing of the public whistle reflects a change in the way we live. We have become a bunch of shut-ins, both summer and winter, living behind closed doors and latched windows. A time whistle very likely isn't even heard by a majority of the people it's supposed to serve, and so has lost much of its value.

I discovered another weakness of the steam whistle as a signal when I left Madisonville and drove on down to Huntsville. Stuck my head in the city manager's office and asked whether Huntsville has a steam whistle that would blow at five o'clock. I was told yes, the prison system blows one, from behind the Walls. Wasn't long until five, so I walked over on the square and waited, about three blocks from the prison. If that whistle blew at five, I sure didn't hear it, because of traffic noise. Even in a small city like Huntsville, by 5 P.M. downtown traffic is making so much racket I don't think you could hear anything happening three blocks away, unless it was about twenty sticks of dynamite.

It was near the end of the lunch hour. I was parked on the Guadalupe County courthouse square in Seguin, waiting on a fellow, when this old green GMC pickup truck came rattling up and stopped across the street. A big, healthy-looking elderly fellow with a shining wide grin got out of the truck. And started talking. Hollered at everybody that passed. Waved at the cars going by. Yelled at people across the street.

He took two boxes of vine-ripe tomatoes out of the cab and propped them on top of a load of watermelons, bedded in straw in the back of the truck. Then he began hawking his melons and tomatoes, shouting his prices, giving testimony about the quality of his produce.

That's the first time I've seen anybody hawking watermelons on a courthouse square in a good many years. But there he was, and having success, too. Doing it right there at the corner of East Center and River streets, with the plush Chamber of Commerce offices sitting on one side of him and the fancy new La Plaza office building on the other. I went over and watched him work a while.

A pretty woman came by on her way into the courthouse, and the watermelon salesman offered to sell her the finest melon on the truck for six bits. She refused the offer. "Have you had a watermelon this summer?" he asked her. She said she didn't believe she had. "Why," he said, "if you don't eat watermelon, you just ain't enjoying the good life."

A white-haired gent in a straw hat walked by, and the salesman tried a different approach. "Judge, I gotta make me enough money to buy some groceries." And it worked. The man bought a sack of tomatoes, weighed out on a little kitchen scale.

Three Mexican-American citizens got out of a car half a block away, and the salesman tried to sell watermelons to them from a distance of 75 yards, shouting at them in Spanish. And a pretty fair accent too.

I went over and said hello. The salesman said his name is Hurley Wilson, that everybody in Seguin knows him, that he's seventy years old, that he's been selling watermelons and tomatoes and molasses around there for a mighty long time. Then he made me the same offer he'd made the woman—best melon on the truck for seventy-five cents.

Hurley Wilson's voice reminded me of the old peddler who used to come by our house long ago. He drove a team of limber-eared mules to a wobbly wagon rigged up with wheels off a riding cultivator. The bed of the wagon was always full of loose hay and under the hay he had all these big juicy Tom Watson melons.

Those mules would creep along, very, very slow, and the peddler sat up there with the lines half-hitched around the wagon brake and sang this two-note song of his. "Wah-a-a-a-da mehlon-n-n." Over and over, lazy and yet so pure in tone. I always thought it was beautiful. We discovered you could run into the living room when the peddler came by and hit middle C on the piano and that was always the pitch of one of his two notes. He used C on the first two syllables of the word *watermelon*, dropped down to B for the third, and back up to C for the final syllable. Those two notes sung by that old peddler came to be a sound of our summers, the same as mockingbirds and locusts. I don't remember that old gent's name. Surely he is gone by now.

"This here's a nice one." It was Hurley Wilson, grinning there by his truck and holding up a melon. "Seventy-five cents," he said. So I bought it. You can't tell, that may be the last watermelon I'll ever buy from a peddler on a courthouse square.

Every now and then a pure-dee city person will ride along with me when I go to the country to work. I always like to see what interests him, and what he will ask questions about. Sometimes it will be something I take for granted and seldom think of.

I had a city rider in the car recently when I drove up to a farmhouse in the woods of East Texas. It wasn't the house of anybody I knew. I just stopped there to ask directions. When I stopped I honked a short honk, and pretty soon a woman came out on the front porch, drying her hands on an apron. I stood at the gate and talked to her and got my directions and we drove on. I have done that hundreds of times.

My rider commented that where he came from it was considered ill-mannered to stop in front of a house and honk people out that way. Yes, but that's in town, in the city. In the country a sedate toot in front of a house is looked on as a courteous warning. It doesn't demand anything. All it says is, "There's somebody out front. You've got company."

So then the people in the house can do whatever they want to do, about somebody coming. Put on a shirt. Comb their hair. Get their hands out of the dough and wash them. It even gives them a chance to go in the back of the house and shut the door and pretend nobody is home, if they want to do that.

Now, honking in front of a country house can, in fact, be done in a discourteous way, and it's important to know how to avoid it. What you want is just a polite little honk. Don't go leaning on the horn and producing a long and persistent noise. It's especially bad to honk long and loud that way and then just sit there behind the wheel, waiting for somebody to come out to the car. It's double especially bad for a young person to do that, and expect an older one to come out like he's giving curb service. Adults in the country expect better manners out of young people than that.

When you toot the horn, you need to get out of the car immediately. An exception to that is, stay in the car if the house has got mean-eyed and stiff-tailed dogs around it. But generally if there are dogs you won't need to honk. The dogs will announce you, and it's all right just to sit silently in front of the house and don't get out until somebody comes and speaks to the dogs.

Many country people have other warnings, about somebody coming. Certain types of poultry make announcements about visitors. Geese are good at it. Guineas are probably the best. I've heard people say a stranger can't walk across a cattle guard half a mile from the house without their guineas will go to potracking about it.

Back in the early thirties I used to ride along with my father when he was selling magazine subscriptions in the country. I never once saw him walk up on a porch and knock on a door. He would first give the little toot on the horn of that 1920-something Chevy, and get out, and if nobody came to the door he would call.

"Hell-oh?" Raising his voice on the "oh" that way, and putting a question mark behind. Then he'd follow with, "Anybody home?" He was so expert at making those calls that when anybody did come, like from around in the back, they would nearly always be grinning at him. Never saw him before in their entire lives, and yet they'd be grinning and friendly just because he knew how to hang over a gate and make those calls in just exactly the right way. It was good for business, sure.

Of course a door-to-door salesman in town, in the big city, would never honk. People would think he was somebody they knew, tooting in front of the house like a car pool driver, and they would resent it. But for friends, I sort of like that little hey-you've-got-company toot on the horn, in the city or anywhere.

Up until the mid-1950s, there was a Red & White Grocery in an old two-story frame building on the town square in Fayetteville. It was operated by Rudolph Mynar and his wife Ludmila, and they lived above the store. Ludmila Mynar continued living up there long after her husband died and the store closed. Bill Rogers of Houston owns that building now. He tells me Mrs. Mynar lived above the store forty-two years, and then went to a nursing home in La Grange.

Fayetteville has long been one of my favorite country towns, and I love to see those abandoned store buildings around that little square open up again for business. Several of them have, including the Red & White. Local folks still call it the Red & White even though Kathy Sturm operates a crafts and refreshment parlor in there now. But the best thing about that old building is that it used to house the Dawn Theater, the last picture show in Fayetteville.

Last weekend I was there and got to meet Joe Mynar, who operated the Dawn through its last years. Also his nephew, Tom Rhode of Houston, who grew up around Fayetteville and sold popcorn at the picture show when he was a boy. The three of us stomped around a while in the dark theater, next door to the Red & White. All frame construction, with the floor sloping down to the screen. A set of winding wooden steps, almost a ladder, leading to the projection booth. Everything properly dusty and cobwebby, the way abandoned theaters ought to be.

The seats have been removed, but Rogers said he knows where they are. Mynar said he sold them, or at least some of them, to the cattle auction barn in La Grange. Anyway, Rogers is thinking about opening the Dawn again, making a little music hall of it. Place where local musicians could play. Maybe show some of the old films that Joe Mynar used to run. I wanted the worst way to find out when the last picture show was screened in Fayetteville, and what the title of it was, and who starred in it. But Mynar couldn't recall. Been too long, he said. Twenty-five years ago.

"The place would seat about two hundred," he said, standing in the middle of the house, looking up, the way people will in empty theaters. "I don't know when it opened. Way, way back, with silent pictures. I was in partners at first with Elo Rhode (Tom's father) and my brother Ignatz. Then I bought them out later. I'd have shows four times a week. Admission was twenty-five cents for adults and ten cents for children."

He remembered the title and star of one film that was very, very popular in Fayetteville. "It was *Steamboat 'round the Bend* with Will Rogers. I kept it for three days. Hoot Gibson was popular, too. And Roy Rogers. John Wayne. Bing Crosby. Hopalong Cassidy. Have you seen the projectors?"

Mynar has celebrated seventy-odd birthdays, but he led the way up the spiral ladder to the projection booth. It was a cold day, near freezing. There's a hole in the front wall of the building that you could fling an eighty-pound shoat through. The wind came sailing in and produced a mighty lot of air conditioning. Which I guess inspired Tom Rhode to recall the winter seating pattern in the Dawn. "There was one oil stove up front and a little electric heater here in back. When the weather was cold, people would bunch up. You'd have 'em sitting way down front by the stove or way back here by the heater, with empty seats in the middle."

Mynar was saying he didn't operate the projectors. Walter Grayson was one of the projectionists. Also Lad Cmajdalka. Mynar would take up tickets. In the last years, Rhode or his older brother Jim would make and sell popcorn. "That old popcorn machine came out of the Catholic church," Rhode said, "and its wiring was old, and full of shorts, and man, it would sure shock you."

Two projectors are still mounted in that booth, just as if they might be expected to operate again. And I really believe Joe Mynar did expect them to. We got an extension cord and plugged one in and Mynar flipped the switch. And behold! The projection bulb came on so bright. I was amazed. Those old machines have been sitting up there a quarter of a century collecting dust and corrosion, likely being rained on through the broken window panes. Yet the lights in them still burn. Remarkable. But Mynar seemed disappointed that the reels wouldn't turn. He monkeyed a long time with one of the machines, trying to make it work. Decided it needed cleaning and gave up. We went back to the fire and I was glad.

In country towns thirsty for excitement, you could generally depend that at least once a year the projection booth at the picture show would catch fire. Mynar can't recall the year, but it happened at the Dawn in a spectacular way. A blaze originated in one of the projectors, and here came the volunteer firemen.

"I tried to keep them from shooting water into the booth," Mynar said. "They did it anyhow and the booth just exploded. But it turned out to be the best thing that ever happened to the theater. I got new projectors, and after that we had very good movies."

What caused the closing of the picture show in Fayetteville? Mynar said "when television came that time." Tom Rhode said yes, but also because the Dawn's equipment couldn't handle modern films. "The last few years he couldn't get anything but old film, and it was always breaking, and it would take too long to fix, and people wouldn't sit still for that."

Before I left the Red & White Grocery I tried to figure what sort of income a full house at the Dawn Theater produced. Seating capacity, 200. Say you had 100 adults at two bits a head, and 100 minors at a dime. A gross of $35. I asked Joe Mynar if he made much money, running that picture show. "I got rich," he answered. I couldn't tell whether he was spoofing me or not.

It was the hour that most working people call quitting time. I was at Seabrook, there on the bay shore near the bridge where all those fish houses are, and gulls, and shrimp boats, and other marine things like that.

The custom is, late in the afternoon, for many of the local folks to gather at the various social centers private enterprise has provided along that shore, and sit about in groups, and discuss the activities of the day. Sometimes if you just pick a place and go in and sit and listen you will hear worthwhile conversation, and sometimes you won't. Anyway, I picked one, and went in, and maybe a dozen customers were in there talking, and shooting eight-ball, and joshing back and forth in a friendly way, and it seemed like quite a pleasant place.

I chose a seat, and got into it, and presently out from under the table next to mine walked a guinea hen. It looked up at me and spoke as follows: "Pot rack!" I looked around to see if any of the other customers were taking notice of that bird, and none were. The guinea stood a while and stared at me, and then went moseying off beneath the tables, just as if it was outdoors and searching around for whatever it is that guineas eat. Then here came a fellow who seemed to occupy a position of authority in that place, and I asked him if he knew there was a guinea in the house.

"Why yes," he said, "that's my guinea. Her name is Pot Rack."

"Pot rack!" yelled the guinea, from over at the juke box.

I swapped names with the guinea's master, and he is Johnny Cates. He runs that place for the owner, Aliene Mills, who at the moment was carrying on a conversation with the guinea at a nearby table. It seems one of the customers made Cates a present of this guinea when it was nothing but a baby chick, or whatever small guineas are called, and it grew up in the place there and is a very popular bird, with friends that come to see it from as far away as Freeport and Texas City.

"I want you to meet Pot Rack," Cates said to the guinea and started to perch it on my shoulder, but I declined. I don't much care about having a guinea roost on me. Let it sit in its own chair, is what I say. Which it did, perching on the back. "Pot rack!"

It is not a custom of mine to go around interviewing guineas at Seabrook or any place else. Still, I will say this bird is above the average guinea you meet in public. It has taste, as it likes Johnny Rodriguez records. And it's got spirit, for it has whipped dogs several times its weight.

In this state a good many small business people will keep animals and birds around their premises, for purposes of entertaining customers and attracting trade. It seems to work, too, although I confess I don't always understand why. I have known them to keep cats and dogs in forty different brands and combinations. I've known them to have owls, pelicans, parrots, snakes, lions, alligators, deer, and once even a buffalo.

Sure, for several years J. B. Choate kept a buffalo named Joe tied out front of his country store at Alvin, and that animal had many friends. At one time Choate made fiscal history by packaging buffalo chips in cellophane and peddling them to tourists at ten cents per. Do not ask me why anybody would buy a buffalo chip. I am only giving you the facts.

J. L. Hayman used to keep a myna bird in a little cafe he had up at Milano. I came to know that bird and liked him pretty well, although I'm surprised he didn't run off more trade than he attracted. When a girl came in, the bird would let fly a wolf whistle so loud and piercing it would pretty near bust a cafe water glass.

Then up close to Lufkin, a fellow whose name I forget used to have a pet coon that would come in his tavern and snitch peanuts off the customers. Many folks thought that was cute, although they might not think it's so cute anymore, on account of the price of peanuts.

To me the most interesting thing about Johnny Cates' guinea is that so many folks who see it don't know what it is, and call it a peacock, or a grouse, or a pheasant. It hasn't been so many years since almost every Texas farm had a few guineas. The ones I knew were all wild and noisy, their meat dark and—unless it was cooked right—tough as a Holstein steak.

This Seabrook guinea is hooked on shrimp and peanut butter, and has a habit of chasing cars just like a dog. Which leads me to the forecast that it will not last to become an elderly guinea. I mentioned that before I left.

"Pot rack!" the guinea said.

Got into Woodville, the county seat of Tyler County, about the middle of the afternoon and went over on the courthouse yard to sweat the domino game. When almost nothing else is going on in Woodville, you can depend that at least a domino game is being held, or if it's not, one has just been completed, or is about to start in a few minutes. In the twenty-five years or more that I've been visiting Woodville I can remember mighty few times I rolled onto the square that a domino game wasn't being played.

In pretty weather the game would be under the big oak tree on the west side of the courthouse. In bad weather the players would move inside the courthouse and set up a table in the women's cell of county jail, there on the first floor. In a town like Woodville women don't get arrested too often, and the cell was almost always empty.

There's an old story you hear on the square at Woodville that if the domino players wanted to use the jail and a woman happened to be in there, they would take up a collection and pay the woman's fine so they could get the use of the cell. I didn't quite believe that when I heard it, but it makes a nice little piece of local color. It's not true but ought to be.

Woodville domino players now have a spiffy new place where they can play, in good weather or foul. It's a county-built domino hall, the only one I ever saw. Nice little one-room house with three domino tables and plenty of chairs, and it sits right there on the courthouse lawn. When I went in, Allen Bingham and Dan Johnson and Louis Hanks were hooked up in a hot game, with Jesse Johnson sweating. Bill and George Barcley came in later. The heaviest play is generally late afternoon, in the hours before supper. Don't look for domino players in action at meal time. One thing you can depend on, domino players quit to eat.

I went to the courthouse, and Ann Fondren, assistant county auditor, looked up how much the little domino hall cost, about $3,600, which came out of federal revenue-sharing funds. So I don't guess you knew that as a federal taxpayer you have helped to build a domino hall on the Tyler County courthouse yard. Ann Fondren showed me a list of categories the federal government has set up. To guide local government in spending revenue-sharing money. One category is capital improvement and another is social services. Don't you suppose a domino hall would fit either of those? Seems so to me.

It's popular to believe that retired men in country towns sit around on benches all the time, whittling and talking about old times. The truth is, they play dominos instead. In some towns the game's at the feed store, or in back of the hardware store, or under a tree on the courthouse yard, like at Woodville before the hall was built.

Tyler County has another service I've never run across anywhere else. Raleigh Lamb at the Tyler County Booster was telling me about it. It's a free bus service. The county bought a small bus and hired a driver and he carries folks wherever they want to go. Mostly it's been old people that don't have any way to get around. Say there's an elderly lady six miles out in the country, needs to come in to the doctor. The bus will go get her and bring her in and take her back. Bus will take a citizen to the grocery store, or even to the courthouse to play dominos.

I was sure sorry that story, about the domino players paying the woman's fine to get her jail cell, turned out to be false. The reason I doubted it from the beginning, though, I never in my time saw a bunch of domino players, at Woodville or any place else, who'd donate much cash to a collection for any purpose—unless it was to buy a new box of dominos.

When I rolled into Wharton the clock was pointing on toward high noon, and I hadn't yet read the morning paper. The reason was, before breakfast I had sat on my glasses again, and popped a headlight out of them, and flattened the wire parts, and put them pretty well out of commission. So I cut north on Farm Road 102 and drove a little way up the Colorado to Glen Flora and stopped at Scheller's Place, my favorite tavern in the world, so I could read the paper with the pair of community eyeglasses provided by that institution.

Well, actually they were provided by Vernon Emshoff, who is a regular customer at Scheller's the same as I am. Vernon became impressed by the number of customers who wander into Scheller's blind, or anyway almost, and unable to read the numbers in the telephone book. So, in a fit of public service, Vernon went into Wharton to the racket store, or some such place where ready-made eyeglasses are sold, and bought a pair of general purpose specs for Scheller's customers. They were Number 24s, I think, or maybe 26s, and they seem to improve the vision of almost anybody who has left his glasses home, or sat on them before breakfast. Pud Joines, who is the owner and operator of Scheller's, keeps these community specs behind the bar, in a drawer below the telephone, and anybody who comes in groping and squinting and wanting to read something can use these specs, provided they are not busy.

Well, they weren't busy, so I was at the back table, reading the news of the world with these community eyeglasses, when the conversation among the customers happened to touch on Mattie Smoot's magic Irish potato, which has proved to have astonishing curative qualities. This Irish potato is peeled, and cut into slices, and is drying and graying in a pint fruit jar on the shelves there at Scheller's, among all the other museum pieces on display in that place.

You remember Mattie, I guess. If I haven't told you before about Mattie I certainly intended to, and I think I did. She is going to be ninety-two, as they say, and lives there in Glen Flora, and every day she walks to Scheller's, and has a couple of soda pops, and eats whatever Pud fixes for dinner, and afterward before going home Mattie washes the dishes. However, it is not proper to call her a dishwasher, because she is a privileged citizen, and has her own chair with her name on the back, and a good many of the important facts I have collected in this life have been told to me by Mattie Smoot.

Anyhow, just lately Mattie has been sort of down in the quilts, sick, with what she describes as a poison in her head. She had been taking that trouble to the doctor without noticing much improvement, until at last she tried the potato cure. She took a regular Irish potato, and sliced it, and placed the slices here and there over her hair, and tied her head up in a towel, and went to bed. The next morning the poison had been drawn out entirely, and she was well.

I wondered where she learned such a cure, and she said, "It just come to me." So Mattie automatically knows such things, the same as she knows that if you get stung by a wasp, to take the sting out you have to rub the place with three different kinds of weeds.

She was good enough to pass along to me two other cures, one for a sore throat and the other for a cold. For a sore throat, just eat half a teaspoon of sugar doctored with a drop of coal oil. Mattie said her mother fed her sugar and coal oil when she was a child and she takes it yet, here when she's going to be ninety-two. For the cold, you might want to try what Mattie calls hog hoof tea. "When they killed hogs they'd save the feet," Mattie said, munching serenely on a mouthful of pork and beans Pud had heated up for dinner, "and cut little pieces off the toes and boil 'em and make tea. It tasted so bitter, but it was sure good for a cold."

A few of the regular customers at Scheller's will say they don't believe for a second that Mattie's sliced potato brought about any cure, despite that the spud is sitting there on the shelf, aging and curing and becoming more famous every time a tourist walks in. They think what really cured Mattie was the doctor going up to $14 for an office visit. Mattie paid it once, and hasn't had a pain since.

Anyway, all I started out to tell you is, if you're down in that country, and lose your specs, and need to read a road map or a phone book, remember you can always stop at Glen Flora and use the community eyeglasses at Scheller's Place.

Way down in the southeast corner of Polk County I stopped at Murphy's Store and heard about the time Deacon Jones' car decided to run away. It happened right there at Murphy's. W. P. Jones, who like a lot of men named Jones is called Deacon, stopped at the store that day and intended to stay just a minute. He was on the way home. He lives in Segno Gulf Camp, which is not far off Farm Road 943, back in behind Murphy's.

The car had been behaving all right, not showing any signs of staging a revolution, and Jones left the engine running when he went in the store. He was standing in there talking to Leora Murphy when she said, "Somebody's driving off in your car."

Jones looked out and said, "Well, who the devil is it? I can't see anybody behind the wheel." But the car was moving, all right. Backward. Somehow it got to vibrating and jumped its automatic transmission into reverse.

Murphy's has a pair of gas pumps out front and a big wide dirt driveway, or parking area, like you see around so many country stores. Jones' car took off at a pretty good clip and backed all the way out onto the blacktop of Farm Road 943 and went over it and turned back across and came curving up to the store front again. "I thought it was going to hit the gas pumps," Mrs. Murphy told me. "But it just barely missed. Could have been bad, if it'd hit one of those pumps." The car completed that first wide circle and started a second, bouncing back out onto the blacktop.

Deacon Jones was at the store the other day, doing most of the telling. I asked him what he did during the runaway. "Mostly I just stood around and watched," he grinned. "Seemed to me the longer that car ran, the faster it went. I chased it a time or two but I could see if I got the door open it would slap me down before I could get inside."

Joe Murphy keeps a pile of creosoted posts outside the store, and once Jones grabbed one of those and when the car came around on about the sixth or seventh pass he threw the post under, hoping to head it off. But it jumped the post and kept circling. "Every time it'd hit the edge of the blacktop," Jones said, "the front wheel would cut a little and throw it into a tighter circle. Finally I decided, well, I'll just let 'er alone, until she runs out of gas. Trouble was, it had a full tank."

Before it was over, traffic on Farm Road 943 was stacking up both east and west of the store and everybody sitting there watching Deacon Jones' car make circles and waiting to see what it would hit. Finally Buddy Wiggins came along and stopped it. He's young and quick and he popped in there and shut 'er down, just like bulldogging a steer running backwards. Give him a hand, folks.

After the telling of the car story I followed Deacon Jones home, and met his daughter Peggy and her husband, Carlos Bolton, who'd brought their children up from Angleton for a visit. Right there in the middle of the day Peggy stirred up a batch of homemade vanilla ice cream and Carlos cranked the freezer and we sat in the shade and ate and talked about how good it was. I believe this is the best job I ever had.

You've been through Kenney, I expect. It's a little town on Highway 36 between Bellville and Brenham. Elmer Freitag is postmaster there, and runs a big country-type store. He's been in that store all his life, and he's sixty-eight now.

I stopped there this past week to visit with Freitag and his wife, Lucille, and to ask about the box on the front porch. It stands by the door, just an old wooden box with a chest-type lid. I always guessed it was one of those homemade soda-pop boxes like we used to see, lined with metal. No, Freitag said, it's a bread box. When the bakery truck comes early in the morning before the store opens, the driver puts the bread in the box so the dogs won't come along and get it.

If you're an early riser, you know that a good bit of perishable stuff is left temporarily on sidewalks in front of stores, before the day's business starts. In country towns where everybody knows everybody else, sometimes you'll see a person stop and pick up a loaf of bread from the sidewalk about dawn, and drive on off. But he'll be back when the store opens to pay for it.

Bread-eating dogs, I bet, are also the reason for the kitchen stove that sits by the front door of the Kenney State Bank Building, next door to Freitag's. Been sitting there a long time, and I've wondered why a stove is parked there at the bank. Well, the bank is closed, liquidated a good long time ago, and later on somebody opened a cafe and tavern in the building. So I expect the stove out front was left there so the bread could be stuck in the oven to shut it off from the dogs.

The little business in the bank building is closed down now. Small businesses in country towns that way, especially cafes and beer joints, are always going in and out. But you take a business like Elmer Freitag's, it's been there so long I doubt you could shut it down with an act of the legislature. It can even *look* like it's about to close, but it'll just keep chugging along.

Walk in the front door and you see a lot of empty shelves, and display cases with just a few items in them, and you have to wonder whether the place is still open. But walk on toward the back, past the post office boxes, and the action begins to pick up. Time you get to the rear, why there is where all the business goes on. Very few of the customers use the front entrance now. They come in the back door instead. The cash register is by the back door, and so are all the groceries, and the wheel of rat cheese, and the slab bacon that Lucille Freitag will slice for you, leaving the rind on or taking it off, as you choose.

Freitag's is the only store I know where a can of baking powder or a box of starch is displayed on a shelf ten feet from the floor. If you want to buy any of the stuff kept at high altitude that way, Freitag climbs his rolling ladder and fetches it down. The store has two such ladders. Some parents visit Freitag's to show their children the rolling ladders because that's how department stores were equipped long ago.

Back in the 1920s, and I expect even earlier, general merchandise stores in country towns issued metal trade tokens to customers. Freitag's did. Say a farmer came in to sell the store some eggs. He might be paid in tokens, which he could then spend for whatever he wanted there in the store. This was a way merchants had of trying to keep the money they paid out from being spent somewhere else. It was common to issue a full denomination of such tokens, from five cents to a dollar, and these would spend just as good as cash. In fact, in some places the tokens would get to circulating from business to business, doing duty as legal tender just like Uncle Sam's coin. A good many of these tokens are still around, mostly in cigar boxes, kept as souvenirs.

Just to see what would happen, I took one of Freitag's old one-dollar tokens and went to the other side of the bank to Laminack's Cafe to see if I could spend it. Truman Laminack didn't even blink when I tossed it on his counter. Sure, he'd honor it, at face value. I decided not to spend it, but I could have. Of course I don't know that Truman was assuming any risk. I expect he could have taken the token back where it came from and Elmer Freitag would have redeemed it, just for old times' sake.

A cold, quiet night at Freeport, I drifted down toward the beach, looking for somebody to talk to. Topped the Surfside Bridge and stopped a while there where Highway 332 comes to an end in the sand. Listen to the wind.

Over the past twenty years I've collected quite a stack of stories along that stretch of sand from 332 to the Jetties, and I've learned a lot from the people who told them. Many are gone now, and I sure miss 'em when I go back.

You remember the night all of us sat in a bunch, just right down the beach yonder a little way, and listened to that young couple sing the "Whiffenpoof Song"? They were as deep in love as Romeo and Juliet and they sang so sweet and sincere, and then walked away in the darkness and I never saw them again. But I have thought about them a thousand times.

On cold nights when business is slow, some of the beach places where you can find somebody to talk to will close up early. But I found lights at Art's Place and went in and there was Art

Himself Margiotta at his own front table, his white hair a shade whiter than when I saw him last. And Booger Red, asleep on the first stool.

No, Booger Red is this tom cat, who has used up another of his lives since I was on the beach. He has now been run over by a truck, chewed up by dogs twice, bitten by a poison snake, and blasted in the stern with a 12-gauge shotgun. So he's got—let's see now—four lives left.

Jim Hilton, charter boat captain, was at the bar. Mack Leeka, looking almost British with his cap sitting so straight and proper, was alone at a far table, and he and Jim and Art were talking about curlews. Beach people will do that sometimes, and I've never figured out why. They'll know each other, and they'll sit in a tavern or a cafe just as far apart as they can get, and carry on a shouting conversation. It's like they want the worst way to communicate, but they don't want to get too close. Art was saying about curlews that they're the best eating bird we've got in Texas, that he'd rather eat one any time over a quail or a duck or a goose. I wrote that down because I'd never heard anybody talk about eating a curlew before. I need to try that.

Then we went to pelicans, when Jim got to talking about brown pelicans he's known. We had a little memorial service for those grand birds, which have just about disappeared from the Texas coast. Even Louisiana, the Pelican State, can't keep pelicans going. We've almost destroyed them, with our everlasting progress. From pelicans we went to mullet, the fish that's mainly a bait item along the Texas coast but is caught commercially as a food fish in some places and considered a great treat.

Paul Johnson came in, wearing a red cap with white polka dots, and Larry McBeth, sporting a fine Apostle Paul beard. You meet some interesting faces on the beach, a grand assortment of eyes and chins and mouths and noses. When I first started going to Surfside I guess fellows like Paul and Larry were just little boys. Now they've been out and seen the world, and they can walk in—even on a conversation about pelicans and mullet—and tell things the old heads haven't heard.

Like Paul Johnson, he worked a while on commercial fishing boats off Florida, and mullet is what they went after, with nets a mile long pulled by power boats. The boats would make a circle, see, gradually closing, closing until the pocket in the net was tight and loaded with mullet. Then the pelicans would come, brown ones and whites both, and actually be a help to the fishermen. Because those birds would get in the pocket, line up just inside near the net, to get their dinner. They ate a lot of mullet, sure, but they were also guards. Their presence at the edge of the net kept many a mullet from jumping over and escaping, so they saved more fish than they ate.

Hey, look here, I'll be dawg, here's a fellow from my old home in West Texas, just walked in the door. Bob Caraway. Bob's about ten years younger than I am but still plenty old enough to be out after dark by himself. We sat around an hour and cut up old scores about life in the old home town and the curious thing is, it wasn't really any different for Bob than for me. The decade between us didn't produce much change. He had the same teachers I had in school, did the same things I did, even worked for some of the same bosses I worked for.

We left and went back toward the bridge and ran into a couple more familiar faces. Lucy Blake and Mabel Helen Warren. You remember Mabel Helen? Piano player? Sure, she's the one played "When My Baby Smiles at Me" in the little chapel on the beach at Dewey Rickenbrode's funeral. While the airplane flew over, and dipped a wing, and scattered Dewey's ashes in the surf. Just the way she'd ordered it done. Just the way she'd done for her husband Rick who preceded her. Didn't I tell you about all that?

Before I chugged over the bridge and back to the main world, I walked a few minutes in the sand and the cold and the darkness, not far from where Mabel Helen played, and where the airplane dipped. Listen to the wind.

On a field trip I took recently, I curved off the trail a little and dropped in at the Deer Camp to see what was going on. There was a mild poker game in progress, which is what goes on most any night at the Deer Camp. So I sweated the action some, and built myself a huge cheese and salami sandwich from the makings laid out, as always, on the rectangle of plyboard laid across a couple of sawhorses. It was good to go back.

The Deer Camp is a place I used to hang out some after dark, to hear stories and sweat card games. At one time it really was a place where deer hunters slept, but the hunting lease was sold to a developer who is putting up homes where the deer used to roam, and I suppose now it would be against the law to fire a gun around there. But the party who bought the land has allowed the cabin to stand, at least for a while, and the hunters go there still to hunt, not for deer but for whatever it is that people search for when they leave home at night.

I must not say where the Deer Camp is, since the gents who deal those cards and build those thick sandwiches and sip those suds would consider it mighty impolite of me to go printing its location. So far as I know, nothing whatever goes on there that's illegal unless you want to count the poker games. But then my goodness, if officers of the law ever set out to raid two-bit poker games in the deer camps of this state, they will need Cox's Army and the Marine Corps to help, and won't be half finished when Gabriel starts tuning up that horn of his.

Still, some of the gents who go to the camp do not wish it known that they go. The reason is, a great many citizens in our state look upon playing poker and eating salami and sipping suds as very bad manners, especially if the party who does it on Saturday night is the same one who shows up in church on Sunday morning to take up collection and lead in prayer.

Which has always hit me as a peculiar attitude. What I mean, it is my personal notion that if a guy can go out on Saturday night and stay up till 2 A.M. dealing cards and popping caps and making sandwiches, he is due credit if he makes it to church the next morning at all, whether he leads in prayer or not. Furthermore, he may even be due more credit than the fellow who watched Lawrence Welk and went to bed and sawed off eight hours. But then as I say that is just my own feeling, and I have noticed that if very many people agree with it, they do not say so out loud.

Listen, I have seen some sweet charity work go on at that Deer Camp, in a curious and gentle and skillful style. I think it's all right to mention it now, without names, since the beneficiary has passed on. He was one of the old boys who used to come to the camp as a regular thing, but then he got sick, and his business went bad, and he stopped coming. He generally always lost at poker, and I suppose he felt like he couldn't afford to play any longer. Sure, his pride was a factor, too.

Well, that gang would go and get this fellow sometimes, and haul him out there, and sit him down, and let him win. And it wasn't easy, because he was very likely the worst poker player that ever drew two cards to an inside straight. In fact, it may be that a part of his money problem was due in the first place to drawing to inside straights, and holding queen kickers, and other bad habits that way. But they would sit with him all night, throwing in strong hands, and letting him rake it in, and I don't believe he ever knew what was going on. It meant so much to him, both to his pocketbook and his spirit.

I admired certain aspects of that charity work. For example, one night I saw the president of a bank, the pain showing in his face, fold up holding a full house over the best pot of the evening. Since then I have tried to think of a more unselfish act I ever saw a banker perform, and I have not thought of one.

When I stopped for a visit down on Galveston Bay at San Leon, the first half-dozen people I met told me about Chester's Dog. As far as I know that's all the name the animal has—just Chester's Dog. He is now alive and well and wagging, and you will understand why the health of this beast is a matter of public interest at San Leon when I tell you that Chester's Dog passed away four days before last Christmas and was buried. Yet he is now back among us.

Chester's Dog is owned by Chester Conn, who is a permanent resident of San Leon. You meet two types of citizens in that community. The permanents and the weekend people. The weekenders are mostly from Houston and have summer houses on the bay. They far outnumber the permanents. The most recent *Texas Almanac* gives San Leon's population as 100.

Among San Leon permanent people you meet a great many dog lovers. They are in fact lovers of all sorts of animals. Chester Conn is one of the most dedicated. Four days before last Christmas, he was up on Lake Livingston and he had Chester's Dog with him, when a really unfortunate thing occurred.

But I must explain why Chester Conn was up on that lake. Just as many Houstonians flee on weekends to San Leon to escape the city, quite a few San Leon permanent people go up into the Piney Woods to escape San Leon. This is just the way people are, that they wish to keep their scenery changing all the time. So several San Leon residents have cabins on the lakes and streams of the Piney Woods. Chester Conn is one of these.

The bad thing that happened at the lake was that he started his car and accidentally backed over his dog and killed him. You know what a high misery that is, if you've ever run over a living thing that you love. Conn was so stricken, as I got the story, he couldn't bring himself to bury the animal, so on the way home he stopped at a nearby store and asked the people there to do it. It was done.

Now then, four days later, on Christmas, two of Conn's friends were up on the lake, and they went by to check on the grave of Chester's Dog. The two were Mrs. Margaret Jones and Arnold

("Robbie") Robinson. Robinson is an electrician at San Leon. Mrs. Jones is, I'm told, the oldest practicing licensed beauty operator in Houston, but I'll not give her age.

While Robinson and Mrs. Jones stood looking down at the dog's grave, they saw some leaves stir at one end of it. Then some soil moved. Robinson hurriedly dug into the shallow, loose grave, and Chester's Dog came forth, not dead at all.

"He was weak," Robinson told me, "but the only thing we could find wrong with him, he seemed to have a hurt leg. We nursed him and fed him and brought him home to San Leon. Only thing I can figure, he'd just been in shock for those four days."

When Robinson and Mrs. Jones took the dog to Conn's house at San Leon, Conn wasn't at home. So they sat out front with the dog and waited. I wish you could hear half a dozen animal lovers there at San Leon as they tell about the reunion between Chester and that dog. As they describe Chester's face. What he said. What he did. I can't tell it right. The reunion in one way was humorous and yet it had an almost religious aspect too. It seemed so absolutely right, such a happy thing, Conn getting the animal back from the grave right there at Christmas.

Anyhow, that's why everybody at San Leon was talking about Chester's Dog.

2

"She's had a good heifer calf ever'
spring of this world
for eight straight years. I can
show you on the
calendars."

Uncle Billy Crockett used to say he could tell it was fixing to rain because the bog was stinking. There was a kind of swampy area of several acres in a neighbor's pasture, and we called it a bog. It was always wet unless we were having a long spell of dry weather. In normal times an inch or two of water stood there and got stagnant and smelled bad. But the stink didn't have much range. You'd need to get up within a hundred feet of it before it hit you. It was true that the bog stunk stronger in unsettled weather, such as just before a squall came through. Then you might smell it half a mile away. This was one of Uncle Billy's favorite rain signs.

I thought about this a while ago when I was going through my files and the stacks of things on this desk, and came to an old almanac that's got a page of folksy weather wisdoms. It mentions stagnant water as a forecasting aid.

Last two or three years I've been trying to collect a few almanacs, and I've ended up with about a dozen. One or two go back into the forties, and all have at least some space devoted to weather signs. During World War II, almanacs changed. They began trying to justify, with scientific fact, the predictions and remedies and recommendations they'd been printing for so long.

For instance, *Everyman's Almanac,* published in 1944 in Chicago, insists that the odor of stagnant water would be stronger just before a weather change because of reduced atmospheric pressure. On a falling barometer, the almanac says, lower pressure would allow an increased volume of swamp gas to escape and stink up the countryside. The same theory seems to uphold the claim that the blooms of flowers give off a stronger fragrance just ahead of rain. The almanac says the reduced pressure allows the blooms to release more of the tiny particles that carry the perfume. Remember that rheumatic people used to grunt and groan and talk about changes coming in the weather because their joints were aching? Justifying that one, almanac editors again argued it was due to lower air pressures, which caused tiny blood vessels to bulge and irritate nerves and produce discomfort.

So maybe those signs were actually our early barometers, partly dependable at least. On the bog stinking, though, I'd think it would depend on where you were located in relation to the stagnant water. If you were upwind as a front approached, seems like the bog would stink less instead of more.

Let's look at a few more weather signs and sayings I've gleaned from almanacs. One of the commonest weather signs that old-timers looked for was sky color at sunset and at sunrise. A red sky at sunset and gray one at sunrise meant a good day of weather. Several little rhymes about this show up in the old almanacs. Probably the most popular is:

Evening red and morning gray
Sets the traveler on his way;
Evening gray and morning red
Keeps the traveler home in bed.

Dew on the grass has special significance to folk weather forecasters. Absence of dew hints at wet weather to come. And heavy dew predicts dry weather:

When the dew is on the grass
Rain will never come to pass;
When grass is dry at morning light
Look for rain before the night.

Those early-times weather people might have been wise to the ways of the elements, but they sure couldn't win any prizes for poetry.

Color of the moon was an indicator, too. A red moon means high winds. Pale moon means rain. White moon means fair weather, no rain or snow. Remember the significance of rain and sunshine at once? Means the devil is whipping his wife and it'll be raining at the same time the next day.

Here's one I like pretty well. It holds that when you go out at night and the snow creaks under your feet, you can expect clear weather tomorrow. That gives me a picture of a fading winter storm of the kind we can get in this country every few years. It'll give us snow, or probably a combination of snow and sleet, with temperatures just enough below freezing that the white stuff stays on the ground a couple of nights. On the second day there'll be a temporary warming that melts a part of the snow and makes everything mushy and wet and messy. Then the clouds blow on out, and the wind dies, and that polar air hangs over us, and everything that melted freezes again, and you go out at night and whatever you step on creaks and pops and cracks. Fair weather the next morning, you bet, but still plenty frigid. You might feel warm in the sun, but you'll shiver in the shade.

Long ago when I was living in the country, I think the weather sign in heaviest use was wind direction. And the biggest weather-maker was an east wind. My favorite east-wind story concerned the country folks who were in a bad drouth, and they decided they'd all go to church and pray for rain. But the old-timer among them said, "Ain't no use prayin' for rain. Pray instead for an east wind. You get the wind out of the east for five days and all hell can't keep it from rainin'."

There's an entire school of folk weather-forecasting based on the behavior of animals and birds. One of my old almanacs says if a rooster gets up on a high place to crow, the weather will clear up. Another insists that if the hens hang around the barn oiling their feathers instead of going out to scratch up bugs, better expect foul weather.

Another bad-weather sign: dishes and cups and saucers sweating in the cabinet. Another still: ring around the moon. Count the stars inside the circle to see how many days before rain. A crow making a solo flight over a cornfield. There's another bad-weather indicator. Two or more crows flying together, that's okay. But watch those lone crows. In winter observe the weather between 11 A.M. and 2 P.M. That's when it'll tell you what it's going to do.

The weather sign that I remember thinking about the most, in my dim past when we were living in the country, was the one that had to do with the Scotchman's britches. Say we'd had cloudy wet weather for a week or more, and the women needed to wash and hang out clothes so bad. They'd go out and look up and come back and start hanging tubs and hauling out scrub boards because "in the northeast there's enough blue sky to make a Scotchman a pair of pants." I always wonder how much blue sky you would need to make a pair of pants for that Scotchman. I ought to have asked Uncle Billy Crockett.

It's seven-thirty in the morning and I am at home, looking out at the first frost that has come to the back yard this fall. Mark the date on the calendar, the way they used to do in the country. November 14. Frost is such a funny business. I can find it in only two places out there. On a three-foot strip of grass near the back fence and on certain dark composition shingles on the neighbor's garage roof.

I remember a storm-cellar door in the country that frost was partial to. We would look there first, watching for the arrival of frost in the fall. There was a little ritual about it. The one who saw it first would come in and make the announcement, "Well, there's a patch of frost on the cellar door this morning."

Those receiving the news would then comment on whether the frost was early or late. It was always one or the other and never on time. If there was a particular date it needed to arrive in order to be exactly on schedule, I never knew it to come on that day. Some would get up and go out and look at the cellar door, as if the report needed confirmation. Next the event would be recorded on the calendar. "First frost," written in pencil by one of those qualified to write on anything as important as that calendar was. After the entry was made, next came the turning back, to compare the date with past years. Several calendars from other years hung behind the current one.

Sometimes when I am making entries on my own calendar, I get to wondering if any of those old calendars that hung on the nail in that farm house still exist, maybe in the bottom of a trunk in somebody's attic. Probably not. Probably they were pitched out and burned. They would be interesting to examine now, just for their weather records alone.

Calendars were a big part of those daily lives and entered often into routine talk. "I believe it was a year ago this week," somebody would say, "we had the blizzard, when the top of the corn crib fell in."

"No, that was in January. Because I know Henry was here. He helped you put the new roof on the crib, and he left on Ground Hog Day. I remember him talking about seeing his shadow in the snow. So the storm was in January."

Somebody would get up then, and lift the pages of the calendars, and check the final authority. "It sure was in January, from the third to the fifth."

Nothing frivolous was recorded in those roomy date squares. Children did not write on calendars, no more than they wrote in the family Bible. Writing on the calendars was the province of family authorities only.

Some of the information was important to the operation of the farm. When the mare was bred. When the potatoes were planted. When the beehives were robbed. I remember a story about an old man, a neighbor who was alone, and farmed a little place to the west, and he died. The neighbors had not seen his chimney smoke for three days and they went to check and he was dead in the barn. So his brother came out from town to take care of the stock and see after the place. The old gent had such a detailed record of what he did and when he did it that the brother actually operated that farm, just the way it had always been run, by following the entries on the calendar.

Family illnesses were often recorded on calendars. They could go back six, seven years and see when Emily had the chicken pox or get the exact day that Ben fell out of the chinaberry tree and broke his arm. Births and deaths in the family were recorded in the Bible. But vital statistics on animals often went onto the calendars. You'd hear statements like this: "You see that old bald-faced cow yonder on the tank dam? She'll be eleven next April, and she's had a good heifer calf ever' spring of this world for eight straight years. I can show you on the calendars."

Calendar records are important to me yet. Without my calendar, how would I ever know five years from now that in the fall of '79 the date of the first frost in the back yard was November 14?

The only thing in the livestock line I associate with now is a miniature schnauzer who is creeping up on his fifteenth birthday. Which makes him old as Uncle Billy Crockett. Around a hundred, figuring seven person-years to each dog-year.

You understand I don't own one share of stock in this animal and don't care to. He merely visits me sometimes during the day when I am not on the road. But I like him well enough. He has one trick he does that I am fond of—he sleeps all the time. I am telling you, this is one slumbering schnauzer.

About the only thing that gets him out of the sack, not counting supper and the routine tours of the shrubbery, is a thunderstorm. So the last couple of days, when we have had these afternoon showers, this animal is way behind on his sleep. A thunderclap will lift him a yard off the floor. When he comes down, he begins digging a hole wherever he lands. He is a digger of non-holes, in places like hardwood floors and wall-to-wall carpet and kitchen tile.

It's sure a phenomenon to see him work so hard and long at digging a hole where a hole cannot be dug. When one of his non-holes gets deep enough to suit him, he crawls in it and makes a curve of himself and goes back to sleep. He'll feel secure for a while, until the thunder wakes him again. Then he'll rise up and dig the non-hole deeper, or move off to the side, stake a new location, and dig an entirely new one. I'm interested in this because his system of hiding in non-holes obviously works for this dog. He finds comfort and security in a hole that isn't there. At first I thought this was pretty stupid, but I've changed my mind. It's at least better than not finding comfort and security at all.

Most dogs I've been acquainted with across the years were the same as the schnauzer about thunder and lightning. I believe this is because they have an instinctive knowledge, that you and I don't have, of the awesome power that even small storms can exert. Maybe they know when it makes sense to be frightened.

Back when my kids were small, they coaxed a huge German shepherd into the yard and he took up with us. In summer he'd sleep on the back step. When a bolt of lightning flashed, he would yelp like a pup and get up and simply walk through the screen of the back door. He'd make a wedge of his nose and powerful shoulders and move the sofa away from the wall and disappear back there. You could depend that he'd stay until the fireworks were passed. You couldn't get him out of there with a pound of ground chuck.

Some dogs appear to grieve the coming of a storm, or suffer physical pain and rigors. I've seen mature hunting dogs, their courage many times proven in combat, cower when a small squall was coming in. One might run into the barn and point his nose at the rafters and mourn, producing the saddest, most plaintive howls.

A lot of humans react to storms in what looks to be a similar way. I bet I've heard this come out of fifty different people, recalling their parents or grandparents: "When a storm would come up in the middle of the night, my grandmother would get out of bed and dress fully and pace the floor, walking all over the house, until the wind died." Maybe a person like that simply has an extraordinary sensitivity to the events that take place in the atmosphere ahead of a storm. Some strange happenings precede storms.

I once watched one, and it sure was a mystery. One of my kids was seven years old, and about two o'clock on a summer afternoon he crawled up on his bed and fell asleep. That had never happened before, not in all his time. He just didn't go to sleep voluntarily during the day. He was classic hyper and it was a happy event when he went to sleep at a decent hour at night. But at two in the afternoon? No. Something had to be wrong. Must be sick, right? But he wasn't. Just lying up there all cool and composed, sleeping like a normal child. He slept without moving for two hours. When he woke up, we had a tornado. It's true. Tornado came walking right across the middle of town—this was up in Bryan—spinning houses and uprooting trees and lifting roofs and you can look it up in the record. That was in 1956.

I've always had a notion things like schnauzers digging nonholes and hounds singing mournful in the barn and hyper kids taking afternoon naps—such phenomena might be useful some way in weather forecasting. For years I said if that kid ever went to sleep again in daylight, I was heading for the storm cellar, but he never did, not until he got about eighteen. Then he began staying up all night and sleeping all day. But I don't think that had much to do with storms.

For some reason or other, lately I've been thinking about the time the Foster girls got trapped in the outdoor toilet. Actually there's not a whole lot to the story, nothing much happened, but as I grow older I see more significance in the event, I suppose because it has the distinction that it won't ever happen again.

The Foster girls had a younger brother in my room at school, a long time ago when we were all growing up out on the T&P west of Fort Worth. Sometimes he'd invite me to go home with him on Friday. That meant I'd stay two nights on the Foster farm, and then on Monday morning we'd go on back to school together.

On Sunday afternoon we'd go to church. It was common then for country people to have services in the afternoon instead of the morning. Mr. Foster had charge of opening up the church, which was just a little old shotgun frame building with a brush arbor by the side of it. We'd go early, and shove up all the windows and put sticks under 'em so they wouldn't blam down and make a bad racket when somebody was leading prayer or reading scripture.

Well, before the service the families were gathered out front, standing around talking and waiting for time, when this big cloud came up. I mean it was tough-looking, all dark and rolling, and it was in the northwest where cyclones came from. (Any strong wind we called a cyclone in those times, whether it was a rotating wind or not.)

The men, at least those who were heads of families and qualified to deliver opinions on clouds, got off to the side in a bunch and discussed what was going to happen and what ought to be done about it. Just like they could take a vote on whether to let it rain or not. Some thought the cloud would pass to the west of us, and some said, no, we're going to get rain and hail too, because the cloud's got a pink tinge.

I promise you it did rain. I don't know if I ever saw chunks begin to float any quicker. Everybody ran into the church and stood at the windows watching the storm. Blow? Mister, that was some kind of wind, bending trees and popping limbs and making that little frame church shudder all over.

The storm had been going on I guess five minutes when Mrs. Foster discovered her two girls had gone to the outdoor toilet just before the blow. And they hadn't got out in time, so there they were, trapped in the privy. (I have changed the family name here; I doubt the Fosters would be embarrassed after all this time, but they might.) I can remember the anxiety in the voices during the discussion of what to do about the Foster girls in the toilet. Should they be sent after, rescued? If they were they'd just get soaking, so why not just let 'em stay until the rain let up? Yes, but how about this wind? Can't you see that privy shaking in this wind? Mr. Foster made a decision. He decided to let the girls stay out there for the present, but if the wind got any higher he'd go and get 'em. Nobody argued, and it didn't occur to me until much later that if the wind got any higher the likelihood is the privy would have blown away and the girls with it.

It was anyway an hour before the rain let up. We had prayer and scripture in the church and the Foster girls stayed in the toilet. They said later on it wasn't too bad. Said the worst thing wasn't the storm but the spiders.

A dark afternoon, broody, the atmosphere heavy and hanging. There is rumbling in the north and west. So it's going to rain. A spring thundershower. There is no way it will fail to come. There are many kinds of threatening skies that never deliver rain, but not this one. Any first-grader on his way home from school could look at this sky and know to hurry on, that it's not fooling.

Reminds me of a place I knew long ago outside the old home town. We called it the cave, and sometimes when we were near it and a thundershower was dead-sure coming, we would go there and watch the show from the shelter of the cave.

It wasn't a cave, really. It was just a cleft in a rock face, a lateral fissure that had opened for reasons that a geologist could easily explain, if he saw the place. The mouth of it was about three feet high and it extended back into the rock only seven or eight feet and horizontally it ran probably ten feet, maybe less. And the interior of it was nice and honest. What I mean, it was free of cracks and holes and projections, so you could look into it and see in two seconds that nothing was in there to bother you. No snakes, or bad spiders, or bobcats, or skunks, or anything else that you wouldn't want to associate with. The top lip of the cave opening overhung the bottom one a bit, so you could lie on your stomach and cup your chin in your hands and prop up on your elbows and look out at a rainstorm. And be so close to it, without getting wet.

I doubt that little cave could be more than a mile and a half from the courthouse. It seemed way out in the wilderness when we were going there long ago. It was in a patch of woods where we did a lot of messing around. Not hunting. Just roving, and look-ing, and smelling, and tasting, and wondering, and talking of matters we didn't know a thing about. These were thin-soiled woods. Mesquite and scrub oak and a kind of elm we knew by an ugly name and by no other. Pecans along the creeks sometimes, and cottonwoods, and briars. And catclaw brush in the flats, and a bush we called chaparral. And lots of cactus, mostly prickly pear.

When the spring thundershowers would march across those

woods, we would break for the cave and line up and enjoy the excitement of what was to come. Everything reacted to the approaching wind and rain. The mourning doves flew in that fast, desperate style, as if the storm was nipping already at their tail feathers. Cattle would stop grazing—every patch of woods or brush was part of somebody's pasture—and point their noses at the rain cloud and walk nervously in little half circles. Over the tops of the mesquite we could see an old poor-boy ranch house. Women and girls would hurry out of it, to take clothes off the line and look back over their shoulders at the cloud, and trot to the door with their arms loaded. Once we saw a haying crew in a little meadow near that house and watched how they rushed against the rain, and shouted, and trotted the mules to the barn with a load, trying to get the hay in before the storm hit.

Young people now wouldn't be apt to find it worthwhile to watch such things. But this was our TV, and our movies, and we were able to see high drama in it. For example, from the mouth of that little cave I watched what I later saw, so many times, on motion picture film. I know you have seen it too, because the idea has fascinated filmmakers always. It has to do with rain coming to a dry land.

The cameraman first gives us a look at one large drop of rain—plop—hitting parched earth. Or—splash—he shows that first drop falling into an almost dried-up pond that has a calm surface, so the drop produces those concentric circles. Next he focuses on a single leaf that's getting peppered with drops, as the rain comes faster. Then we're shown three or four leaves, wet, with the water beginning to drip off their edges.

The camera follows the drops to the ground, shows them making dry dirt wet, shows them filling cracks, producing small puddles. Shows them spreading, joining, making tiny rivulets and streamlets, picking up speed, building into larger, bubbling bands of muddy water that melt clods and tumble pebbles, and fill gullies and small ditches and channels and creek branches and then creeks. Then boiling and foaming into rivers, and over waterfalls, and rapids, all turbulent and wild, and finally then, with the music booming and crashing, these millions of raindrops collected into a torrent pour back into the sea where they came from.

This exciting process, the early stages of it at least, we could see from that cave. And it always pleased me that moviemakers found out, later on, it was worth putting on film.

At this minute I am looking out the window into the back yard at home, and something plenty nervous is going on with the weather. I think a thunderstorm is wanting to take place, but it hasn't yet managed to happen. There is lightning and thunder and not much else. So this isn't a thunderstorm if you take the word of the American Heritage here on the desk. It says a thunderstorm has heavy rain.

There is no rain here, and the sky doesn't even threaten any. The cloud cover is solid as far as I can see, but it's light gray and not very thick. There is absolutely no wind. Not a whiff. But the air has that peculiar metallic smell that means a lot of electrical business is going on. Then once in a while—ka-pow!—a clap of thunder will pretty near move me out of this seat.

When I am talking to myself about it, I call this kind of weather a thunder-and-lightning storm, or a dry storm. When I'm close to one this way, I get awful edgy. I had ten times rather sit through a good honest storm with the wind whipping the trees and the rain flying horizontal. The threat of lightning doesn't seem so great then, when so much violence is already taking place.

Probably these dry thunder-and-lightning storms are common, and occur when most of us are shut away in air-conditioned buildings.

I hated the dry storms out on the South Plains when I was going to school long ago at Lubbock. Most buildings on the Texas Tech campus then were separated by great treeless expanses of real estate. Walking to class across one of those broad flats in a dry storm, you could get to feeling like a target. The smell of lightning would be all around, and nobody talked much as they walked along. They were waiting for the next ka-pow and hoping the bolt would hit the chemistry building instead of their noggins. Sometimes you would see students, and faculty as well, walking sort of humped over, wanting to pull their heads inside them the way a turtle can. Just like it wouldn't hurt as much when lightning struck if they weren't standing up straight. I did it myself, because I couldn't help it.

Then there's the summer I spent up in Swisher County in the Panhandle, mostly riding a tractor. On Saturday sometimes we'd go into Tulia or Amarillo. We'd get a paper and read where a tractor driver was struck by lightning while plowing on such-and-such a wheat ranch. It sure gave you a personal interest in the news.

That's when I learned to hate dry thunder-and-lightning storms the most. You'd pray for it to go ahead and rain, because then you could knock off and go to the house. But they wouldn't let you quit just because the weather got like it is right now—still, and overcast, and smelling of lightning. So you'd drone ahead, across that grain stubble, and—ka-pow!—you'd end up stretched across the steering wheel, trying to lower your profile. The odds on getting hit may have been pretty long, but they sure weren't as long as if you'd been in a forest with a lot of nice tall trees for lightning rods.

On those plains, the head of a guy riding a tractor was often the highest target on the landscape. There he'd go clodding away at one mile an hour, in the center of a 320-acre wheat field, and not a tree in sight that wouldn't be proud if you called it a bush. Bordering that 320-acre field on the east would be another 320-acre field precisely like it. And another on the south, the same as the west and north—320-acre fields as far as the land went. If you were working close to the house, you might be able to spot a windmill two miles off, the only other item on the surface of the planet that a streak of lightning would care anything about hitting.

The worst thing would be if you had read a little bit about lightning and how it loves tractors in empty fields. You would get to thinking you could hear the negative charge building up in the clouds above you, sizzling, looking for a courtship with something positive. Here would come the positive charge out of the earth, engulfing that tractor, creeping up your arms and legs and making your ears tingle and your hat tremble. And you felt so sure that inside the next thirty feet here would come the two charges slamming together, finding relief from their stress by melting a tractor in the middle of a 320-acre grain field.

Saturdays in town I would mention that feeling to other tractor drivers. Most of them thought I was overstating the danger, even when I would shove in front of them the obituary page out of the Amarillo *News-Globe* and point to the account of another tractor driver's funeral.

I never entirely recovered from plowing among all that thunder and lightning. About two years after that I was in Europe. People were shooting at each other over there then. Dropping bombs on towns, and firing anti-aircraft shells at planes passing over, just like in the movies. I used to ride with my eyes shut so I wouldn't see anything dreadful, and while I waited for the next explosion I would think, "Oh well, at least it's not any worse than riding a tractor across 320 acres of wheat stubble in Swisher County."

You hear people talk a lot about watching the weather, but it means something different than it used to. Now they mean they watch the weather report on television. Watching the weather once meant standing outdoors and looking at the sky and trying to figure out when a norther or a thunderstorm was going to hit, and how bad it would be when it did.

Once in a while, driving through the country, I'll see somebody standing on the front porch looking at the sky. But it's not common any longer. I suppose they figure they can tell more about what's coming now by keeping up with the TV weathercaster's radar. It was once mighty important, to a great many enterprises, for people to look at the sky and make a good guess about what the weather was fixing to do. Sure, it's still important, but we have so much help now from the weather forecasters that sky-watching is not practiced as a skill the way it once was.

The other morning I was talking to A. A. Callihan, lives down at Freeport, about watching the weather, and the matter of blue northers came up. Callihan has a good deal to say about blue northers. He says the term is widely misused now in newspapers and on television weather programs, and I think he is right. At least it is not being used in its traditional sense. It now seems to mean just a severe cold front. Callihan says the reason a blue norther was first called blue is that its most awesome feature is visual.

He argues that to experience a blue norther and appreciate it fully, you've got to be out on a prairie where you can see for miles. He insists there's no way to see one if you're in a city or in hilly or in timbered country. Callihan grew up on prairie, where he could look out the back door and see halfway to town. No, not out in West Texas. Right there on the coast prairie in Brazoria County, at Liverpool. Lot of West Texas folks imagine they've got the market sewed up on flat land. But I don't know where you would go to find land any closer to dead flat than this coast prairie.

Anyhow, Callihan wrote out for me his description of a blue norther. Here is a part of it: "The classic setting is a mild, sunshiny day, with a gentle breeze from any direction other than north or west. The first sign is a low dark streak on the north or northwest horizon. It rises rapidly, with upper cloud layers soon obscuring the sun. At that stage, a closer look in the direction from which it is coming will reveal an ominous, low-hanging roll of blue-black clouds, spanning the horizon. The lower edge appears to drag the ground, tumbling toward the observer. There is no lightning or thunder—only a dead calm immediately preceding the impact. Usually there is no rain with the first onslaught, but the wind is gusty, and the clouds writhe and seem to be just overhead, and loose things tumble on the ground. It's as if a refrigerator door has been jerked open."

Yeah, well, I've watched a flock of northers like that, out in the west part of the state. To me the most impressive thing was that you didn't know anything spectacular was about to happen until you looked up and saw it barreling down on you. But now, a real blue norther will be tracked by the weather people from the time it's still passing polar bears, and Mexicans in Tampico will be watching it on TV while it sails over Lake Winnipeg.

All this talk about northers, here in the spring, may not sound too timely. But Easter is still two weeks off. According to tradition, we could still have a blue norther. The old Easter Spell, that is. The greatest believer in the Easter Spell I ever knew was my own mother. She began talking about it the first of March, and if the weather did turn up wet and cold near Easter, it seemed to please her. If it *didn't* happen, she was disappointed. And she mistrusted sunshine on Easter morning, if we hadn't already had something that passed for the Easter Spell. Easter Sunday could come in shimmering and bright with sunshine so beautiful it seemed enough to resurrect all twelve apostles and Moses to preach. But if we hadn't had the Easter Spell, she would stand at the window and study the sky, just as if the Spell was lurking right yonder under the horizon, and would come whistling in and put out the sun before church.

The world was so small then, when people watched the sky that way. On weather, it wasn't any bigger than as far as they could see.

3

*"We didn't have to spell it.
We just had to do it."*
TOM TYLER

My idea of something worth doing is to sit in a comfortable seat, in surroundings pleasant and quiet, and listen to a friend talk about what he loves—such as a person, or a place he once knew, or an event that marked his life long ago and glows bright in his memory. So it was good to visit with Phil Weathers, up on the Colorado at Kingsland. From Phil's front door you could throw a rock with a sore arm and hit the river. We sat and watched the water and I got Phil talking about his father, Seab Weathers, who was a farmer in McLennan County when Phil was a boy. They lived near Mart, out east of Waco. He's talking here about the 1920s and 1930s:

"You know how mules and cows get the colic, usually in the spring from eating so much green grass. Nearly every year we'd have a mule catch the colic. My dad would tie a knot in the mule's tail, and then wrap the knot around with binder twine so it wouldn't come out. When I was a kid I helped him do that, but I never thought much about it until I got older. One time we had a vet come to our place, and he had a colored boy with him, and he had the boy put a halter on our mule that had colic and walk him around and around. I told the vet about my Dad tying the knot in the mule's tail and asked him if that wasn't just a superstition, and he said no. He said, 'You see that boy out there walking that mule? Reason I'm doing that is to keep the mule moving, because if you let him lie down or lean up against the barn he'll die. He works that gas off, moving that way. Your dad tying that knot made the mule uncomfortable and restless and he kept moving, and it's the same thing.' Well, I don't know whether my Dad knew why the knot helped or not. I guess he saw his own dad do it."

Phil Weathers spent a good many years in oil fields, and a good many more in an oil company office building in Houston. He and his wife, Ruth, are now in this pretty house there on the river bank, gardening and doing the country scene. They say they work hard, but it looks like pretty soft living to me. I've noticed this, that when a man gets it all made and sits down in whatever shade he's picked, what he likes to talk and think about are times past, when things were tough.

"We lived about three and a half miles out of Mart, toward Battle," Phil said, leaning back in his big soft chair. "We were right on the edge of East Texas. We called McClennan County Central Texas. We would talk about East Texas folks. We considered that East Texas began about Mexia (about twenty-five miles away). When you went to Mexia you went to East Texas. We were tenant farmers. When I was seven years old my dad put me on an old wiggle-tail cultivator, and I worked in the field until I left home."

Phil's father was a high-tempered Irishman who had some curious habits: "He always carried a big old stock knife with a bore on it for punching leather. He had a way of timing when a sow would have pigs. When the sow got bred, my Dad would take that knife and bore a little hole in his thumb nail, down to the quick, at the base of the nail. Then when the nail grew out to where he could comfortably trim it off (trim off the hole, that is), he knew the pigs were due and he'd start keeping the sow up . . .

"Another thing he did that always interested me. He'd go around the wash pot and different places on the farm and pick up rusty nails and put 'em in a fruit jar and pour vinegar on 'em, and let 'em set for two or three weeks. Then he'd take a dish rag and strain the liquid off those nails, and every day he'd drink about half a cup of that. Said it was to get iron, that he got iron out of those nails . . .

"He always kept a half-gallon fruit jar of Black Draught tea, and no matter what your ailment was you got a dose of that tea, and it was sure awful . . ."

Seab Weathers had this explosive temper. One time Phil saw him get mad at an old Oakland sedan he was working on and take a sledge hammer and pound the engine "until there wasn't a piece of it left big as your hand." Then this: "He gave me some fearful whippings. But I never held it against him because some way or other, without really saying it, he'd always tell me he was sorry."

We talked about country religion, in the twenties and thirties, how adults used to put such withering pressures on children to "join the church." I can't help resenting that, even now. Phil told this one out of his own boyhood: "I was about ten, I guess, there at Mart. We used to have camp meetings, the Methodists and the Baptists. We went to the Baptist. They'd try at those revivals to get all the young ones converted. I was holding out. Everybody in my Sunday-school class had been converted but me. At the revivals they'd give that—well, what Billy Graham does, that just-one-more-chance, that play-another-verse, that I-know-somebody-out-there's-just-hanging-on-the-edge. Then's when the Sunday-school teachers and the leading church women would catch a holdout. They'd come over to your pew and start working on you.

"They were working on me and my sister Johnnie. She was four years older than me. Johnnie was always ashamed of me, because I was ragged and dirty and generally raising hell, and in town she wouldn't recognize me, didn't want anybody to know she was kin to me. (Grinning at the memory of that.) Well, at the revival one of the church women had a hold of me. She took me by the arm and she said, 'Looka there, looka there, there goes your sister.' (It was Johnnie, walking down the aisle to join up.) She's saved, and here you are, the only one left in your family.' Well, that did it, for me, seeing Johnnie go down that sawdust trail. It's an emotional thing, you know. They get you all worked up.

"Johnnie hadn't any more than sat down good than here I came, and they sat me down right beside her. She had her head bowed but she kinda turned and saw it was me. Well, of course she didn't want to be associated with me there, and figured I'd just followed her, which in fact I had. Anyway she reached back of that pew—Johnnie always had good fingernails—and she got a big pinch of my tail, about an inch of it, and I came up out of that seat, and hollered, and everybody thought it was religion. I guess they said, 'Boy, he's really got it now.'" So that's how Phil joined the church, and I expect a multitude of other Texans, of many denominations, had similar experiences in that brush-arbor revival era.

"Funny thing," Phil said. "Later on, when we got older, Johnnie and I were real close."

We got onto country schools. There's the tendency to remember country schools from half a century ago as pretty dull places. "When I was about seventeen we moved to Delia (up toward Coolidge, a few miles west of Mexia). Mart had a good school, but Delia was a little old country place and the school had ten grades and four teachers and it was pretty backward.

"I remember a history teacher there talking about George Washington and he made the remark, 'Hit didn't make no differents to Warshington.' Well, I passed a few words about Delia being a backward school compared to Mart, and the superintendent heard about it, and jumped me. And I sassed him. I forget what I said, but I sassed him. In those days, all you had to do was get out of line a little bit and they just slapped hell out of you. I'd seen two or three of 'em get slapped that way.

"He (the superintendent) walked over to me, and raised back (his hand). Well, I was riding a horse to school, and to keep from getting my spurs stolen I'd carry 'em in the room and hang 'em up under my desk. When the superintendent started over to me, I took one of those spurs and ran the shank up through my hand and when he drew back, I came out of that desk and I roweled that SOB from here clean to there. Blood spurted out of his head. I ran out and got on my horse and went home . . ."

Phil went back and graduated from that school, but not until after it had a new superintendent. He received his diploma under the following circumstance: "I never had any patience for any kind of arithmetic. Too damn iron-headed to learn it. One day (when all he had to do to graduate was pass the courses he was taking) I was crossing the Navasota River on a horse and I had an old geometry book strapped on the saddle. I said, hell, I didn't have any use for that, and I just threw the book in the river. That geometry teacher told me (when the book showed up missing that way), 'Well, it's just so hard on the taxpayers for you to come back to school, and you're not gonna learn anything nohow, I'm gonna give you credit in geometry.'" So Phil became a Delia School graduate with his three classmates.

Here's another incident about Phil's father: "There at Delia, there was a fellow named Jenkins had a good bull. Of course we were on a party line, the same as everybody else out in the country. My dad had a cow in heat and wanted to talk to Mr. Jenkins about breeding her, so he called on the telephone. In those days, around women, you didn't say 'bull,' you said 'male.' Well, Dad said 'bull' on the phone. Old Miz Scott had fallen and broken her hip and was in a wheel chair, and all she did was listen in on the party line. She broke in and she said, 'Mr. Weathers, you ought to know better than to use language like that on the telephone. You said a wrong word.' And you know, the funny thing about it to me was, he apologized. Instead of telling her to go to hell and get off the line, he apologized."

My Aunt Minnie Hale lives in Fort Worth. Next August 14 she'll be ninety-one. I believe she's my oldest kin now. All my life, when I thought of a pioneer Texas woman, I pictured Aunt Minnie. She was small but strong (she weighs 110 now), she worked hard, and wore her hair combed straight back and done into a knot at the back. She still wears it that way.

She is the widow of my Uncle George Hale, who was a constable and deputy sheriff at Thurber, a little coal-mining town out west of Fort Worth. I went to see her this past week and put a tape recorder in front of her and she talked for two hours. I thought maybe you'd be interested in a few of the things she said. Here she is on how she met Uncle George:

"Well, I met him out at Number 8. You know Number 8 mine, west of Thurber? That's where Grandma Hale lived when I was about ten years old (in about 1894). We went to Strawn to school. George drove the buggy that we went to school in. He was four years older than me. My family got the buggy and Grandma Hale furnished the horse, because she wanted George to go to school. So that was the first time I met him . . . "

Aunt Minnie's family name was Cox. Later the Coxes and the Hales lived on farms near Gordon, close to the Palo Pinto–Erath county line, and all the children went to a country school called Fitzgerald. It didn't even have grades. Students just went there until they quit, usually when they got married. Aunt Minnie talked about spelling bees held at Fitzgerald and about studying "high history." She said high history was United States history.

In about 1898, Aunt Minnie and George Hale got married. "Well, we run away and got married. Just run away. We went to Stephenville (about thirty-five miles). We traveled all night. Two or three other couples went with us. The next morning we went to the courthouse in Stephenville and got a license and got married. I was going on fifteen . . . You talk about your honeymoon (laughing at this memory): We got back from Stephenville on Monday evening. Tuesday morning we went to the cotton patch and picked cotton . . ."

That was on the old Hale farm where my father grew up. Uncle George brought Aunt Minnie into a small farmhouse that had eight sons and daughters in it. I'm not sure they were all at home then, though. One of the children was my father, Fred, two years younger than Aunt Minnie. What she remembers best about him is that at school, he was always dancing.

Aunt Minnie and Uncle George farmed a while and then moved to Thurber and went to work, as everybody at Thurber did, for "the TP." That's the Texas Pacific Coal Company. The name was later changed to the Texas Pacific Coal and Oil Company. That outfit owned everything at Thurber. It owned the house Aunt Minnie and Uncle George lived in. I used to be taken there on visits. A fine place. Full of good smells. It had a picket fence. The yard was hard dirt swept clean as the kitchen floor. A branch full of crawdads was close by. I always loved to go to Aunt Minnie's. She had a dog named Penny.

Her three children were born in that house and her husband died there before he was fifty. Aunt Minnie lives now with her daughter Gertrude Willet. "When I had Gertrude," she told me, "I was sick in bed with the measles. Gertrude had them too. Had the measles when she was born . . ."

I've always thought of Thurber as a pretty tough town, in its early times. Aunt Minnie doesn't think of it as tough, though. Said Uncle George, as a peace officer, never shot anybody or got shot at. "I never did think of locking up my house at Thurber," she said. "But, my land, you sure better lock up here now."

Aunt Minnie's got some arthritis and some eye problems and some hearing difficulty, but overall, I'd say her health is remarkable. She talked about it: "I said I thought my age, and me alivin' as long as I have, was due to a lot of my outdoor work. I always worked in the garden, and we raised chickens and turkeys and milked cows. I had three cows to milk sometimes and I tended to 'em myself . . .

"When I was sixty-five I developed this arthritis in my hands. It began to get pretty bad. The joints got big. Doctor said well, there's not anything we can do about that. That'll just have to go to your grave with you. He said probably I'd get to where I couldn't use my hands. He said, 'I don't see how you milk a cow.' I said, 'Well, I do.'

"I couldn't get my hands together, like this (closing her fists). But I can now, and I did it by keepin' aworkin'. I'd milk cows this way (with thumb and forefinger), sort of strip 'em. A lot of the time when my hands hurt so bad, I'd keep 'em in a pan of real hot water with epsom salts and a rubber ball, and I'd squeeze that ball . . ."

She kept milking cows until she was seventy-five. Her son Harvey—she always lived with Harvey after Uncle George died —Harvey moved away to Denver City and Aunt Minnie left Thurber and got a house in Strawn, where she "kept on aworkin'. I had the awfulest yard there. A big lot that was full of these old sand burs. I told Harvey—he was here yesterday—I told him I fought those sand burs for three years, just dig 'em up in big piles and let 'em dry out and burn 'em. And when I left Strawn, I had a pretty yard. For about a year I mowed that yard myself, with a push mower. Then I hired me a man to do it. I was eighty, and didn't mow after that . . ."

From Strawn Aunt Minnie went to Gertrude's in Fort Worth where she lives now. She's been sick but she battles back. She's even come back from a broken hip that put her into a walker.

"I never was in a hospital in my life until I broke my hip, be three years ago in June. When I fell I had tomatoes this big, and ripe, in a garden out here behind Gertrude's garage. (She was eighty-seven then.) But now I can't even wash dishes. I get kind of blue sometimes when I feel so bad, but I like to watch my TV programs, and all the newscasts. I want to know what's going on. And I've got some pretty African violets I take care of . . ."

About the state of the world's affairs: "It's pretty bad. I just don't know what to think, hardly. The war in Vietnam, and Cambodia, it's been terrible . . ." Aunt Minnie stayed with the Watergate TV hearings down to the last witness, and thinks Watergate is the worst thing that's ever happened in American politics in her time. Her opinion of John Connally: "I think he was a good governor, but for him to turn and go with the Nixons, I said I bet he wished he'd stayed away from the Nixons . . ."

A relative came in and brought Aunt Minnie a little glass of wine, and she sipped and said, "I got to reading about some country where people drink wine with their meals, and there was some of 'em 106 and 107 that was still aworkin' ever day. And there was some that lived to be 140 years old. (Laughing now.) I said though I didn't want any of that . . ."

Her big trip: "In May, before I fell in June and broke my hip, I went to Houston and went to the Astrodome. It's something awful nice to look at . . ."

And finally, her great regret: "I can't garden. I can't get out and dig. It sure does make me feel bad, to look out and see so much that needs to be done."

At Wharton I went to see Tom Tyler, and we talked a long time in his little two-room house at the edge of town. That house tells a lot about the man who lives there. It has a pickup and a trailer at the front door, and a dog tied to the porch post. What you'd call the yard is fenced off for a horse, which has a shed out back pretty near as big as the house. It's a bachelor's camp, and no mistake. Not a frill anywhere. Tyler's wife has been dead since 1934. He has spent his time on ranches and roughnecking in the oil fields. He's a big, friendly grinning fellow, still looking strong. He was born in 1902.

"I tell 'em I'm forty past," he said, grinning at me from the foot of his high bed where he sat. "It's like these fellows will tell you a horse is six, seven years past. But they don't tell you how much past."

What Tyler loves most is "bein' ahorseback." He still gets ahorseback sometimes and picks up a day's work cowboying on a ranch somewhere. Used to keep leopard dogs and hunt wild cattle for Wharton County ranchers. But that's rank work, and not for a fellow past seventy with a little heart problem and a bum knee.

Right away the conversation settled on horses and mules, and Tyler talked about Old Kit, a mule his father owned up in Hill County long ago: "Papa's business was hauling freight from the depot to the stores, at Hubbard (near Waco). Every morning he'd hook Old Kit to a little two-wheel cart and take her to work with him. They'd use her sometimes for light hauling.

"She'd always come home for dinner, by herself. Then she'd go back to town and park in those big cottonwoods between the depot and the hotel. She'd stay till quitting time. Then she'd come home, and somebody would put the barrel on the cart and Kit would go to town again and back the cart up to the door of the hotel, and the cooks would pour the slop in the barrel. Then she'd come on home and bring that slop for the hogs. She did that every day. Finally the city council up there voted Kit free. Free, to roam around town, and nobody bother her."

Tom Tyler broke his first pony when he was ten. He's still got a picture of it. When he was maybe thirteen, one day his father put him on a mean green horse and let him get a lesson in how to survive, by being tough and not quitting. "That horse throwed me, saddle and all, high as a telephone pole. I'd be alayin' there on the ground and Papa would come up and say, 'What you layin' down there for, boy? You ain't gonna learn nothin' layin' down there.' So I'd get up, and get back on. By the time Papa died, I had that old horse pretty well rode out."

Tyler's father spent six weeks in a Waco hospital and died, in 1916. Tom wasn't yet fourteen. He went to work. He got work plowing, and hauling. He'd haul cotton from the gin to the depot, and load it in box cars. He could handle mules, and he was strong.

"When I was fourteen I'd take four mules and go to the gin at Eldorado and get in the seed house—be hot as a burnin' stump in that house—and I'd load up about a ton and a half of cottonseed and haul it to the oil mill at Dawson, and scoop it all off. Then I'd go home to supper, and then I'd take my weights back, and get my check." And so that way and other ways, as so many country boys did when their fathers died early, Tyler helped his mother "pay off the place."

By the time he was sixteen he was six feet tall and could pull his hat over his face and walk into a saloon and drink whiskey with the men. One day he was getting half a day's work on a road-building crew up in Limestone County. The gang could look over yonder and see a drilling rig on the horizon. "That was the discovery well in the Mexia field," Tyler said. He drifted into oil field work and never entirely left it until he got to having too many birthdays. From Mexia he made the rounds of the oil patches—Luling, Mirando City, Cross Plains, Orange—pretty well all over the state. Even did a little drilling, on small rigs and shallow holes.

The conversation worked around to fighting somehow. You've heard, I guess, that roughnecks are known to throw a few punches on appropriate occasions. "I never did enjoy fighting but it didn't bother me, either." Tyler made that remark without expression, just like a boy might be stating his position on eating spinach.

"I worked for a driller one time named Charlie Grider. On the rig, every time I'd pass by Charlie I'd hit him, just hard as I could. I'd hit him here, on the shoulder, and try to knock him down. He'd do the same to me. Charlie would hit. He'd knock me winding."

Grider had a rule that a crew member couldn't quit while angry. He would fight to enforce it. "Maybe a fellow would get mad about something on the job and threaten to quit. Charlie would tell him no, he wasn't going to quit mad. Then they'd go off and fight about it. After a while they'd come back and go to work. At the end of the day Charlie would tell the fellow, 'All right, now you're calmed down. If you still want to quit, you can.'" Usually he wouldn't.

Tyler said the worst he was ever hurt fighting was by a girl, back in Central Texas when he was young. A bunch was walking home from school, and Tyler and another boy got in a scrap. "His sister was there," Tyler told me, and rubbed the back of his head. "She had a Good Luck Baking Powder bucket she carried her lunch in, and she hit me on the head with the edge of that bucket, and it sure hurt."

Tyler's got some mossy memories of the oil fields, and he talked about them some. For example, about fishing for a string of almost 3,000 feet of drill pipe that'd been dropped in the hole back when those wooden derricks weren't always strong as they needed to be. So they'd move the controls, the throttle and the reverse lever, way out here maybe 75 feet from the rig so they wouldn't get hurt if the derrick collapsed, and they'd have the derrick sway-braced, and wind-legged, and they'd have a luff line rigged and . . . I stopped him to ask how to spell *luff*. He looked at me real level and said, "I don't know. We didn't have to spell it. We just had to do it." That quote may say a lot about Tyler and Texans of his pattern. It may state their values: If they have a choice, they'd rather be doers than spellers.

Tyler's been around Wharton since the middle thirties, in the oil fields, and "doin' things ahorseback" on ranches. He still hankers to get up every morning and ride out. I wondered if he ever just rides for pleasure, say along the road there near his home. I felt a sadness in his answer: "No, I'd like to, but the traffic's too bad. You go out on these highways ahorseback and they'll run over you."

"ALL UH-BO-O-OH-ARD! The Texas Eagle, northbound Missouri Pacific train . . . for Conroe . . . Phelps . . . Huntsville . . . Lovelady . . . Jacksonville . . . Longview . . . Texarkana . . . Hot Springs . . . Memphis . . . St. Louis . . . Chicago . . . and New York. All uh-bo-o-oh-ARD!"

That's Willie A. Stewart, calling a train the way he used to do in the lobby of Union Station, at Texas and Crawford. Stewart was a train caller for thirty years, until 1961.

One of the first things I learned to love about this city was going to Union Station and sitting in that lobby, which seemed so cavernous then, and hearing the train caller. I remember Willie Stewart and I remember the late Charley Denman, who called at Union before Stewart did.

Denman's song was sure musical. It had the sing-song quality of a New Orleans street vendor, and I worshiped the sound of it, even though the station names were sometimes hard to hear. Stewart came along in Denman's path and drew immediate praise for his beautiful baritone voice and his good enunciation. People could understand the stations he called and he kept calling thirty years and that's all he did, for Houston Belt & Terminal Railroad, was call those trains.

Before sound systems were installed in railroad passenger terminals, the train caller was a showman and an attraction. Generally he was a black man with a distinguished look about him. He'd stand out in the middle of the lobby floor and perform as if he were on stage.

A few months ago I wondered if any of those train callers were still around in Houston, and Maurice Higginbotham found Willie Stewart for me. Higginbotham works for Houston Belt & Terminal and he knew Albert Evans, also a HB&T employee, who happens to be Stewart's nephew. So we ended up in Stewart's living room on Arbor Street in the southeast part of town. I took a recorder so we could get Willie Stewart calling a train one more time. I hate to see fine old sounds like that disappear.

Stewart said he hadn't called since he retired, after a heart attack, in '61. But without even tuning up (unless he did it before we got there) he called the Texas Eagle, and it was so beautiful.

Look, here's a man who went to work at Union Station as a redcap in 1921, when he was fifteen. Is he doing all right? I guess so. One reason it took us so long to find him, he was down in Miami on a wedding trip.

Here he is again, calling a different train: *"All uh-bo-o-oh-ARD! The Texas Chief, northbound Santa Fe train . . . for Richmond . . .*

Rosenberg . . . Sealy . . . Bellville . . . Fort Worth . . . Gainesville . . . Oklahoma City . . . Topeka . . . Kansas City . . . and Chicago. 'BOARD!"

When Stewart retired in '61, he began another career as a businessman. Coin-operated laundry. Obviously he has done mighty well, and come a great distance from being a redcap at Union Station, carrying a bag for a dime. Been around the world twice. Traveled over Europe. Sailed on the *Queen Mary II.*

He's studied trains from Houston to the Orient. "I've always been fascinated by trains. I've ridden fine trains in other parts of the world. I don't know why we can't keep our trains over here. I think it's pathetic." Stewart told us one of the most exciting places he's ever seen is Houston's Union Station, when he was a boy. Trains going and coming from all over the country. New York. Chicago. Denver.

"That building itself was beautiful to me," he said. "And the acoustics seemed especially suited to my voice. Once they put a sound system in, but it wasn't satisfactory except when I would speak over it. So they took it out. They said they already had a sound system." A Willie Stewart sound system, that is.

Something I remember about Stewart, and Charley Denman as well, was that they couldn't be rattled. A smart-alec boy could take a stance in front of Stewart while he was calling, and the boy would make faces, and dance jigs, and get no notice whatever from the caller. Not just boys. Adults, too, even railway employees, would walk up to Stewart while he was performing and wave their hands before his eyes and ask questions and try to distract him. He'd just keep on calling, as if they weren't in the world.

If train callers are still working, except on public address systems, Willie Stewart doesn't know where to go hear them. Before we left his house I asked him to call one more train into the recorder. The final train call, maybe, who knows?

"All uh-bo-o-oh-ARD! For the Texas Zephyr, Burlington–Rock Island northbound train. For Teague . . . Corsicana . . . Waxahachie . . . Fort Worth . . . Dalhart . . . Colorado Springs . . . and Denver. 'BOARD! Last call!"

"No, I didn't build this mill for profit," Lorenza Driver said. "I'll never live long enough to get my money out of it. I built it because serp making draws a lot of company, and we love that." At that moment he ought to have been happy, then. Because the rain had stopped and a fire was swooshing beneath his syrup pans and the cane juice was bubbling and that sweet steam rising up, and I guess a hundred folks or more had come to watch Lorenza Driver make syrup.

Driver is a tall and thin man, with big round gentle eyes and a friendly little grin for everybody. He lives in the Odell community of Angelina County, out east of Lufkin and Huntington toward Sam Rayburn Lake. And that's where his syrup mill is. The day I was there, Driver and his helpers were making syrup from a cane crop raised by H. D. Matthews, who lives a little way west of Lufkin. He was firing the pit while his cane juice was being cooked.

I hadn't been to a country syrup making in a long time. Back during the fifties and sixties I thought syrup mills were going to pass completely out of the rural Texas scene. But now they've made a comeback. When I was at Driver's I heard of four mills in Angelina County alone. Some say the reason for this is the high cost of sugar, but my guess would be a greater influence is this strong interest in old-fashioned things that has lately spread over the entire nation.

For country folks, going to the syrup mill was once a sort of adventure. The children always wanted to ride along when their folks hauled cane to the mill. It was an exciting, sweet-smelling place, and the young ones would get to drink some of that cane juice, and it was good.

Syrup making has not changed a lot from the way I remember it. The main way is the source of power. Driver's mill—that is, the machinery that squeezes the juice out of the cane—is run by the power takeoff on a big tractor. The old mills were mule-powered, like the early hay balers.

Everything else is pretty much the same. You need a lot of help to make syrup. Especially skimmers. When the juice bubbles out of the mill, a lot of green scummy-looking stuff is on it, and this needs to be skimmed off. You always have four or five folks standing around with skimmers, dipping and shaking. The skimmings are generally fed to livestock. The old syrup makers used to keep hogs to eat the skimmings. When that stuff would ferment, those hogs would sometimes get wobble-legged drunk on it. Maybe you've heard the old saying, "Drunk as a syrup-mill hog." Driver feeds his skimmings to his cows. They stand at the fence and fight one another for it.

A syrup-making setup comes in two basic parts. The mill where the cane is juiced, and then the pit and the pan where the juice is cooked. From the road I expect Driver's setup is mistaken for a barbecue pit sometimes.

Making syrup is a simple process, but you've got to have at least one man on the job who really knows what he's doing. He'll be the one on the plug. That is, he is standing at the low end of the pan, and he decides when a batch is ready to run off, and he pulls the plug to let the finished syrup drain out.

The cooking pan is long and narrow and has a baffled bottom to guide the flow of the juice. Raw juice goes in the high end and moves slowly through the maze of baffles, cooking all the way, giving off clouds of steam. The syrup maker decides by color and consistency when it's time to pull the plug. Good ones always have long experience behind them, and are highly respected for their skill. Driver told me, "I've been foolin' with serp a long time. I imagine forty years." When it comes out of the cooker, the syrup is strained through burlap into a tub. Then the bucket brigade comes in and pours the finished product into syrup cans.

So all you do in making syrup this way is to cook just the proper amount of water out of the juice. Nothing is added. Quality of the syrup depends on the quality of the cane and the skill of the syrup maker.

I had a little visit with Matthews, who raised the cane being processed. "This is Cuban sugar cane," he said. "For makin' serp I put it above all the old Texas ribbon canes that there are. It'll give you a better yield and make you a better serp."

Only thing Matthews will use to fertilize his syrup cane is cottonseed meal. He won't put commercial fertilizer on it. "I don't want any kind of nitrates on my cane. It'll ruin your syrup. Make it so strong it'll burn your mouth."

There are certain little threats to a person's health that it's good to know about when you go to a syrup mill. One, you can get stung. Bees are always hanging around syrup mills. Or you can get your hands burned trying to pick up a harmless-looking bucket of fresh syrup. Mister, that can stays hot a long time. Or you can get sick, from drinking too much cane juice. Satan himself couldn't devise a more desperate nausea than a country boy can suffer under these conditions: He's already sick from that juice, and now he's got to ride home five miles over rough road in the bed of a steel-tired wagon.

I stayed at the mill until Driver ran off a batch or two and called Matthews up to the peg for a tasting. They each dipped a finger into a cooled sample, and stood tasting and smacking and looking at one another, and then Matthews said, "Now that's good serp."

Driver nodded. "I think so," he said.

This past week I spent some time along Farm Road 1725, in that Sam Houston National Forest area of San Jacinto County, and I had a little visit with Arthur ("Skinny") Boyd. I'd heard that Boyd lives alone in an interesting old house back in the woods. So I went to see, because I like country houses where a man has lived by himself a long time. Nearly always such houses take on character that you won't find in a home where you have women to keep things clean and straight.

I'd heard also that you want to be careful how you walk up to Boyd's house, because he keeps mean dogs. So I didn't go in the yard until Boyd came out and said it was all right.

Here came a dog, just asailing, a sweet-faced little border collie bitch, black and white, wearing a small cowbell on her collar. "Come on in here!" Boyd shouted from the porch. No dogs in sight except the collie, who wagged and rang her bell and said it was all right to get out.

The house is frame and unpainted and looks old. A dog run separates its main parts. A porch all the way across the front. Close to one end, a well with a new rope in the pulley and a foot-valve bucket hanging alongside. Chickens everywhere. Gamey-looking birds, mostly black. Droppings on the ground indicated the chickens roosted in the cedars by the front fence. One old hen stood on the porch steps and looked out, her neck stretched to see who was coming.

Boyd sat on the battered couch on the front porch in bright sunlight. He said he'd been there most of his life in that house, "and I'm still here, with the help of the Lord and a few of the women. I'm not a bit over 200 years old." Laughing a bit, at his little spoof. A tall man, with dry pink skin, coarse gray hair standing at attention, thin face, sharp features, and the palest blue eyes. Wore work shoes and blue cotton pants and two flannel shirts, both buttoned at the neck. Chewing tobacco, and spitting into an empty green bean can.

"No, I haven't got the bad dogs anymore," he said, talking loud. "This collie is the only dog I ever owned in my life that wouldn't fasten onto a man. I always had old cur dogs, stock dogs, mister, and they were so mean they'd even bite *me*." He never did say what happened to the mean dogs.

Granny Boyd. You still hear Granny Boyd's name mentioned in Cleveland stores. She was Skinny Boyd's mother, known and talked about as a salty Piney Woods pioneer-type woman who knew how to milk a kicking cow. Who was still making thread on a hand-carved spinning wheel long after spinning wheels were museum pieces. "Mama's been gone now twenty-five years," Boyd said.

53

Is it true, as I heard, that Granny Boyd's spinning wheel is still in that old house, and that its spindle holds thread she was making when she died? Boyd said it's true. Then he got off on how he traded a glass nest egg to a feed store man in Cleveland for that new well rope. It was an antique nest egg, one that didn't have a hole in it. Boyd said you can't find new nest eggs made without the hole. He still has one of the old types, and got up and went into the dog run to get it.

Country bachelors always produce the most marvelous clutter on their front porches. Boyd's has two refrigerators. That old couch with a mosquito net hanging in a frame above. A fifty-five gallon oil drum. A sick baby chick in a pie pan. Iron skillets and pots hanging from rusty nails. A stack of stove wood. A rickety wash stand propped up with a hickory pole.

Boyd got the nest egg out of the dog run and showed it. Several nests for his hens are fixed in cardboard boxes there in the dog run. "Sometimes chicken snakes come up on the porch after the eggs. Pole cats, too."

Suddenly the collie exploded and streaked out of the yard down to the gate, her cowbell jangling, and Boyd stepped to the edge of the porch and watched and yelled, urging her on. "It may be a fox," he said, "or a wolf. Something bothering the chickens."

I asked why the bell on the dog. "She's trained for taking care of chickens," Boyd said, "and that bell scares wolves. Wolves don't seem afraid of the dog, but that bell seems to run 'em off."

The old part of the house was built in 1909. Boyd's bedroom is in that part. He opened the door and we went in. You talk about austere living. An iron bed. A wood stove. A table with a kerosene lamp. An old rocker and a straight chair with a rope seat. Two calendars on the wall. "I've done a little of everything," Boyd was saying. "I've sawmilled. Railroaded. Made ties. Hauled ties. Raised cows, and hogs . . ."

Granny Boyd's spinning wheel is in a smaller room adjoining Boyd's bedroom. We looked at it in the gloom, the half darkness, and it was strange, Boyd standing there showing how his mother turned the big wheel with one hand and fed the cotton to the spindle. Thread she made is there, all right, on the spindle. Boyd said she loved to crochet with the thread that came off that old spinning wheel. "That's Mama's room over there," he told me, indicating a closed door the other side of the dog run. "I don't ever go in it."

Before I left I asked Boyd to let me watch him draw a bucket of water out of his well. I wanted to see that foot-valve bucket work. It doesn't look anything like a bucket. It's more like a three-foot length of downspout off a rain gutter. You let 'er down and sort of bounce it on the water's surface, to open the valve and admit the water. Then the water's weight closes the valve as you draw the bucket up. Finally you have to jerk a wire in the top of the bucket that opens the valve and out comes the water into the trough or whatever container you're filling. I remember when country folks who had such a well bucket were considered prosperous. Because it meant they had a machine-bored well, instead of a jug well or a hand-dug well. Or a cistern.

I think Skinny Boyd considers himself prosperous, I really do. I asked what he needed that he didn't have, and he said nothing. He has a little pension, and once a week a friend drives him into Cleveland to get what he wants to buy. He said that night for supper he and his little dog would have some biscuits and barbecue and "a couple or three eggs," so what else would they need?

"I hadn't made any whiskey now in about two years," he said, "but there's still a lot of it made around here in these woods. I've got my riggin', if you want to see that. They tell me the only thing the revenue people will arrest you for is having a worm, a copper coil . . ."

We were way back in the woods of East Texas, never mind exactly where, this moonshiner and me. He said he'd talk about making whiskey if I wouldn't put his name in the paper, and we shook on that. Like every moonshiner I ever met, this one said he no longer makes whiskey, that he just used to make it. Yet he told me he now has, on hand, 200 pounds of sugar. Of course he might be intending to make up a very large batch of cookies, I guess.

"I started at it back just after World War II," he said. "Old C—— come and stayed with me one time, fishing, and he drank so much whiskey he kept us all broke so I told him we'd just make us some goddang whiskey, and that started me.

"What you have to do is get you some grain. Wheat, rye, corn. I like rye best. First you wash it, get all the dust out, and pour off that dirty water. Then have you a container you can put a fire under and cover your grain with clean water and bring it to a boil. Then let it cool and settle out, and add your sugar.

"Put about a pound of sugar to two gallons of water and add your yeast. The way we do it, we'll have two barrels hold about forty gallons, and put about twenty-five pounds of grain in each one and about half a box of this powdered yeast in each one, and stir it up good with a boat paddle.

"All right, that's your mash. You let her sit about seventy-two hours, or until it quits workin'. When it's workin' it'll bubble and boil, look like a big old fish swimmin' in there. When it stops workin' and all your grain settles to the bottom, you pour off your liquid. It's beer then, really. You can drink it, sure. Make you high as a two-tailed cat. But to make whiskey you got to distill it.

"You want to be real careful what you cook that stuff in. Anytime you make it in anything metal, except for stainless steel or copper, you're subject to gettin' metal poisoning. Might make you blind, or kill you. Real dangerous. Now, some of these fellows around here make it in old fifty-five gallon drums, and go right on. But I wouldn't want to do that . . ."

I asked if he'd take a drink of moonshine whiskey if he didn't know anything about its source. He said no, he sure wouldn't. Remember that, Mel. That's the authority talking.

He showed me his whiskey-cooling vessel, a big copper container that tapers toward the top. "You pour the liquid off your mash into something like this," he said, rapping on the copper kettle. "You get a fire under it some way, and you cook your fumes off. You have your riggin' with your worm, your copper coil, on top. I rig mine with a glass reflux tube up here, and a thermometer. The reflux tube lets the alcohol vapor go into the worm, and it collects the water and lets it flow back into the barrel. You've got to watch your thermometer. That's the key.

"The idea is, alcohol vapor cooks off a lot sooner than water vapor. Of course water boils at 100 degrees centigrade, so you don't want your temperature to get over about 95. If it gets over 100 centigrade you'll just be boiling water, and you don't want that. Your strong alcohol vapors start comin' off at about 87 degrees, and go into your worm. You've got your worm in water to cool it, and you keep the water circulating. So the vapor in the worm condenses and comes out alcohol. That's your stuff, that comes out of the worm. That's your product, right there. They call it white lightning.

"When that son of a gun comes out of there it's about 180 proof. It's possible to drink it, but it'll take the hide off your mouth. And believe me it's explosive, at that point. You can put it in a gasoline engine and it'll run like crazy. Now, you need to cut the white lightning back. To do that you use distilled water. Ordinary water won't mix with the alcohol. If you don't have distilled water you can put the alcohol on the stove (very, very carefully, right?) and put plain water in it and bring it to a boil just a second and it'll mix up. But it's best to have distilled water. For one gallon of white lightning you can mix in about half a gallon of distilled water and that'll cut it down to about 95 proof. You can take a little hydrometer and tell what you're doing.

"To make your sure-enough good booze, cut back to about 95 proof and buy some of these little wood kegs, charred inside. They come from Arkansas. I used to get 'em in Houston, anywhere from ten-gallon kegs on down to two. You put your whiskey in there, and seal it off, and put that son of a gun back for about six months, or as long as you can leave it alone, and you got something better'n you can buy in a liquor store.

"The charcoal takes out your foreign stuff, enzymes they call 'em, and ages your whiskey. Some of 'em put a little lye in it to age it, but charcoal's better. Another way, if you got the right kind of container, is put that charred keg in a barrel of water. You got to seal the keg tight and put a band around it to keep it from blowing the cap. Then just boil the whole keg, and overnight you've aged whiskey ten years.

"That charcoal is where you get the amber color to whiskey. White lightning is clear. And the flavor, it comes from grain. You can make alcohol out of sugar and water and yeast, don't even need grain. But grain gives you flavor . . ."

I asked where he went to get rye, to make whiskey. At the feed store? He frowned. "Well, you got to be careful gettin' it that way. These feed stores have all got orders, if you buy rye you got to leave your name and address and tell what you're gonna do with it. That's just how close these revenue people are. Best place to get it is off these old box-cars that come through, shippin' grain to Russia . . ."

He talked about costs. Said if he used fifty pounds of grain he'd probably pour fifty-five or sixty gallons of liquid off his mash and distill ten to twelve gallons of alcohol out of that. "I used to make a gallon of white lightning for two dollars, but that was before the price of sugar went up. I haven't figured it since then."

My host entered into many of the finer points of whiskey-cooking that we'll skip here. You'd not want to hear them unless you're going to make whiskey, and I know you wouldn't do that.

It won't surprise you that my friend doesn't think too highly of the law against making whiskey at home. "It's the worst law they ever passed. Look at all this grain being sent to foreign countries. Farmers could make alcohol out of it and burn it in their equipment. With research, maybe it would solve the fuel shortage. Of course these old women think the men are gonna drink all the alcohol made, and they're against it. But you don't have to make grain alcohol. You can make it out of wood, bark, limbs, almost anything."

You don't necessarily need fancy equipment, either. "Long time ago these old country folks poured the beer off their mash and cooked it in a pot on the stove and put a cloth over it to catch the fumes. Then they'd squeeze the cloth into a jug, and have alcohol. You've heard of corn squeezin's. That's where it came from."

There's the tendency to consider that moonshining is pretty well a thing of the past. I asked my friend if moonshine booze is hard to find. "You can get it most any time you want it," he said, "if you know the right people. And if they know you."

A drowsy afternoon. I was sitting in Dan Wilson's shop at Tomball, watching him lock-stitch a piece of leather around a saddle horn, using that stout linen thread treated with beeswax. I love to see a saddlemaker work.

Dan's been at it a long time. First at Wharton. Then he had a shop at Sealy. Even did saddle and harness work in the army several years. Now he's out there on Brown Road west of Tomball. But I never had heard where he came from. "El Campo. I grew up at El Campo, or a little way outside of it in the country. My Dad was D. B. ('Watermelon') Wilson." He looked up from the saddle and over the top of his glasses and grinned. "My Dad died in '44 but right today you can go to El Campo and say 'Watermelon' Wilson and they'll know who you're talkin' about. He raised many a melon down there. Man, I packed so many of them things when I was growin' up I can look at one now and get sick.

"I got started in the business there at El Campo workin' for Old Man W. J. Rudder, when I was a boy. I had him make me a pair of chaps and they cost $6.75. He put me to cuttin' saddle strings to pay for those chaps. I stayed in that shop all summer, cuttin' saddle strings, and that's how I started."

Louise Fisk came in to pick up a pair of shoes. Lot of saddle men do shoe repair. Dan wouldn't take any money from her. "You ought to let me pay you for your labor," she said.

"Nope. I can't take your money for somethin' I'm not sure it's gonna work."

Good rich leather smells all around the shop. Old boots with new heels and soles, waiting to be picked up. Hard-used saddles with new leather here and there.

Dan was talking about his twin granddaughters, three years old. Has he made them saddles yet? Up came the eyes again. "No, but I'm lookin' to. You know what Dolly wants? She's just dyin' for me to get those twins a couple of them burros you've read about in the Grand Canyon." Dolly is his wife of thirty-eight years.

Randy Shaw was there in the shop watching Dan work, hoping some day to learn how to make saddles. He offered me a dip of Copenhagen, the label torn away from the tin the way they do, so the top will go on and off easier.

It says something about Wilson that he won't have a telephone in the shop. He says all a phone would do, it'd just ring all the time.

He showed me a rebuilt saddle he's proud of. A calf roper had brought in a beat-up saddle he loved because the tree it was built on felt exactly right for him. Dan took another saddle with a broken tree and put a lot of its leather on the old tree and made a saddle almost good as new, he said, and a whole lot cheaper. You get Wilson to make you a new saddle and you're talking about $700, somewhere around there.

The calf roper came in before I left. He sat in the rebuilt saddle and grinned and seemed pleased. It didn't *look* anything like his old saddle but he knew the old tree was under there, because of the feel. How much Dan gonna charge him? "Oh, two-fifty," Dan said.

The cowboy, Steve Cook, nodded. But he said, "I can't pay you all of that today. I can give you a hundred."

"How long you gonna make me wait for the rest of it?" Dan asked softly.

"Monday," Cook said. "If I can win me some money this weekend I'll come back and settle with you. But I know I can get it Monday." Dan's turn to nod. He made out a receipt for the payment and had Randy bring the saddle around front, and I think Cook was surprised. "You gonna let me take it now?"

"Sure, I ain't afraid of you. Now you get out there and get in them ol' boys' pockets. And don't throw that saddle in that trailer and let it get beat up like the other one." Cook promised he wouldn't and went out grinning. When he was gone Dan said, "He's a good boy. A fine roper."

Dan Wilson's name once meant something in professional rodeo. A steer wrestler. A bull rider. But mainly saddle broncs. He stayed on the circuit from '34, when he was only seventeen, until '43. He has the usual box of pictures to show, and the scars, too.

"The worst I ever got hurt," he said, sewing again on the saddle horn, "was at Rosenberg on the ninth day of May in 1939. The Texas Kid had set up his Wild West Show right in there behind the old Sylvan Club. I drawed a horse named Overall Bill, and they turned him out on me. (That means the bronc was let out of the chute before the rider was ready.) When he came out I had one foot hung in the stirrup and he dragged me around that arena. I don't know how many times he went around, but I think my head hit ever' post in that fence.

"Finally Melvin Harper, from down here at Buckeye, stepped into the arena and grabbed that old horse and pulled him down. Melvin was just a spectator but thank the Good Lord he came to that show, because if it hadn't been for Melvin Harper I wouldn't be here now. I was unconscious nine days, and they had it out at El Campo that I'd been buried."

Several customers came in, and I drifted toward the door to leave. I hung back just a minute, to see if the newcomers would produce any bits of talk I wanted to remember. There was one fellow who was about to move, and Dan had heard about it and he asked, "You fixin' to leave us?"

"Yeah, got to go."

"Well," Dan said, "I sho' hate that."

The day I visited Carolyn Svetlik in the farm home where she grew up, she had put out a big washing. We stood in the back yard. Sheets and pillow cases and cup towels and denim work clothes flapped in the wind on the clothes line. I asked her if she'd explain to me the way she had washed.

She laughed about that, about somebody coming to see her and wanting to hear how she washed. I said it might be interesting to women in Houston. "Well, the first thing I did," she said, "was cut up two bars of my homemade soap in the wash pot." She nodded at a big black cast iron pot sitting over a bed of ashes. "I still make my own soap, and it's just as pretty and white as snow.

"Then I filled the wash pot with rain water out of the barrel (caught off the roof of the house, the way wash water was once caught at most homes in Texas). I like to use rain water because it gets clothes whiter and I don't have to use so much soap. Our well water here is so hard.

"Next I built a fire under the pot and sorted my clothes while the water came to a boil. I let it boil long enough to dissolve the soap, and then put the first batch of clothes to boil . . ."

To a lot of young homemakers, washing that way may sound like an ancient and quaint ritual, boiling clothes in a pot with homemade soap. To others who aren't so young, it will sound mighty familiar. My guess would be we've got hundreds of fashionable women in Houston who once punched clothes in a wash pot with a bleached stick.

The house where I visited Carolyn Svetlik is at Gleckar, a rural community near Schulenburg. She grew up in that house with a brother and five sisters. She does not live there now. Her brother Fred Rode does. Rode (pronounced *road-y*) is a bachelor, and his sister comes once a week and washes for him and cleans house. That's what she was doing when I saw her. She is married to Louis Svetlik. They live also at Gleckar not far from the old Rode home.

The reason Mrs. Svetlik washes in an iron pot is that she thinks some clothes have to be boiled to come clean. There is, in fact, an electric wringer-type washing machine in the wash house of the Rode home, and it is used along with the wash pot.

So some of the rural Texas domestic practices survive through habit and personal preference. You might be surprised at how many bright and happy people live in the country without conveniences we think of as necessities in the city.

The Rode family, some time along the way, piped water into the kitchen, converted it into a bathroom, and built a new kitchen on the side of the house. But at the Svetlik house nearby this was never done. So when Carolyn Svetlik washes at home, she carries the water from the well, and out of the rain barrel. There is an electric pump on the well, and television in the house, but no telephone.

And no bathroom. When Louis Svetlik washes up for dinner, he uses a pan and a bar of homemade soap on the back porch. Taking a bath means filling a washtub from the well and bathing in the kitchen. Going to the toilet is a stroll out the back door, to the privy.

Yet I like that Svetlik house. There is nothing about it that suggests hardship or underprivilege to me. For one thing, it looks so orderly and clean. I especially like the big wood stove in the middle of the living room. For the summer it is covered with a pretty print skirt, starched and ironed. And green plants hang everywhere, watered out of that rain barrel. Rain water does good and secret things to plants.

Carolyn Svetlik knows what it is to be surrounded by conveniences. She worked long years in Houston, before she married, as housekeeper for some of the city's most prominent families. But if she considers it any come-down to be living in the country without running water, she sure has got it hidden well.

For some reason I'm not sure of, it pleases me to run across people in the country doing old-fashioned things like washing in a wash pot. Say, remember what the women would do with the wash water after the clothes were all rinsed and hung out? Mrs. Svetlik had just finished when I walked in the yard. With the hot soapy water left in the pot she had mopped the house, including the back porch and steps. And poured all the rest of the wash water in the flower beds.

Listen to Wiley Price, talking about walking to work in the mid-1920s when he was a log cutter with Long Bell Lumber Company in East Texas. He lived near San Augustine then.

"When I was sawin' logs for Captain Bannister, the way I'd get to my job, I'd walk eighteen miles through wooded country, and eighteen miles back home, every day. I'd leave home about three o'clock in the mornin'. A log cutter could always make his day by two o'clock so I'd have plenty of time to walk back . . .

"They was a lot of wolves back in that country, and sometimes they'd howl-l-l-l. Once I was about halfway to the camp, in that timbered country, and I'd holler, just to see what would answer. Well, an old panter (panther), he answered me. And so he followed me, he come on to me, and he caught up. He wouldn't come right up to the road, just close enough to look at me. It was starlight. I'd walk along, and he'd follow me. I'd stop, and he'd stop. I'd done picked me up two clubs, pine knots. I had one in each hand. One to throw, and one to fight with.

"He got in a kind of starlight place where I could see him good, and I threw at him hard as I could, but I didn't hit him. About a mile and a half this side of the camp, I hit the main road. He followed me along there somewhere, and then he turned back. He looked to be . . . aw, you measure him from nose to the end of his tail, looked to be about eight or nine feet."

He paused a while, and then surprised me by saying panthers are still seen in the Piney Woods of East Texas. "They's two of 'em around here, that we got a history of. They're over on Harvey Creek. Ever once in a while you hear tell of one catchin' a calf over there. I was talkin' to Mr. Allbritton a few days ago and he said they hear 'em squall."

I mentioned that most folks will say there are no panthers in East Texas now and Price answered, "Well, of course that's somebody talkin' that don't know."

The Harvey Creek Wiley Price mentioned is the one that flows into Rayburn Reservoir, near Broaddus. Price has been in that country all his life, more than seventy-eight years. I visited him at his home on the east shore of the lake above Broaddus. "I've been on this place here since 1927," he said. "I raised my family here. I think in all there was fourteen of us . . . seven for myself and seven for other folks. Seemed like every time a boy or a girl would leave home they'd come here, and stop, and they never would leave . . . times were pretty hard, and seemed like their folks couldn't make a support for 'em, so they'd come here."

Price farmed and raised cattle almost half a century on land that's now flooded by Rayburn Lake. He sold out of the cattle business when the water rose. He and his wife Myran live in a white frame house close by an old unpainted cabin where they raised most of those children.

Price is still straight and tall and fit looking. He carries Indian blood. "My great-grandmother was a slave," he said. "She was an Indian. I guess practically all Indian. Seemed like to me, the best I remember she told me Choctaw."

He has a deep interest in Indian things, not so much because of his ancestry but because the land he once farmed and ranched is loaded with Indian artifacts. "All up and down this area here, at these knobs and sandy places, you'll find where Indians lived oncet a time. For years I plowed up bones. Jaw bones. Leg bones. Arm bones. I thought it was deer. Then one day I was plowin' on a knob over here and I plowed up a head. When I come to find out what I'd done, why I was sorry." Price told me government archeologists dug up three whole Indian skeletons on his land before Rayburn Lake filled, and he dug up one by himself. "But I was sorry I did it. The thought come to me, I wouldn't like for somebody to dig up any of my own folks."

Story-telling is Price's strong suit now. I love to listen to him. He's got one buried treasure story that would fill this page in small print. It's about him trying to dig up a whatever-it-is while some most astonishing circumstances combine to keep him from digging. Like the wind will blow up a hurricane, just at that one spot while everywhere else the weather is calm. And once a great bull-like beast charged him, all blurry and vague and he couldn't really see anything except the steam coming out of its nostrils.

As you'd expect—seeing he's a man who will call up a panther on a starlit night and face it with a couple of pine knots for weapons—Wiley Price is a big hunter. He told me several hunting stories. My favorite was the one about the bobcat. You need at least to know that it's customary with some hunters, when a cat or a coon is treed, to try to shake the quarry out of the tree and let it fight the dogs. Price spoke about his dogs treeing one night and he went to them and looked up and "there sat a big old bobcat. I had two young dogs and I sed I'd been wantin' to see a fight, so now's my time. I set my gun down and up the tree I went. I stayed on the opposite side of the tree (from the bobcat) until I got to some limbs.

"I was standin' on the first limb and that cat was out there lookin' back at me and growlin'. Another little limb was growin' out there, so I caught it and pulled it to him and slapped him with it and it throwed him ten or fifteen feet from the tree. He jumped up when he hit the ground and got the lead on the dogs. They went out across an old field there, dogs abarkin' and makin' a pretty song, and I said well, I can hear the race up here a lot better than standin' on the ground so I'll just stay in the tree.

"Well, after a while I heard 'em comin' back. They ain't treed him yet. They swung across above me, and then turned back toward me and I said, they're comin' straight back so I better get down from here because a cat's bad about climbin' the same tree twice.

"Well, I got back to that first big limb, and something hit that tree—kuh-wap!—I thought another tree fell against it. But it was that cat. He jumped about eight feet and caught that tree again. So I'm standin' on that limb, and he come right up close to my foot, and he looked up and lowed at me—ahr-r-r-r-r—well, he asked for that tree, and I gave it to him. I jumped over him, and when I hit the ground them dogs just covered me."

No, he didn't get chewed up, but he gained an experience he still laughs about. A lot of hunters have jumped bobcats out of trees, but Wiley Price may be the only one who was ever jumped out of a tree by a bobcat.

Grace and Albert Garcia wrote me from Bay City to say that Joe Lozano is dead, that he died of a stroke back on August 3. I hadn't heard. Well, the record may show that Joe died of a stroke, but that's not really what killed him.

After I got the letter I went to Bay City to the Garcia home on Doris Street and sat at the kitchen table with Albert and Grace and with Joe's younger brother Paul and his wife Lucy. We talked about Joe and his astonishing life. It was a little bizarre, all of us sitting around there giving testimony to each other about Joe. It was sentimental and cornball, I guess, the kind of thing people did back in the forties after they'd lost somebody they loved in the war. But you mustn't think we weren't sincere.

"I wish I could build a monument to Joe," his brother Paul said. "And put on it all the things that happened to him, and how he took them, and then when anybody thought they were having troubles, they could read about Joe."

I met Joe Lozano in Bay City in 1968. He was forty-eight then, and husky, and full of grins. He certainly looked healthy. He did have a limp, because of the artificial leg. Then there was a hurting in his dark eyes that showed through if you looked deep.

Go back to September of '41. Joe was eighteen then. He walked into the army recruiting office in Bay City and said one of those things chesty young guys were saying then: "There's going to be a war, and I want to be in it." He had six younger brothers and sisters at home, and his father was dead. "You'll never have to go into the service, Joe," the recruiting sergeant said. But he did, with special permission from his mother. Mrs. Lozano told him, "If you must go, then go." By the time we got into the war in Europe, Joe was a tank commander. He lost five tanks and six crew members in that war. Came home with a Silver Star and a Purple Heart.

In 1950 he was a warehouse manager there in Bay City, and his first son, Paul, was two years old. Joe was called back in the service and sent to Korea. On April 22, 1951, afted he'd picked up another Silver Star as a tank commander, he was blown twenty-five feet high by a land mine. He didn't wake up for sixteen days. By June he was in Brooke Army Hospital at San Antonio. He would stay there two years and three months. His right leg was useless. His left leg broken in nine places. His sixth and seventh vertebrae were shattered. He had no fingers on his left hand. Doctors told him there wasn't much point in amputating his right leg, since he'd never walk anyway.

"Take the leg off and get me an artificial one," Joe said. "I'm going to walk."

So they took the leg, and in 1953 Joe was back in Bay City. He walked in his front door on an artificial leg. Within a year he was climbing houses and fixing roofs. He became manager of a furniture store and coached a little league baseball team.

In 1960 Joe's wife Alicia got sick. Diagnosis: cancer. In six weeks she was dead. She left Joe with seven children, from eleven to one. Relatives and friends offered to take the children. Nothing doing. Joe kept them together. He even sewed dresses for his little girls. "I can do anything anybody else can do," he'd say. "It just takes me a little longer."

In August of '66 Joe's oldest son, Paul, turned seventeen. He asked his father for permission to join the army and become a tank commander. Joe tried to get him to stay in school, but the boy begged to go. Joe signed the papers and let him go. He went to Vietnam. On May 13 of '68, Paul had only a month to serve on his tour of combat duty. That's the day a Viet Cong shot him in the head, at close range, with a sawed-off shotgun. Joe always liked to give the combined total of military decorations he and his son were awarded—twenty-six, for Paul and Joe Lozano.

In 1973, when Joe and his family were living on Avenue M in Bay City, their house burned. Total loss. Joe saved the clothes he wore and nothing else. He spent one night with his brother Paul and went out the next morning to start over again, at age fifty.

One of his married daughters and her husband, Louis Rodriguez, were living with Joe last spring. On March 1, here came more heartache—Rodriguez was stabbed and killed in a tavern.

But the blow that wounded Joe the worst, even deeper than the land mine long ago in Korea, came last April 29. Exactly what happened, and how and why, is yet to be unraveled in court. Anyway, there was an argument among some youths in the neighborhood, and when it was over Joe Lozano's youngest son, Raymond, lay dead. Shot in the head, as the oldest boy, Paul, was in Vietnam.

Through all his years of trouble and hurting, Joe was a cheerful and a life-loving man. At least up to the time of Raymond's death.

One of his friends, Odie Sweeny, came by the Garcia home while I was there. "Joe dedicated his life to helping people," Sweeny said. "I don't believe I ever knew a man who loved people so much."

Paul Lozano is executor of Joe's estate. "Since I started working with the estate I found out things that he did that we never knew about." Maybe not big things, just helpful. Joe had a total disability income from his military service and spent most of his time working for nothing. He'd haul sick people to Austin or Galveston or Houston to the hospital. He worked with Boy Scouts. Counseled with disabled veterans. He'd do volunteer carpentry work. Tend bar. Paint houses. Mow grass. He bought this big riding mower, and he'd roar around mowing, baseball fields especially. He loved baseball, and umpired thousands of games in Bay City, both boys' games and girls' games.

Don Ferguson came and sat at the kitchen table with us a while. He worked a lot of ball games with Joe. "He was a fine umpire," Ferguson said. "The kids all loved him. I know when they'd pay us, Joe used to turn the money back. He did a lot of hurting. He'd never complain, but you could tell."

He didn't complain about anything, not even that he was plagued with bad luck, or that tragedy seemed to follow him everywhere. "He just kept calm," brother Paul says, "and took it. But I think Raymond's death is what killed Joe." The stroke hit him last August 2, and he died the next day. He was fifty-three.

Now his friends in Bay City are wanting something more for Joe than just a death notice in the paper. They want to put up a marker, or get out a little book about him, or name a baseball field after him—so people will remember. Around the kitchen table we talked about the last thing Joe did. What it was, he got out his needles and his thread and he made a flag for one of the Boy Scout troops there in town.

When I got to his house at Dolen, Warren DeSpain told me that everything he intended to do that day he'd already got done that morning. Which was a nice way to be greeted because it meant he had plenty of time to talk.

It was early afternoon and we sat down to get the talking done and DeSpain's wife brought us each a tray with coffee and sugar and cream. DeSpain took up his cup in one hand and his saucer in the other and held them like that a long time, waiting for the coffee to get the right temperature.

Dolen? That's a little place in North Liberty County, east of Cleveland on State 105 toward the Trinity River. DeSpain was saying over the coffee cup that as far as he knows his family is the only bunch of DeSpains in that part of the country. Back in Cleveland, or down the river at Liberty, when people who know him talk about DeSpain they come down hard on the first syllable and make the name sound like this: *Dee*-spain.

He poured some coffee from the cup and drank it out of the saucer. I never saw it done in a neater style. You know that takes a steady hand, to drink coffee out of a saucer? You just try it.

We talked about outlaw cattle and wild horses and cooking cornbread on a camp fire. And about fences. "Been a time," DeSpain said, "I could ride from Shepherd to Dayton (thirty-five or forty miles, maybe more the way you'd have to go on a horse) and never hit a fence except on the Southern Pacific Railroad."

The way that sounded, you'd expect he was talking about another century, but Liberty and San Jacinto and Hardin counties and all that timbered country north and east of Houston were still pretty much open and free range, right up into the 1940s. That ride DeSpain talked about, from Shepherd to Dayton without fences, he could do that in 1935. Fences were mighty slow about coming to Southeast Texas.

I don't expect any man has ridden more miles in those woods than Warren DeSpain. Surely not in Liberty County. In the 1930s he was a range rider for the government during what veteran Texas cattle people still refer to as "the dippin' days." Those were strange times, the dipping days. A lot of nervousness and hard feelings.

There was this law that said that cattle—horses, mules, and donkeys, too—had to be dipped every two weeks to kill the Texas fever tick, which was threatening to wreck the livestock industry of the state. The government built dipping vats and hired inspectors and range riders to enforce the dipping law. This went on a long time. "About five years, here in Liberty County," DeSpain said.

He was one of the range riders. Rode mostly with Willie Wright, "still lives down south of Cleveland." Their job was to comb the woods and see that the cattle were dipped. Livestock would be marked when it was dipped, so a rider could look at a cow and tell how long it had been since she went through a vat. "We worked Liberty County and the edges of all the other counties Liberty touches," DeSpain said. "We camped in the woods. Willie Wright and me would leave Highway 59, say about Splendora, and ride across our territory (that is, across the Trinity and through Liberty County to the Hardin line), and it'd take us about three weeks." The most DeSpain ever got paid for this work was about $128 a month, furnishing his own horses and equipment and cow dogs.

A few ranchers resisted the dipping law. When a man wouldn't dip his cattle, they had to be dipped for him. That is, riders like DeSpain and Wright would have to round the cattle up and get 'em to a vat. Then the owner was charged for the work.

You can see that if a man owned a few old outlaw cattle running free range in the woods, they'd seem a mighty lot of trouble for him to go out and catch. So maybe he'd just not fool with them, which meant that government riders like DeSpain and Wright had to do a lot of mean cowboying in the woods.

Some people would even hide their cattle to keep from dipping them. "We'd have a good bit of trouble in the towns," DeSpain said. "We had a lot of milk cows in towns like Cleveland. I've seen people hide their milk cow in the smokehouse to keep from dipping her. Sometimes you'd have cow men trying to hide a bunch of calves on you."

These were individuals who just didn't want the government messing in their business, telling them what to do. Then others didn't understand the necessity for dipping. So you hear a lot of stories about some mighty touchy confrontations in those times between government man and rancher. DeSpain still doesn't care to talk in detail about a few in which he was involved.

The dipping days had a deep and abiding influence on the Texas livestock industry, and therefore on the state itself. In Southeast Texas, in that Big Thicket–type country, it put an end to free-range days. "Here in Liberty County," DeSpain said, "most of them began building fence in about 1940. When a man got his cattle cleaned up (that is, free of the fever ticks), he didn't want 'em running with cattle that hadn't been dipped, so he'd begin pasturing them, build fences to keep 'em separate."

Those mean years in the woods also put a permanent mark on Warren DeSpain. He's had both legs broken, a flock of ribs cracked on both sides, and is generally banged up about as bad as a rodeo-circuit cowboy. Been in the cattle business for himself now, a long time. But he's still mighty steady. Since I was at his house I tried drinking coffee out of a saucer with one hand, and I just can't cut it.

On a recent trip into the Big Thicket country I was privileged to make the acquaintance of Savan Caruthers, who lives at Hull and is seventy-five years old and one of the best old-time fiddlers I ever heard.

He told me this: "I was born way back in the woods between Sour Lake and Batson, and until I was seven years old I didn't know there was anybody else livin' in the world except just my own family. When I was about four those older brothers of mine sent off and got 'em a fiddle. They never did learn to play it, but they wouldn't let me touch it, because I was too little. It laid around there for two years. Finally one day when they were gone I got hold of that fiddle and I could play a tune on it the first time I picked it up and that's the truth."

A little bunch of us was standing around there listening to Caruthers talk and somebody asked, "Savan, can you play 'The Devil's Dream?' "

He said, "I ought to can. I was under the bed when he dreamed it." So up came the fiddle and we had "The Devil's Dream," which caused feet to pat and hands to clap, and when it was over I asked Caruthers if he can read music.

"Naw," he said. "You hold a piece of sheet music up in front of me and it just looks like a wire fence with a bunch of junk hangin' in it."

Then he played "The Port Arthur Waltz." After that he talked about going into Houston to a fiddling contest one time. "They asked me where I was from and I told 'em I come out of a holler log in the Big Thicket. I went to school just three days in my life and I can't read or write." I never did decide whether Caruthers was serious about that, because he does kid around a lot, but when I asked him if he meant it about not being able to read, he grinned and said sure he meant it. And took off on "Arkansas Traveler."

Then he stopped a while to say: "One day Dr. Gibson (the late Dr. Royce Gibson of Hull) came to my house on a sick call and when he got through he asked me if I could play 'Arkansas Traveler.' I said I could and he picked up the phone and called a friend of his and told him to listen. And I played into the phone and when Dr. Gibson started to leave I asked him what I owed and he said, 'You already paid me.' " How about that? A doctor bill, and a house call at that, paid for with a fiddle tune.

Next we had two of Caruthers' own compositions, "Big Thicket" and "Daisetta." And while he rested up, he told about his first public fiddling appearance, in a saloon at Batson when he was seven. Said his daddy brought him in and tied him to a table and made him play for the men, who'd pitch him coins. Why was he tied? "To keep me from runnin' away," he grinned. "It was the first time I'd ever been to town and I was scared."

Caruthers certainly managed to conquer stage fright. He has played for country dances in East Texas for more than sixty-five years, and he loves the work. "I've been livin' a long time," he'll say, "but I'm still full of fun." And he'll dance you a jig, to show how spry he is.

Caruthers' old fiddle came out of a player piano, one of those forerunners of the juke box, which had built-in instruments played mechanically. He first saw the fiddle in Batson in 1910 but didn't get it until much later. Said he paid five dollars for it.

Caruthers doesn't go to old-time fiddling contests any longer. "They got too many rules now," he said. "I went up to Crockett to that big contest they have and I got up and put the fiddle behind my back and played like this, and stuck the bow in my mouth and played, like this, but they've got rules now, about the way you hold the fiddle. I can't play good, either, with these modern bands like they've got in Houston. They want you to stay in the same chord all the time, and it's not natural."

I thought maybe he meant in the same key, but I never did get straight on it. I promise you there's nothing sloppy about Savan Caruthers' fiddling. He's good, still, at seventy-five. You don't have to be an expert to tell that. You take fine old country tunes like "Cotton-Eyed Joe" and "Leather Britches," they've got some pretty intricate passages, and even a fair ear is offended if they're performed sloppily.

When I went to see him Caruthers played I guess thirty tunes, including "Snowbird in the Ashes," "Beaumont Rag," "Horn Blossom Special," "Eighth of January," and "Wednesday Night Waltz." Said he once named more than 200 numbers he knows but got tired counting and quit. "If I can just remember them," he said, "I can play 'em."

In the Big Thicket, Savan Caruthers is just about as well known as a homegrown comedian as for his fiddling. There's been an insurance policy story going around about him lately. He claims to listen faithfully to Radio Station XEG in Monterrey, from which you can order anything from insurance policies to prayer cloths to cures for prostatitis. Other day Caruthers' insurance man came to him and said, "Savan, I got notice you cancelled your burial policy? How come you want to do that?"

Caruthers said, "I don't need it any longer."

"How come you don't need a burial policy?"

"Oh," Caruthers said, "I done ordered me a new kind of policy from XEG. All I got to do is keep it paid up and I ain't gonna die."

The sign across the front of the building is in big white letters. It reads, "In God We Trust—Grimes County Jail." Travelers who haven't ever seen such a sign on a jail stop and take pictures of it when they pass through Anderson. What they ought to do is go on in and meet the man who caused the sign to be put there. He is W. O. ("Dick") Johnson, Grimes County sheriff. You're not likely to meet another Texas sheriff like Dick Johnson.

He's a man somewhere around sixty, I'd guess, with a kind round face and a little smile that's—well, almost tender, you'd have to say. It'll embarrass him to see that in print, but it's so. He's the sort of fellow who'll say, "If you're ever around here at dinner time, why just come right on in and eat with us."

I did that. Went with him over to his living quarters that join the jail. A few others who just happened to be around there at dinner time ate with us too. County Judge Joe Haynie and Elliott Goodwin of Navasota and John ("Chiney") Darby, who is Johnson's chief deputy. We sat down and the sheriff said, "Chiney, you ask us a blessing, will you?" So we all bowed and Darby thanked God for the day and for all our blessings, and he asked Him to bless the food to our bodies and to bless the hands that prepared it, in Jesus' name amen.

The blessed hands that prepared it belong to Mrs. Johnson and Mattie Lee Mitchell, the sheriff's sister-in-law. Mrs. Johnson cooks not only for her husband but for the prisoners over in the jail and apparently anybody else who's hungry. After we started, Claude Wren from up at Iola came in and Mrs. Johnson fed him too.

It was the kind of meal you may remember getting in an old farmhouse somewhere, the kind Dick Johnson ate when he was milking cows down on Wallace Prairie a long time before he went into politics. We had chicken and dumplings, a big platter of sliced beef, fresh blackeyed peas, sliced tomatoes, potato salad, corn, hot biscuits, fried hot-water cornbread, and big schooners of iced tea with the sugar already in it. The women didn't eat with us but stayed in the kitchen and came out now and then with more hot biscuits.

Johnson isn't the sort of sheriff who'll sit and tell tales about his experiences. But others do it for him. They tell you how he'll go out in that calm way of his, say to a house where there's a big family squabble, and he'll sit there for hours, talking, calming everybody down, getting them in a good humor. The voters of Grimes County obviously like his style. They've kept him in office since 1953.

He doesn't carry a gun. He told me he tried to wear a pistol once but it kept getting in his way.

"Where's your pistol now, Dick?" Judge Haynie asked at dinner.

"I think it's back yonder in a dresser drawer somewhere."

He does carry a shotgun in his car. "I figure it's the only kind of gun I could hit anything with. I'm not much of a shot. I never owned a gun of any kind until I got elected." He never has taken a shot at anybody. Said he's been shot at a time or two, though.

We plowed through all that food, stopping just at the border of gluttony, and the women brought out peach cobbler and coffee. The sheriff doesn't drink coffee. "I don't even know what it tastes like," he said. "I tell these policemen, just to rile 'em up, that I might try a cup of coffee if I ever had time to let it cool off."

"Tell him how you lost those finger joints, Dick," somebody said.

The sheriff held up his right hand. The ends of the middle and index fingers are missing. And I thought, at last, here comes a hairy lawman story about getting his fingers shot off. Then he said, "I wore those fingers down, soppin' syrup, during the depression when there wasn't anything else to eat."

We all got up rubbing stomachs, groaning, grinning. I started to get Deputy Darby, since I ate so much it was probably sinful, to say another prayer and ask forgiveness. But the sheriff was saying, "If you're ever around here again at dinner time, why . . ."

The other day when I was running around in the woods close to Segno in Polk County I stopped by to see how Hardy Cain was doing. Found him out behind his house, drawing a bucket of water out of a new seventy-foot well he just got through digging. He dug it by hand and by himself, and I expect Cain is now seventy-five. He says he's not sure, that he may be anywhere from seventy-two on up.

"Ain't that the best water you ever tasted?" he asked, when he'd handed me a dipperful out of the bucket. The day was hot and dry and the water was cool and sweet, and I don't think I ever did taste any better, at that.

I asked Cain if he'd take me down in the woods and show me the pond he was building the last time I saw him. That must have been—good gravy, it's been almost ten years. Calendars just don't last the way they used to.

Before we went to the woods we had a little music. When you go to see Hardy Cain, you almost always have singing. He builds fiddles and guitars and makes up songs. He sang me a couple he'd composed since I was there last. One named "Good Luck for Me" and the other "I Like to Hear Myself Sing."

Cain is a small man with rusty-colored hair and red skin and sharp features and eyes so blue and clear and young they're just outrageous. Sometimes you catch him looking deep inside you, studying you. "I'm glad you came," he'll say, about half an hour after you get there. "I just wish you could stay here and be with me all day. Studying other people helps a man to see himself."

Hardy Cain is a problem to understand. Sometimes he says things that don't make sense to me, but then other times he seems really deep and wise and full of valuable thoughts. He's a man of the woods and the thickets and the creeks and what he says doesn't reflect much formal schooling, but I'd be last in line to call him uneducated. Because, like he says, "A man can keep aponderin' around and aponderin' around and sort of educate himself." And he has tender feelings about a lot of matters. "I get heartbroken a heap of times," he told me.

After the songs, when I was following him down through the woods, I had to marvel at the physical strength of this little gent. The pond he built appears to have maybe two acres of water in it. The horseshoe-shaped dam has to be at least 300 yards long, and although it's low in most places it rises to a height of about twelve feet at one point. I wish an engineer would go there and figure how many thousand cubic yards of dirt are in that dam. Because you hear this: Hardy Cain built it alone, using a shovel and a wheelbarrow and a couple of old buckets to carry the sand in. And he packed it into the dam with his feet. I watched him work at it one day, back when he first started.

No, he wasn't paid to do it. The pond isn't even on his own land, and so of course a lot of people think it's peculiar, to do all the back-wrenching work to build something that can't belong to you. I followed Cain around the dam. The little pond has a hushed, swampy Big Thicket kind of character. Dark water and cypress trees and cattails and lily pads and big goggle-eyes flouncing around sunken logs. Cain is proud of it all, you can tell. To him it's a mighty important pond.

He'll tell you now that the only reason he built it was so he'd have water where he could seine fish bait and kill moccasins. But I know why he built it. He told me why, that first time I visited him. Said he'd like to make a pretty place in the woods, where people could come and fish and sit under trees, and the place would be there long after he's gone, and finally somebody who came would ask, "Who fixed this place?" And the answer would be, "They was an old man here, that fixed it."

A good many visitors have enjoyed the pond, and if Cain really owned it, I'd print directions on how to get there. But it's on private property and I'm afraid sending crowds there might result in its destruction.

I bet you'll agree it will be a good thing if one of these times, maybe years from now, people will unfold a great and detailed map of the Thicket and there in southeast Polk County, labeled in important letters, will be Hardy Cain's Pond.

Katie Hattan lives near Wharton on a country road that hooks up Egypt and Spanish Camp. I found her house about three o'clock in the afternoon. She was out in the back, swinging a big hammer and fixing a hole in the hog pen. I thought that was newsy, considering that she turned 100 on December 18. She's such a small, narrow woman. I bet she wouldn't weigh ninety, not even holding that hammer.

Zennie Ray Hattan is her son. He was in the house. He took me out back to see his mother. He explained I wanted to talk to her. "I got to fix this pig pen," she said. I didn't think she was going to talk.

"I'll fix it myself," Zennie Ray said. "You go on in the house and talk." He took the hammer and hit a couple of licks.

His mother said, "You won't fix it the way I want it fixed. Just go on back in the house."

Zennie Ray looked at me and grinned. But he did as his mother said and went on in. Finally Katie Hattan stopped working and walked with me toward the house. "That boy's been gone all day," she said, talking about Zennie Ray, scolding gently. "I don't know *where* he goes off to."

I asked how old Zennie Ray is. She said he was born on the sixth day of August 1901, so he'd be seventy-six.

She took a chair just inside the front door, out of the wind, in a kind of entryway. Her face looked so small beneath the heavy knit cap she wore. But such a strength showed in that tiny face. A knowing, a confidence in the eyes. Here was a person accustomed to being in control, to giving orders, and being minded.

"I was born December 18, 1877," she said, "this side of Glen Flora. All my foreparents were slave people. I didn't miss slavery far myself. Well, you caught me fixin' a pig pen." She smiled about that, and it was one of the most special smiles. I caught myself being so glad to see it, and for a few seconds I wondered why it affected me that way.

Zennie Ray came to the front door and picked up a full gallon of paint and a brush and went back in the house, and his mother said, "What you gonna do now? I want you to fix that place where the wind comes in." Zennie Ray said he was going to paint now, that he'd fix the place later. Said he was going to stay there and work all night.

"I helped my father on the farm," Katie Hattan said, when I asked her to talk about her childhood. "I chopped cotton, and picked cotton, and worked and plowed like a boy. I still work, now. Every day I do things. I hammer. I nail. I do what a carpenter does. I milk my cow every day, and fix my milk. Zennie Ray!? What you doin' in there?!

"I had three children. I've got grandchildren, and great-grandchildren, and great-great-grandchildren. I don't know how many, but it's into the fifth generation.

"I piece quilts. Zennie Ray! Bring me those quilts here." He came with quilts his mother had made and spread them out to show. "I read the Bible," she went on. "Do you read the Bible? Do you believe what it says? I do, yes, I believe every word of it. Well, I watch TV sometimes. I watch news, but I don't see no use in watching it all the time."

She talked about her health. She has been in the hospital once in these 100 years. A gall bladder attack. So now she can't eat onions or cabbage or greasy things. "The doctor wanted to operate on me for gall bladder," she said. "But I told him God put that bladder in there for a cause. I asked him, 'If you take it out, what you gonna put in its place?' " Then she prayed about it, and she said the Lord talked to the doctor, and told him what to do, and the doctor changed his mind about taking out the gall bladder.

"Zennie?! I want you to fix that light! What's that boy doin' in there now?"

She talked about the state of the world, about the condition of humans, and she wasn't able to say very much good on the subject. "The world's gettin' worse. Somethin' bad's gonna happen if people don't change. They've gone off into idolatry. You go to church now and you don't find many people, unless there's a funeral. The sport has taken over. You want to find a crowd, go to the ball game, or the rodeo. But not in church. The Lord ain't pleased. If people don't change, He'll do something about it. He made that flood, in Noah's time. When you go too far, He'll stop you that way. He's the head. He's supreme. Zennie?! Zennie Ray!"

I stayed long enough to see her smile again. I think the reason I liked the smile, I saw hope and encouragement in it. Not for Katie Hattan, but for you and me. I find comfort in the fact that a person can live in this world for a century, and work so hard, and plow, and fix holes in pig pens, and even see bad things ahead. And yet still produce a smile like that.

4

*"Them ain't
your hawgs, Mr. Groves.
Them's your mules."*

Do you notice that men don't have the high shine on their shoes that they once had? I believe the reason is that we have so few shoeshine stands now. Most men are shining their own shoes, and there's a tendency to be lazy about it.

The past several years I have not had a good shine parlor along the paths I travel daily, and I miss going to one. It makes a man feel good to have a hot-shot shine on his kickers. My father, who was mighty particular about his duds, used to say that a good shoe shine would do more than any other one thing to dress a person up. He'd say a gent can have on ragged pants and two days of beard, but if he has a shine on his shoes he won't look like a bum. A nice store-bought shine was always more than that to me. There was something therapeutic about it. Relaxing. Then at the best shine stands I've known, getting a shine was often a social event that I liked.

For example, when my kids were growing up I lived in Brazos County, and every Sunday morning a lot of citizens would go downtown in Bryan where Jesse (I never knew his last name) would open the barbershop next door to the picture show and shine everybody's shoes. Doctors and lawyers and other professional people who were busy and hard to see during the week would often show up at Jesse's stand on Sunday morning, to visit and get a shine before church. I used to find out things there I couldn't find out on an ordinary Tuesday work day.

An experienced shine man can make your feet feel better, with his style of using the brush and the cloth. When my feet felt the best and my shoes stayed the nicest was during the two and a half years I worked in the old Humble Building in downtown Houston. The custom there was that the employees would make an agreement with a contract shine man. You would pay him so much a month, a flat fee, and every day he would come around to your office and shine your shoes while you sat at your desk. I suppose this was done in other buildings as well, and may still be.

Those fellows were marvels of speed and efficiency. Good businessmen. They contracted to take care of whatever you wore to work in the way of shoes. If you wore your top pair that stayed nice, the shine might not take twenty seconds. If you wore a pair that weren't quite what they should have been, the shine man would invest whatever time and effort it took to get your feet looking right.

I always imagined those shine men knew more about what went on in that company than anybody. They moved freely throughout the building, in and out of the offices of big shots and little shots. Even if you were having a conference, as every meeting between two or more people was called, the office door might swing open and here would come a silent shine man to break out his brush and polish and go to work on your shoes.

Back in the sixties when I was going down to Mexico a lot, I learned a lovely way to relax. Relaxing has always been a problem for me but this one method never failed me after I got it perfected. I would go to the central plaza of whatever town I was in, because that's where the shine boys would be. They really are shine boys, not men. Some are only seven or eight. For about an hour I would stroll around, among the trees and shrubs and statues and bandstands and fountains, and every ten or fifteen minutes sit down on a bench and get a shine. At that time a shine cost usually a peso, which was about twelve cents, so four or five shines wasn't any extravagance at all.

The reason I got so many was that it felt good to get one, and they had a sort of cumulative effect, and the relaxation climbed and spread all over me. I have spent fifty dollars at a doctor's office and gotten less benefit.

The interesting thing is that I never once saw a Mexican shine boy who seemed to find it peculiar that a gringo would walk around in the plaza getting four or five shines on the same pair of shoes. In fact I once tried to bet a friend two dollars that I could come into the plaza wearing a pair of sneakers and the Mexican shine boys would work on them as if they were made of the finest leather and never blink one of those dark solemn eyes. The friend wouldn't bet with me.

I do miss getting shines, foreign and domestic both. And I wish shoe shining was still an industry here, as it is in Mexico and other nations.

When I am traveling down the coast on U.S. 59 and need some ice for my soda pop box, I will hold off until I get to Wharton so I can buy it from Wharton Fruit Market. That's my favorite place to buy ice because to get it you go into Soupy Brandl's old-style walk-in freezer, with the thick wooden doors and the heavy metal latch that makes such a satisfactory noise when it opens and shuts. On a hot day about four o'clock I like to go in there and just stand a while and let the coldness envelop me.

It's something like going to the ice house, the way we used to do, and the fellow in charge would play the little joke on you, and stick you in the freezer room and let you stay till it didn't feel good in there. Maybe you remember then how nice the heat felt when you were out again.

Most places where I buy ice now I don't get any satisfaction out of it. Pay nearly a buck for a little dab of ice in a plastic bag. At Soupy's, if you want it he'll come and grab the ice pick that's stabbed into the two-by-four block on the outside of the door and he'll chip you a twenty-five pound block, the way they used to at the old ice houses. Or if you want it crushed, you get it in a nice big heavy-duty paper bag that's good for litter.

Small towns aren't likely to have ice houses any longer. Wharton doesn't have one. Soupy has to get his ice out of Houston, and even then can't get it delivered. Has to send up the highway, to Richmond I think, and meet a truck there and take it off.

Hasn't been long since practically any country town big enough to have two filling stations and a football team also had an ice house. I am talking about an ice manufacturing plant and not an open-air tavern of the type that is called an ice house now. The ice house was always in the ragged end of town, near the railroad tracks or next door to the wholesale grocery warehouse or back in behind the blacksmith shop.

The ice house was a fine hangout for country-town boys who didn't have anything much to do. We used to go there and crawl underneath the loading dock and let the cold water drip on us, and bury bare feet in the wet dirt when the temperature out in the street was around 100. What a delicious feeling that was. But the best thing about ice houses was the men, who were big and grinning and friendly and carried the great chunks of ice on their broad backs. And they were artists with ice picks. Chip chip chip, and a piece just the right size would fall away from a 300-pound block.

Some of the ice houses I've known used to sell watermelons. They'd take customers in the cold-storage rooms to pick out melons, stacked high as your hair-do and chilled to the heart. It was something special to have a watermelon from the ice house. This method of retailing produced a figure of speech I haven't heard since my early times. People would say, "Cold as an ice-house watermelon."

We used to sit under the loading dock and watch the ways people carried the ice they bought. A popular method was to put a block of ice on the car bumper, back when bumpers protruded more and made a sort of rack. Some people would stick fifty pounds on the bumper and drive ten miles out in the country, and the block would be half melted before they got home. There were marvelously old people who would come, with canes and on crutches and limping, to buy the least amount sold. The man would tie binder twine around a nickel's worth, and those old folks would shuffle back home in the heat, carrying their pitiful little hunks of dripping ice.

Then the ice deliveryman, one of a steady procession of retail tradesmen who came in and out of houses as if they were neighbors and friends. Ice man. Grocery delivery. Sometimes even the milkman would come in, if you wrote a note and asked him to put the milk in the ice box. The ice man would call softly at the back door. "Ice man!" Then come on in, without waiting for an answer, and other deliverymen would do the same, and it seems strange now, in these times when we live behind locked doors. But then we *knew* the ice man. Knew his family, and probably saw him every Sunday in church.

The barnstormers would come on Sunday afternoon. They'd land their old biplanes in the pasture out north of town, scattering scrub cows and barefoot boys.

Everybody would go out to watch after church. We'd go out there on foot, or on bicycles, or in stripdown Model Ts, or 1934 Chevys with knee action, or maybe even brand-new 1936 Fords with V-8 engines and marble knobs on the steering wheels.

"Dare-Devils of the Skies!" shouted the posters the advance man put up in the barber shop a week ahead of the show. "See Ace Morgan Perform Death-Defying Wing Walk! See Lovely Marilyn Fox, The World's Only Lady Parachutist! Take a Ride in The Clouds! See Your City as the Birds See It!" It wasn't true, that part about the woman (her name was always Marilyn Something) being the world's only female parachutist. But who cared? Nobody cared.

We'd all crowd around Ol' Ace and inspect him like he was a creature from another world. He was tall and lean and chewed gum in a sort of crooked, go-to-hell way. His calves encased in the slick black leather of what we called aviator boots. One flap of his helmet cocked up so he could hear. The big goggles across his forehead. I tell you he looked keen. And the Lovely Marilyn, who was pushing forty, dressed just the same way, all in black. A lady aviator, who flew that biplane while Ol' Ace walked around among the wing struts and held on sometimes with just one hand.

Then here came the Lovely Marilyn floating down to earth in that milk-white parachute, like some kind of an angel, waving at the crowd and making a rough landing that turned her a double somersault. And you'd hear, "Oh my law, she's hurt! Is she hurt? Did she hit that bob war fence? I thought she hit the fence! No, look, she's gettin' up! She's all right! She missed that bob war by about this much!"

The tension relieved temporarily, Ol' Ace would climb, to do us some stunts way up there. And a couple of the smart alec boys in the crowd would make it up to pull the airplane joke we all learned in the cotton patch and thought was so funny and so wicked. "Say," one would yell, "is that a mail plane up there?"

"Naw," his confederate would answer, "that ain't no male plane. That's just the wheels hangin' down." All the boys would roar, and the girls would stay quiet because they didn't get it, or pretended not to, and the joke would be pulled again and again until nobody laughed anymore.

Finally then came the airplane rides, two dollars a head for a circle over town. Prohibitive for all except a few of those driving the new Ford V-8's. But Ol' Ace would have some unexpected passengers.

"Hey, look at that. Guess who's goin' up? Ol' Man Groves! Can you feature it? How old is he? Why, don't nobody know. Paint wasn't dry on Noah's Ark when Ol' Man Groves was born, and here he's goin' up in an airplane!"

And he did, and when he got back down he climbed out all wobble-kneed, wearing a silly little grin, his glasses hanging from one ear, and telling about it. "I got 'im to take me over my place, way up high, and I looked down and thought I seen some of my hawgs. And that aviator said, 'Why, Mister Groves, them ain't your hawgs. Them's your mules!' " Oh, how we laughed about that.

When it was over we'd stand there in the pasture and watch Ol' Ace and the Lovely Marilyn and the airplane until they were a dot in the east, leaving us, headed back, nonstop, all the way to Fort Worth.

The last time I went back home I drove down to the depot and parked and walked across the tracks to see if the hobo jungle is still there. It is not.

Long ago at sundown we would see them sometimes, back in the brush on the side of the tracks opposite the depot. Never many in a bunch. Two or three, most times, hunkered around a little fire. More often we would only see that they had been there and gone. We'd circle the ashes of their fire, and talk of where one had slept and flattened the weeds.

We'd look for signs that they had marked the homes in town where a tramp could go and get a meal. It was told that such houses were somehow marked, that a tramp could walk the streets of our town and find the signs and nobody except other tramps could read them, or even find where they were. We doubted that the houses were marked. Because if they went only by a mark, surely you would have tramps off the railroad walking the streets all the time, looking for marks, and we saw no sign of that.

We guessed, then, that in the jungle where they slept we might find some sort of map, or crude address list, that the tramps would leave behind after they'd been fed. We found no such system, ever, or even a clue to it. There were stories of how you could go down in there and turn over an old plank or a piece of tin and find addresses scrawled. But we never found anything like that. Probably the location of the houses was passed by word of mouth. Or not passed at all, and the tramps would come up from the jungle and hit the back doors at random. Or pick them by some private clue system of their own, without any help from signs or other tramps.

Something else that added weight to the hobo legend that houses were marked (this is just my opinion)—people enjoyed thinking that theirs was one of the marked houses. They tried to pretend that feeding railroad tramps was a bother and an expense. When in fact they enjoyed imagining that they were known throughout the hobo world as generous and compassionate folks and that their house was marked with five secret stars, or some such brand of distinction. They liked to tell how the tramps could find them even if they moved all the way across town. Even if they moved three or four times, still the tramps would come to their back door, so the houses *must* have been marked.

I think it's more likely that tramps knocked on every back door in town. Because listen, *nobody* in that little town moved more than we did. In fact I expect my family set a record in towns with population of between 2,000 and 4,000, for moving more often than anybody else. The tramps would always find us, but I doubt that was because they knew us. Still, we were like all the others and enjoyed feeling special, being people that bums knew and appreciated.

I liked to imagine that one of the tramps would walk into the hobo jungle, rubbing his stomach and chewing on a toothpick and saying, "Well, boys, the Hales have moved again. They've given up the boarding house on Daugherty Street and moved over to Mulberry, a block west of the Church of God. You can tell the place by its porch swing, and the horseshoe-pitching stakes alongside, and a Jersey milk cow in the back yard."

Hobo jungle. First time I ran across that term I classed it plenty romantic, just oozing with adventure and freedom. But I had a hard time connecting that romanticism with the sorry lot of men who knocked on my mother's back door to ask for food. They had sad, dark faces and broody eyes and thin, tight mouths. I never heard one laugh or even speak with a grin in his tone. They all seemed to be nursing some private torment. And I expect they were because those were terrible times.

If that's what being a hobo meant, I didn't want any part of it. When it came my time to roam I roamed, but not on the railroad, not as a bum. Up until I watched those old boys sitting on our back steps, scooping up pinto beans and wolfing down cold cornbread and Jersey butter, up until then I had a notion it would be fine just to take off, and go, and be a bum, and not follow any rules or maps or take any orders. But those sad faces changed my mind.

Jungle was a good name for that place by the depot where the hobos stayed. It was a thicket, a tangle of briars and catclaw bushes and oak underbrush, and it was close by the creek where the mosquitoes were thick, and the water moccasins. I can think of a lot better place to sleep.

Of the vanished Americans we hear so much about, the one I really miss is the milkman. All my time I've liked milkmen, the guys who used to get up so early in the morning and rattle those bottles on the front steps.

The first milkmen I knew drove rubber-wheeled wagons in Fort Worth in 1928. My family had moved into the city from the wilderness for a while, and the milkman was a link to the country that remained after we'd left the cows behind.

I used to lie in bed early in the morning and listen for the milkman's sound. Klop-klop-klop-klop. That was his horse, making that klop sound. He drove a great big dappled gray work horse with feet the size of pie plates, and on a quiet morning you could hear him coming fifteen minutes away. I loved that sound, that klop-klop-klop. It was rich and crisp and made echoes along the damp streets.

This was in simple times when a young person didn't have far to look to find a hero. He could just look out the window at six o'clock in the morning and see a man to admire. A man who could stand on your front porch and softly call, "Whoa," and that great horse would stop and wait.

Later on I got on a hello basis with milkmen who cared, who

knew about people. I remember milkmen who could look at houses even before good daylight and tell nobody was home, that they'd gone off again to Grandma's and forgotten to leave a note. A milkman who recognized a situation like that wouldn't leave any milk, because it would just stand there and sour. He'd know that the bunch wouldn't be back from Grandma's until Sunday night.

I liked the signs of milkmen times. Signs like bottles on front porches with notes scrawled on tablet paper and rolled up and stuck in their necks: "Mr. Bailey, Jimmy is home for a week so please leave an extra quart until Tuesday. Tell Elsie to come see us." Those were times when doors didn't need locking and you could leave a note and tell the milkman, "We won't be back until three o'clock so please come in and put the milk in the ice box. Try a piece of the devil's food cake. Audrey made it."

Times when people passed judgment on the quality of milk by how much cream rose to the top. Times when you'd look across the street early on cold winter mornings and see if the milk had frozen on the neighbor's front porch. And if it had, it might have pushed the little cardboard stopper out and two or three inches of frozen cream would be poking out the top of the bottle.

Back in '48 and '49 I got to know a whole squad of Houston milkmen. I was getting up early to go to work at KPRC when its studios were in the Lamar Hotel, and on the way downtown I'd stop at a little all-night restaurant out on West Gray. This bunch of milkmen stopped there too, the same ones every morning, about five o'clock. I got to sitting with them. They were milkmen in the old tradition. Good old grinning boys, strong and good-natured and full of jokes, and they liked their jobs, you could tell. They were all men around forty then, and they'd talk about times when it was hard to keep steady work and so getting up in the middle of the night to deliver milk wasn't any punishment to them.

The last milkman I knew was a fellow about thirty. He seemed in a bad humor all the time, and came awful late. Then he stopped coming altogether, and disappeared, along with the ice man and the delivery boy from the grocery store and the man who drove the panel truck from the tailor shop.

Handy men, they were called, with the emphasis on the first word. *Handy* men. I remember several from long ago, in country towns. Maybe they were the same gents who were called hired hands on the farm, the ones who'd come walking up the lane looking tired and empty and asking for work. But I never heard them called handy men on the farm.

In town you'd hear a woman tell her white-collar husband when he went off to work, "I wish you'd send me a handy man. I want to get the garden spaded up."

The white-collar men I remember from my early times didn't do much manual labor around the premises. Today you'll find even company presidents going home and spading up gardens and rewiring lamps and such. But they didn't do that at the time I am talking about, because there were handy men for those jobs.

I am now able to see in fairly good detail a composite of all the handy men I once watched, and talked to. He was about 5'10" and maybe forty-eight years old and somewhat stocky. But bent at the shoulders, probably from doing so much stoop labor. Flaming red skin that did not get along well with the sun. Yellowish stubble on chin and jaws. A broad round face. And teeth missing, right in front, so when he grinned he looked mighty snaggly. He smelled, ever so bad. You wanted to keep upwind of him.

His pants didn't fit because they were cast-offs somebody had given him. Sometimes he would wear a rope to hold them up. The pants were always too long, and the bottoms of the legs would be frayed where his heels stepped on them. If he wore a coat it would be cast-off also, and it would be the coat of a suit. I see him most often in a beat-up felt hat of gray, a brown coat, and a pair of old dark blue pants. He walked, worked, so slowly. I never saw a handy man who was quick. Even the best of them worked slow.

He accepted, without question or complaint, whatever working conditions he found. If children were where he worked, he accepted that they would be following him around, getting in his way, asking questions. He was a kind of babysitter. He seemed neither to enjoy that position nor to object to it.

He came to work empty-handed. Never a tool of his own. He used what tools he found on the premises. I can see him coming to the back door about the middle of the morning, and knocking, and asking, "Ma'am? Is there a hatchet?"

He was good at jobs like breaking a garden, cleaning out flower beds, digging post holes, fixing fences. In his time it was common for town people to have milk cows and chickens, and there was always fence repair to do. He might even be pretty good at finding where the roof was leaking and putting in extra shingles to stop it. He could fix a sagging step. Make a cotter key out of a nail and put a wheel back on a scooter or a tricycle.

If the woman wasn't too particular she might let him prune the shrubs or clip the hedge. He was not any 'count with electricity. He was a hammer and saw man, and grubbing hoe, and shovel, and ax man. And paint brush, on jobs that didn't matter, like cow sheds and chicken houses.

I wish I could remember, because it seems right, that the handy man told great stories and spouted folksy wisdoms of high educational value. But I don't think he did. I can remember, though, something about the handy man that would just as well be forgotten. It has to do with what he ate. It's a special talent of mine that I can accumulate in my noggin a great amount of practical information, and inside a week I am able to forget every trace of it before I can convert it to anything of value. Yet I can remember, from fifty years ago, a meal that was served to the handy man. He ate it on our back steps.

It was served to him in a big platter, not a plate. The platter was heaped. Navy beans. Black-eyed peas. English peas. Pinto beans. Boiled cabbage. Leftovers, don't you see. Cold sausage from breakfast. Cold biscuits. A stray hunk of yellow cornbread. Pickled beets. A big raw onion. Buttermilk in a quart jar. He ate it, every bite in silence, sopped the platter with the last biscuit, rolled a Bull Durham smoke, and went back to work.

Nearest thing I've seen lately to a handy man, a fellow with a pickup full of power tools knocked on the door, asked if we had any kind of work we needed done. We did, in the yard, and he went around and looked it over. Said he wanted to do some figuring, and he'd stop by the next day and give us a price. He never did come back, though.

5

"It's got the gear shift
up on the steering post and
it's got four-wheel brakes
and it's been in town
since last Thursday."

About 4 P.M. I drove into Round Top and spotted this beautiful blue pickup truck parked on the town square. It was exactly the kind of truck I had been searching for, and I was certainly pleased to find it. It looked to be close to its fifteenth or sixteenth birthday and had a spectacular multiple fracture of the right windshield. It was also showing a fine assortment of dents and scrapes and bruises. But best of all it was loaded, inside and out, with the magnificent clutter of stuff that makes a Texas pickup genuine.

Genuine pickup trucks in this state are a minority breed. Most pickups haven't really got any business being trucks, and would serve their owners better by being passenger cars. I have done my share of griping about pickups in Texas, but I know a genuine one when I see it, and I have a respect for it.

I went around the square asking until I found the fellow who admitted he belongs to that old blue truck. He was sitting in the Round Top General Store. His name is Kenneth Levien. Lives there at Round Top. Man of maybe twenty-seven or twenty-eight, stocky, with pale blue eyes and a fine rusty mustache. He's a heavy equipment operator. Drives a bulldozer. I asked his permission to take an inventory of everything he was carrying in the truck. Told him it would make an important story for the paper, and I believe that's true. I have filled up acres of space in this journal with stuff of far less significance to the Texas scene than the contents of a genuine pickup truck.

Levien seemed pleased that somebody besides himself admires that pickup. We went out to start the inventory, and he gave me a little history on that grand vehicle. "It's a '64 Chevy," he said. "My daddy bought it second-hand in '65 when I was about thirteen. In '68, I bought me a car, but I was driving the truck more than the car so my daddy and I just traded, even. From '70 to '74 I was in the Marine Corps, and my daddy drove the truck while I was gone. There's no telling how many miles it has on it. The speedometer stopped in '68, and it was showing about 84,000 then. I use it now for hunting and fishing, and I drive it to work. About all it needs is a new transmission. It's a good old truck."

We made a list of its contents, starting with the seat and the floorboards: A .410 shotgun. A tool box. A roll of toilet paper. A pair of binoculars. A hard hat. A curious crooked stick. "I use that," Levien drawled, about the crooked stick, "to hold the hood up because the prop is broken."

Pair of old Marine Corps coveralls. Some safety glasses. A thick cushion to sit on because the foam rubber of the seat is just about gone on the driver's side. A box of .28-gauge shotgun shells. A nine-ounce jar of mustard. Mustard? "Sometimes I buy bread and cold cuts to take on the job, and I need something to put on it."

Several kinds of headgear, mostly caps, both summer and winter styles. A heavy-duty electrical plug, with lead-in, the kind used for wiring a mobile home for power. And half of a gun rack, on the seat near where the driver sits. "I use that," Levien said, "to hold the shift lever in gear. This truck jumps out of high gear when it gets going good." He discovered the hook of the gun rack held the shift lever nice and snug when braced against the dash. Works fine.

Genuine pickups always have interesting stuff riding up on the

dash. This one had several plastic holders of rifle cartridge cas-
ings, empty, being saved for reloading. Ashtray full of cartridges
of various calibers. Box of points for tuning the truck. A hunting
knife. A radiator cap. A hatchet. A brown teacup. "I got it out of
the kitchen at home to use as a cuspidor," Levien said about the
cup. "Now I don't use it, because I found this real little brass
cuspidor here. My wife knows where the cup is, but she doesn't
want it back."

A piece of blue lumber crayon he uses on the job. A pair of
pruning shears. A shaker of seasoned salt. Notepad and pocket
calendar. A Prince Albert can full of beans (seed for planting). A
dozen empty Copenhagen snuff tins. And a whistle for calling a
bird dog. I asked about the whistle and Levien said, very quietly,
"Last Labor Day weekend somebody poisoned my dog. No, I
don't know who did it. If I did I probably wouldn't be standin'
here talkin' to you."

Riding in the bed of the truck: A fish basket. A tool box. An ax.
Two tackle boxes. Two plastic coolers. Four outboard motor oil
bottles. An iron pot with a basket for deep-fat frying. The air
cleaner off the truck's carburetor. A long-handled back brush. The
gas tank off a lawn mower. A cane pole. The remains of a carton
of fishing worms. A six-pack of king-sized soda-pop bottles. A
jack. A hammer and a sack of staples. And seven empty beer
cans. Now I want to defend seven empty beer cans in the bed of a
pickup. Just remember that's seven beer cans that weren't flung in
the ditch along the road. Say the same for those dozen empty
snuff tins, too.

Levien gave me a short ride, to show how the hook of the gun
rack braces the shift lever so the truck won't jump out of high.
And how he always shifts from low to high and skips second
because second gear is shot. "I've had another transmission I
guess for about a year, but I just haven't gotten around to puttin'
it in."

Before we parted we looked over the pickup's contents again, to
be sure we hadn't missed anything of importance in the inventory, and Levien made the most remarkable statement of all.
"Wasn't but just a few days ago I cleaned this old truck out."

It's hard to imagine that the spirit of a young man could soar
higher than it does on the day he receives his first automobile.

I've watched several of them go through that day. They enter into an uplifted condition, and it may last a month.

During this period of gladness, a boy of sixteen has been known to show genuine affection toward a little sister. He may also hug his mother without warning and say out loud that he loves her and send the old girl into a state of pleasurable shock almost equal to his own. It's possible he'll have a seizure of generosity and make a sudden gift of his old bicycle to his younger brother, who hasn't been anything in past years except a punching bag.

It's not at all hard to spot a young fellow who has lately gotten a car. He'll be out in the driveway washing that vehicle at 7:30 A.M., before school. Thousands and thousands of teen-age males wash automobiles every day in this country, but I challenge you to find me one washing a car at 7:30 A.M., unless it has just recently started belonging to him.

I don't know, in the long run, whether it's good for sixteen-year-old boys to have cars. Maybe it isn't, for some of them. But those males who didn't get a car at sixteen—and there are millions of us—were deprived of a mighty sweet experience. It comes the first time the young fellow backs out of the drive and roars off while The Girl Is Watching.

I suppose you have seen it. The Girl may not be fifteen, but she already knows how important it is for her to watch, and she will take a little stroll around the neighborhood at just the right time. He will seem not to see her. But he sees her, don't you worry about that, because he's been in the house watching the street half the afternoon. When she turns the corner he hustles to the mirror, to make sure his hair is hanging over his forehead and ears in just that proper groovy way, and then he exits the front door, whistling the tune he has picked out in advance.

He doesn't just get in the car. He swings in. Floats and flows in. And settles behind the wheel the way your best cowboys board a horse, and while his left hand is yanking the door shut his right is already on the ignition. "Gah-room!" The engine must start on the first turn, else everything is spoiled. "Gah-room, gah-room, gah-*room!*" Leaning just a bit forward, you know, listening to the engine the way the masters do. The way Cale Yarborough listens. The way Junior Johnson listened. The way Barney Oldfield listened.

And now backing out at the right second. Coming down the drive a little faster than he ought to, spinning the spokes of the steering wheel with his right index, the left hand lying casually on the dash to show he doesn't need it. Then like a concert pianist, three fingers of the right hand extend and pull the shift lever down into drive and there is just the suggestion of rubber burning, only a slight squeal, a token peel-out, to show her what he would do on the open road.

And finally the wave, slow and cool, almost a salute, that he gives her when he goes past, pretending he just happened to see her at the last second. Now that's got to be a sweet experience, folks.

The only thing that surpasses it may be to hear the roar of a car that you build, yourself. I never built one, but one of my former dependents did back when he was in high school, and it pretty near put me and his mother in the nut house while he was about it. Some of the neighbors, too. It took months. Years, I guess, I don't remember. Studying manuals, catalogs, magazines. Working weekends and after school for money to order parts from Honest Charley out of Kansas City. Hours, days, weeks, months out there in the carport on freezing nights and sweltering days.

And then finally came The Time. To see if it would run. We stayed in the house and peeked through the curtains. Maybe a dozen of his friends out there, looking doubtful, grinning. He raised the trunk lid and connected the two great batteries to the ignition system and then got behind the wheel and took a deep thoughtful breath and punched the button. The starter ground. And ground. And ground. And the dozen guys grinned. And I said silently, "Lord, let it start, because he's worked awful hard on it and spent every cent of money he's ever earned on it. Let it start at least for a little while." His mother confessed later she offered up the same supplication.

And it started. Oh, how it did start. It made such an awful racket I bet they were able to hear it at that place in Kansas City where the cams and the connecting rods came from. And later on, especially the day the police called and said somebody was complaining about the noise, I was almost sorry I'd asked the angels to help him start that monster. But I don't regret it now. The neighbors forgave us the racket. And I know he'll always remember his fine hour, there under our carport, when a machine he put together with his own hands sprang to life, and made that great noise.

Last Tuesday the odometer on this little station wagon I'm driving now turned 35,000 miles, and I have not had a flat tire since I bought it. I hear other traveling people talk about running a set of steel-belted radials 40,000 miles and more without ever having a flat but 35,000 is a record for me. My father wouldn't believe that. He would just snort at the idea that a car could roll 35,000 miles without a flat.

A long time ago when my family was living at Stephenville, on Sunday my father would drive us to Grandma Hale's farm, about thirty miles up near the Palo Pinto–Erath county line. When we would get to the farm several of the kinfolks would be sitting on the front porch and one of the men would ask, "Well, when did you get off?" Meaning what time we left Stephenville. My father would say we got off at seven, or whenever it was. Then watches would be pulled out and consulted and one of the uncles would say, "Well, you made fair time."

And he would say, "We didn't have but one flat." Which explained why we made fair time. Because it wasn't uncommon for him to spend more time fixing flats on that thirty miles of country road than he spent driving. I have known him to fix three and four without even losing his temper or using a word that made my Methodist mother mad at him.

I think of this: We have got traveling men now who are past forty and have been on the road more than twenty years and they don't know what it means to fix a flat. Change a tire, yes, but not actually fix a flat. The fact is I have never had to fix one myself, and I started traveling in 1946. I've fixed a flock of bicycle flats but not car ones, not the way my father and his contemporaries fixed them.

It meant jacking up the car and taking the tire off the rim and pulling the tube out and finding the leak. To find the leak you had to pump the tube up and listen for the air coming out the hole. It was best to find water in a ditch somewhere and dunk the tube and look for the bubbles. And look for more than one hole because you might fix the most obvious leak and put the tube back in the tire and pump it up and get it remounted and discover there was another leak that you'd missed. Then you'd have it to do all over again.

You fixed the inner tube with cold patching that everybody carried. The women sat on the running board and watched while you buffed the surface of the tube around the hole. You buffed it with the lid off the cold patch kit. That lid was metal with a built-in roughness, sort of like a kitchen grater. Roughing up the spot on the tube made the glue work better.

The glue was in a little tube in the kit. You spread it and let it air a minute and then stuck the patch on. You cut the patch to accommodate the size of the leak. So you needed scissors or a razor blade or a mighty sharp pocketknife. You pressed the patch on and held it and held it and hoped it stuck. You pumped the tube up again and went to the ditch to test your patch. Or if you couldn't find water, you spit on the patch to see if any air was coming from around the edges and making bubbles.

You understand this might have to be done several times a day when you were on bad roads with weak tires. And it seemed to me then that all roads were bad. It was the nature of roads, as I first learned them, to be bad, all rutted and infested with rusty nails.

Here was a bad thing: Sometimes after a tube was properly patched, it would be pinched while you were remounting the tire, and all the air would bleed out. When this happened the women would take the children and walk a little way up the road and pretend to be interested in the wildflowers. This was so the fixer of the flat would have room to cuss. The first two or three flats might be fixed pretty smooth, but it is my belief that there was no way to fix a fourth one without cussing. Then for the fifth and sixth flats, a man would even need help with the cussing.

You can still buy those tube patching kits. I bought one a few days ago for bicycle tires for only fifty-nine cents. I may not ever fix another bicycle flat, but I am glad to have the cold patch kit. Just holding it in my hand enables me to see a lot of scenes that happened long ago, and helps me appreciate driving 35,000 miles without having a flat tire.

The high school and college students that I know don't talk about new cars the way their mamas and papas used to. In my own green times, one of the big days of the year was when they took the sheets off the new-model car on the showroom floor.

Crowds of us would be waiting out on the sidewalk to get that first pop-eyed look at what marvels of power and beauty Detroit had created for the coming year. When the wrapping fell away, there would be a moment of near-silence while we drew breaths, and then we would whistle and say, "Boy, that's really keen!" *Keen* was our word then. Sometimes *neat* and sometimes *swell* but mostly *keen*. The keenest thing of all was a new car.

There was a special triumph that a lucky young citizen could score, on seeing a new model. It came to few of us, and it almost never came twice to any individual. You had to know somebody important, like the son of a mechanic who worked in the service department of the dealership. One day at school he'd say to you, looking over his shoulder to be sure nobody else could hear, "Hey, guess what's down at Bell's. A brand new '38. Just got it in. My dad's gonna take me to see it after supper. You want to go?" Which was similar to asking a dog if he'd like to visit a meat market.

The mechanic was a big gruff fellow with solid black arcs of grease under all his fingernails. The grease was there even on Sunday when you saw him in church. He would take you in by the back entrance at the car dealer's and say, "Cost me my job, anybody finds out." I doubt that was true, but the idea made the adventure more delicious.

So then for an hour, you were privileged to view the new '38, crouched back there in all its gleaming glory. It would be three more days before the public could view it, so you were seeing something truly forbidden. "Now don't tell anybody," the mechanic would say, when the secret viewing was over. You'd promise not to say anything and then run pretty near a mile and a half looking for somebody to tell. Not telling—what a ridiculous notion.

The experience stirred your sleeping sense of possession. You felt you knew things about the new car that nobody else in the world knew. It was almost as if you owned it, then. Which was a completely outrageous idea.

Perhaps that was the main difference, between then and today. All young men, now, know that eventually they will be able to have expensive things like new automobiles. Even a person living in the suburbs of poverty can, by the wonders of our credit scheme, drive a new car. But back there when the new '38s were coming out, I don't believe the high school gang that trooped down to admire them thought they'd ever own anything so fine. Oh sure, you had grand fantasies about cars, the same as about romance. You trumped up tasty visions of running off in a new convertible with Betty Grable. But you knew the car was impossible, same as the girl. So getting to view that forbidden automobile was a huge moment. You felt it was the nearest you could come to possessing it.

When the rest of the world was permitted to see what you'd already seen, you acted mighty smug. You went down to the dealer's, sure, but you stood back in the fringe of the crowd, arms folded, legs spread athletically, and tried to look bored. When the fact was, you were bursting to tell what you knew. When anybody came in the front door, you wanted to walk up to them and say, "It's got the gear shift up on the steering post and it's got four-wheel brakes and it's been in town since last Thursday."

You've noticed, I suppose, that it's no longer popular to brag that you've bought a new car. Just the reverse, in fact. The people who used to talk about their new cars are now going around telling everybody that they're driving battered compacts with 97,000 miles showing. Maybe one of these times the energy situation will improve and you will be allowed to talk about your new car, but not now. It's almost unpatriotic, especially if the new car is a big one that burns a lot of gas. So this is another of the bad aspects of the energy shortage—Americans are deprived of the pleasure of showing off their new cars.

Back when I was growing up, the best thing that could happen to a family was getting a new car. I used to dream that it would happen to my own family, that one day my father would come home in a brand-new sparkler straight off the showroom floor. But it never came to pass. He died without ever owning a car that had not belonged to somebody else. The closest he came, he showed up with a big Willys-Knight that had a burned-out clutch but only one previous owner. Evidently he sensed that this was it, this would be our finest hour with respect to cars. So he put us all to washing and polishing that vehicle, and when we got it looking good we piled in and he drove us around town. Past all the best houses so people could see us. We even parked in front of the drugstore on the square and honked for curb service. My father wouldn't do that in the car we had before the Willys-Knight, because it was held together with baling wire and had a chicken coop on the back, and he didn't want us to be seen in it downtown.

A new car in that little town was a municipal event. Everybody knew about it by supper time. They would know how much it cost, too, and whether it was financed or whether cash was paid for it. That drew the most notice of all—somebody hauling off and paying $700 cash for a new car. Didn't even have to go ask the banker for permission.

The first new car I bought—well, I never did own it entirely, it was a partnership between me and one of those big sets of initials like CIT or GMAC—my first new car was a '49 Ford with a gun-metal-gray paint job that went bad, and an overdrive. First thing I did was drive 225 miles to show that new car to my father. We got in and rolled around town, past all the best houses, just as we did in the Willys-Knight, and we parked on the square, too, and waited for people to come by and look us over. That was mighty rural, sure, but then I think Americans everywhere have always acted rural about their automobiles, and do still.

Back in the fifties I served a sentence working in a downtown Houston office building, and off and on I was a member of car pools. It was almost like 1938 when one of those guys would roll up in a new car. Man, you were expected to ooh and ah and issue congratulations and make cornball jokes about crop failures and it reminded me of the old home town. One time one of the car-pool drivers was due to buy a big new sedan. He'd been making the deal for a month, so we knew about it and we cooked it up between us to pretend we didn't notice.

So when he picked us up in the new car, we said good morning as usual and talked about the ball game last night or politics or the weather, anything but the new car. All the way to town, not a car word said. Driver sat up there in about half a huff. That evening on the way home, same thing. Just standard talk, nothing about the automobile. We'd talk about *our* old cars, but not his new one. About three-quarters of the way home he exploded. Pulled over and turned around and yelled, "All right, you smart-bleep bunch of bleepers, I want to know what you think of this new car!"

Don't you imagine certain new-car owners are feeling sort of that same degree of frustration, right now? Say here's a guy who's been driving economy cars forty years, out of necessity. Then suddenly something really nice happens to his financial circumstance, and he yearns for what he's always dreamed of and worked for, a truly fine luxury automobile. He can afford it. He can afford the gas it'll burn. If gas goes to two dollars he can *still* afford it. So he buys, at a time when buying big cars is considered the first cousin to a dark sin. That must take a lot of the fun out of it.

Did you know this? That there are people old enough to vote, and who have held driver's licenses since they were fifteen, and who have never driven an automobile as much as a mile in the mud? I consider that sad. They've missed a lot of fun. Why, I bet you that today there are cars five years old and showing 60,000 miles on their speedometers that never have been stuck, unless it was in the mud of a parking lot at a football stadium. Driving in mud is not only fun but educational. You get on a good crooked stretch of muddy road, and get stuck a couple of times, it teaches you something.

Sometimes in weak moments I feel a little pain of regret that by the time I got started traveling this state you could drive all the way across it on pavement. My father used to have a perfect passion for driving under all conditions, but especially in the mud. Up until World War II he was a traveling salesman, beginning in the mid-1920s when there was still adventure in driving around over Texas. When I'd go to see him in his last years, he'd bring out a map and get me to show him where I'd been lately. He'd ask about "road conditions" everywhere. Then he'd sit back and talk about how he made that same trip, to the very one I'd just made myself, but he made it in 1927 in the mud.

He'd pretend it was a terrible hardship, and the truth was he loved every mile of it. Didn't really mind getting stuck, because that generally meant he'd get to meet new people. He'd walk up to a farm house and get somebody to come pull him out. He remembered them all. "Man's name was Riley," he'd say. "He had a big patch of roasting ears by the side of the road and a mare with twin colts and two big red mules named Luke and John. He had a boy, a big old freckled-face, snaggle-tooth boy must have been six foot and two inches. He harnessed the mules and went down there and pulled me out. I offered him fifty cents but he said, 'Naw, we don't want your money. But you'll never make it into town tonight. Creek's out. You may as well come on in and spend the night.' And I did. The next morning the creek was still out so I stayed over and helped 'em fix fence."

He knew people like that everywhere. People who'd pulled him out of mudholes. He always kept in touch with them. He'd write 'em post cards from the Rio Grande Valley or from up at Wichita Falls, and when he got back that way he'd go to see them again and take something that country folks weren't likely to have, like a sack of oranges or some storebought bread in wax paper.

On short trips I'd get to go with him sometimes. I was just a shirt-tail kid then and thought he was the world's most important man, because he drove all over Texas and sold overalls to dry goods stores.

On a rainy day he'd stop at a crossroads and he'd say, "Well, I'd like to cut across here, to Itasca, and save a little time. But it's ten miles of mud. Do you reckon we can make it?" And I'd say I didn't know. Then he'd say, "We'd probably get stuck." And he'd grin, and push the brim of his hat up and say, "Let's give 'er a try." And off we'd roar, spinnin' and splashin' and slippin' and weavin' and laughin'. Save a little time? Ha. Time didn't mean any more to him than it would to a hog. All he wanted to cut across for was to see if he could make it through ten miles of mud.

You seldom see little boys hanging out around service stations now. It used to be that just as quick as a small kid was allowed to roam around out of his mama's sight, he went to the filling station up on the highway and sat on the edge of the grease pit and hoped the filling station man would let him run an errand. The first filling stations I remember were mighty educational places. Some of the education was good and some of it bad, but it was all valuable.

The men who ran those stations were lonesome guys. They had no help, and I suppose that's why they didn't mind little kids hanging around. They were generally smeared with grease and smoked Bull Durham and had tattoos on their forearms. One I remember had been in France during the war, and he told the grandest stories. He had a helmet there in the station. He claimed he killed the German who wore that helmet. Killed him with a bayonet, and he would tell us all about how it felt, to kill a man.

The station where we hung out the most had just one pump, with the gallons marked off on the glass part above. We would stand in line and take turns, pumping the gas back in the tank. I thought it was a beautiful thing to watch that foaming gasoline come gushing in the big glass cylinder. At that station we learned to recognize cars—the Chevys and the Fords and sometimes a Willys-Knight and maybe even a Pierce Arrow. We thought the filling station man knew everything right and proper there was to know. We considered him a genius, and strong as Charles Atlas. "You ought to see him crank a Model T," we'd say at home.

He would let us put water in radiators sometimes. He'd teach us to test the radiator cap before we unscrewed it, so we wouldn't get scalded. We learned about cold-patching an inner tube, and how to put a boot in a tire with a hole in it, and how to pump a quart of oil out of the tank into the copper can with the marvelous spout that bent in all directions. We would work around that station just as if we were getting paid. We'd sweep the oily floor and pick soda-water caps up off the gravel driveway, and we'd go to the bakery and bring back a fried pie for the filling station man. As a reward we might get a free soda water, and we might not get anything.

The greatest thing of all was when the big trucks would stop.

We considered a truck driver a greater hero than the filling station man. Not a one of us dared speak to a truck driver or ask him a question, but we'd creep close and listen when the filling station man talked to him.

"Lookit them big ol' casins," we'd say, eyeing the truck tires.

"That truck driver claims he come from Corpus Christi!"

"Man! All the way from Corpus Christi."

Sometimes we saw and heard things we didn't tell about at home. The first time I ever saw a man take a drink of whiskey was right there in that station. He turned up a pint bottle and gurgled down a few swallows and then walked out, and we marveled that he didn't stagger or fall down, because we'd been taught at home that as soon as you swallowed any whiskey you'd be drunk and on the road to hell. Occasionally the filling station man would have adult visitors, and they'd get behind stacks of tires in the back and have a crap game. It was wonderful to watch a wicked thing like that, with nickels and dimes and now and then even a quarter being gambled at one roll of the dice.

The last time I went back to the old home town I drove out the highway where the station stood. It has been torn down and a new little house built on the lot. In the front yard I could still see some of the red gravel left over from the driveway. The grease pit has been filled in with topsoil and it is now a zinnia bed.

Hey, guess what I saw, gliding sweetly south on the West Loop. A '52 Merc, green with red wheels, just like mine. Just like the one I bought in '51, I mean. The car I loved the most of any I ever owned. The very best of them all. I yearn for it yet.

I first saw that sweetheart on a golden October day when I was driving on South Main. Driving a rusty '49 Ford with 110,000 miles on it, and bad wheel bearings. Suddenly I heard mystic music. I heard sirens calling. Felt them tugging at my shirt sleeves. I pulled over and stopped and there it was, so splendid, so cool and green and beautiful. It was beckoning to me, from the showroom floor of old Turbeville Motor Company, which is no longer in business.

I went in and walked around it and smelled of it and loved on it and told the man in charge of it that I had to have that car. He named a price, an impossible figure. I could never pay that much for a car. "I'll take it," I said.

But not right that minute, because I didn't have the money for the down payment. But I would get it. I would rob liquor stores. I would snatch the purses of nice old ladies. I would go to the Blood Bank and sell as many pints as they'd take. I would get the money because I had no choice. Do you understand that?

Before I left that day I tried to get a promise out of the man that he wouldn't sell the car to anybody else. He wasn't able to make such a promise. He did say he wouldn't try very *hard* to sell it. He was a nice man. Every day, while I was searching for the money, I would go by Turbeville's to make sure the car was still there and all right. I would go in and pat it and rub up against it and whisper to it and tell it to wait for me.

I had to keep the payments below $80 a month. That was an established budgetary imperative and wasn't negotiable. You know what they agreed to do? Take the heater out. If they took the heater out the payments would run something like $79.65. I went home to wait. I got a call from Mr. Turbeville Himself. He said, "Nice car like that, I sure hate to see you driving it without a heater. I tell you what, it'll cost me about $20 labor to get that heater out of there. I'll knock $20 off the price, and leave the heater in." No, I said, take it out. The payment's got to be under $80 and $20 off the price of the heater won't quite cut it. So they took it out. I drove that lovely automobile many hundreds of miles with cold feet and a time or two with chattering teeth. But always with a warm heart, because I loved it so.

It was four-door, and that bothered me some. Because we had a knob-twisting, handle-yanking, button-pushing, mountain-climbing, left-handed two-year-old then, with his baby sister due on the next Christmas Day. I ought to have bought a two-door car, so they wouldn't be pulling up rear lock buttons and stepping out of the back seat. Some fellow in the back shop of that Merc place had the answer for that. He installed special locks that couldn't be opened when the ignition was on. You turned on the key and *click-click*, two solenoids snapped and two bolts drove home and the rear doors wouldn't come open, for a child or anybody else. Not unless you thumbed a release button beneath the dash. That sounded gadgety, and I wondered how long it would last. Well, it lasted something like 200,000 miles.

I thought that '52 Merc had one of the classiest of body styles. It set patterns, especially, for rear-end style. I look now at some of the new luxury cars, sell for $25,000 or more, and they've got the same classy rear end the '52 Merc had.

That old lover had a standard transmission with an overdrive, and on the highway it would sit on seventy, and clock off twenty-one miles a gallon if you knew how to keep a light foot on the gas pedal.

Both the babies who rode in that back seat learned to drive in that car. Getting rid of it was another of my mistakes. Its last year it sat on blocks alongside the garage. The St. Augustine grew a foot tall up its red wheels. A man came, at last, and said he'd tow it off. For nothing. For its parts. I went around the house because I didn't want to watch it leave. That night he called. Said he was just curious. Wanted to know what that *click-click* noise was in the back doors when you turned on the key.

6

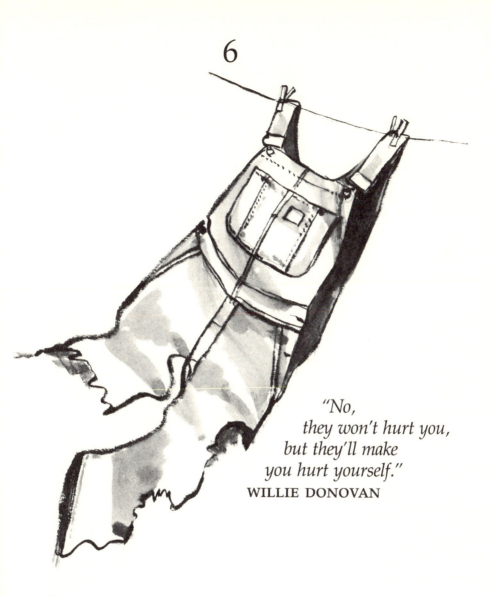

*"No,
they won't hurt you,
but they'll make
you hurt yourself."*
WILLIE DONOVAN

Every now and then I take a spell of chasing down folk tales. Comes on me like a sickness, the way a person breaks out with a food rash or the chicken pox. I've had a bout of it the past few days. While it was running its course I was up in Trinity County and heard the story of how the preacher drank the poison in the pulpit. A true story, now. Folk tales don't necessarily have to be polished up and exaggerated, although many of them are.

Some people who are particular about the definition of folklore might argue that the poison story is not old enough to qualify as a folk tale. It happened, the best I can find out, some time in the

1920s. But it seems plenty folksy to me. Happened at the country community of Pagoda, not far from Trinity. This name is commonly pronounced as if it's spelled "Pegody."

Taylor Cemetery is a landmark in the Pagoda community. It was named for a pastor of a church nearby. When the poison-in-the-pulpit incident took place, a revival was being held at that church. A protracted meeting, as they used to call 'em. I guess you know what a protracted meeting is. Exactly what brand of church that was I never have heard, but the members found it appropriate to stage demonstrations of faith. They handled snakes, and things like that.

In my early times in the twenties and thirties we didn't have interesting action of that type in the churches I was taken to. Oh, we had shouting, I guess you'd say. We had plenty of Amens, and a good many Praise the Lords, and a few Hallelujahs. And once in a long while we had something called Testimony, where completely grown people would get up and confess sins before the entire gang. (Nothing specific, though. Just general stuff like, "I'm guilty of coveting." Well, shoot, who's not?)

But we never did have anything as good as handling snakes, or speaking foreign tongues, or rolling in the sawdust due to religious ecstasy. Churches who had activity of that sort, we always called 'em Holy Rollers. I once thought Holy Roller was a denomination, that if a member was filling out a form and it asked for church affiliation he would write "Holy Roller." I found out that's not true. Well, the reason I get into that, I think the revival at Pagoda must have been the kind of meeting we'd have called Holy Roller.

The snakes were handled (as I got the tale), and nobody was bitten or harmed, and a lot of converts were converted, and everybody got all emotional, and the preacher leading the revival must have felt he was just about Sitting at the Right Hand because he made the congregation a mighty rash promise. He offered to drink poison in the pulpit. He said he'd drink this poison, and then the congregation could pray it wouldn't kill him, and if it didn't then that would show the power of prayer.

A lot of folks still alive and well in Trinity County remember when this happened. A young fellow went into Trinity and got the poison from a drugstore. Storytellers insist that the druggist pasted skulls and crossbones all over that bottle, and instructions saying, "Do Not Drink." The preacher stood up there in the pulpit, and he drank the poison. And the people prayed. And the preacher fell down and died.

I tried to find somebody who remembered that preacher's

name, but I couldn't. He is buried there in Taylor Cemetery at Pagoda. I got some instructions and went to look for the tombstone but darkness came before I could get there.

Leonard W. Chappell, rancher and rice farmer, sat in his living room at El Campo and talked about the time he saw Madame Annie Blackley, in 1917. Madame Blackley has been dead now for about twenty years. She lived at Victoria. She had a wide reputation as a clairvoyant, and many a rancher along the Texas Coast Prairie consulted her. To those who had faith in her, she was considered dependable on predicting weather and at helping find lost things.

"When I was seventeen," Leonard Chappell told me, "we were living five miles west of Nada. It was in the spring, and we were putting in a rice crop. This was before tractors. We had a big old horse named Charlie that we used pushing levees. He was black, and had four white feet and a star on his forehead. And he got lost.

"Now my Dad never did believe in fortune telling or anything like that, but when we lost the horse he asked me, 'Leonard, you want to go to Victoria?' And we went, to see Madame Blackley. Sometimes they called her Aunt Annie. We went in a Model T, and I drove. Madame Blackley lived down close to the Guadalupe River there in Victoria. Her house was what they called 'under the hill.' She was on the front porch, sitting in a rocking chair. There were vines on the porch. Honeysuckle, I think it was.

"She was a big woman, six feet tall or better, and had this long face. And she had curly hairs growing to the side of her nose. The hairs were curled up so they made you think of a watch spring. I've seen hair like that, on the faces of mulattoes. She kept her eyes about half closed. She said to Dad, 'You've lost a horse.' And then she said, 'I have a presentiment. I see your horse in a village with white houses. He is grazing in grass up to his knees, and he is in a pasture with a gray tick mare and a pair of line-backed dun mules. You will hear from your horse by Friday.'

"Then Dad asked her how much he owed her, and she said, 'Whatever you think it's worth.' He laid down a five-dollar bill and we left. On the way home I teased Dad. I told him, well, all you have to do to catch that horse is just cut out the gray tick mare, and Old Charlie will follow her. We laughed about the horse being in grass up to his knees. The fact was we were in a drouth, and there wasn't any grass growing knee-high to a horse.

"Well, it was on a Monday, that we went to Victoria. On the next Friday, I went with my brother Earl into Garwood. We traded at a store there. While we were in town, a fellow came around asking about a horse. He'd say, 'Has anybody lost a big black horse with four white feet and a star on his forehead?'

"That sounded like Charlie, so we got in the Model T and crossed the river and went to that fellow's place. I can't call his name now, but he had leased the pasture on what was called the Englehart Potato Farm on the Colorado. When we got there we could see Old Charlie. He was grazing beside a gray tick mare. And in the pasture with him was a pair of little old line-back dun Spanish rat mules.

"We caught the horse and when we were bringing him back we met a Negro we knew, they called him Big Boy Charlie. He told us the horse had been through there the day before, and he had tried to catch it but couldn't. Earl and I looked around, and there at that place was a bunch of little white houses, like Madame Blackley said.

"And that pasture, where we found Charlie with the mare and the mules, it was in the river bottom, and the Colorado had over-flowed there, and the soil had plenty of moisture, and Charlie was grazing in clover and grass up to his knees."

In a little restaurant on U.S. 59 near Cleveland I heard a big fellow talking about doing some bulldozer work, and he said he dug up a tarantula that was eight inches across.

That's sure some spider. I never saw a tarantula that big near Cleveland or anywhere else. But what interested me about the tarantula conversation was the remark made by the cafe's cook. He came out of the kitchen to get a cup of coffee and he said, "Well, you better watch them things. Tranchlers can jump forty feet, you know."

The bulldozer man laughed and said he knew that. The laugh meant he knew a tarantula can't jump forty feet. But at one time, the notion that tarantulas leap great distances was held by a great many folks, even those in the country who saw tarantulas often.

Myths about the creatures of nature survive so long. Even after they're disproved, they'll live on, and get repeated for purposes of entertainment.

The length assigned to the leap of that spider is remarkable to me, the way it has hung constant at forty feet. More than fifty years ago in West Texas I was taught that a tarantula can jump forty feet, and now an East Texas fry cook repeats the myth and uses the same number, forty feet. I wonder why forty, instead of twenty-five or thirty?

Hearing about those long-jumping spiders again reminds me of coachwhips and prairie runners. Those are names that we assigned long ago to a variety of fast-moving snakes. Any time we walked up on a snake that went scooting away at a swift clip, we said it was a coachwhip or a prairie runner. I have no idea now what the proper name for these snakes is, and don't much care.

We believed that coachwhips and prairie runners could chase whatever they were after at a top speed of sixty miles an hour. Of all the misinformation that took up space in my head, the most sensational portion had to do with snakes, and one of the foremost examples was this 60-mph coachwhip. Sixty! That's really going, for a snake.

We believed this because people who were much older than we were said it was so. We went along then on the belief that you were ignorant when young, and wise when old. Therefore, when one of your elders said a thing, you knew it was true. At night on front porches there was always somebody ready to give us testimony about watching a coachwhip chase and overtake the fastest of horses or dogs. I can see now that the best part of such a story ought to have been the reason why a snake would chase a horse, and what happened when it caught up. But in those dim old story-telling times, we didn't entertain doubts. The ignorant were not entitled to question the voices of wisdom.

That myth about the swift-running snakes was branded into my hide so deep that even today, when I think of the word *coachwhip*, I am able to see an automobile going along a country road at fifty-five miles an hour, and being overtaken by a snake doing sixty.

We believed then that the outdoors was infested with the awfulest, most exciting dangers. Imagine walking across a prairie where you might at the next step encounter a snake that would chase after you at sixty miles an hour. Or you could set a foot, and never know what hit you, inside the forty-foot range of a tarantula which would leap and get you in the neck and that would be the last of you.

We knew ill-tempered lizards that lived in rocky places and were called mountain boomers and they would run you down and their bite, as we thought, was the same as a rattlesnake's. There's a large, ground-nesting wasp with bright orange wings that we knew as a cow killer. What a name. Cow killer! We surely believed its sting would stretch out a full-grown cow. Why else would it be called a cow killer? We could easily see, then, that a wasp able to kill a cow could also knock off a lightweight human being with nothing but a near miss.

So we went forth into the woods, and over prairies, in a heavy fog of false and stimulating information about nature. When I think of it now I wonder that we weren't afraid to go outdoors.

"Some of this I've seen, and some of it I've just been told," said Oscar Childress. "But I want you to understand, everything I'm gonna tell you is the gospel truth."

I said I understood. So Childress leaned back in his rocker, looked at the ceiling, and began to talk about hoop snakes. He is a big man, with heavy eyebrows and craggy features and the bull-toned voice of a railroad section foreman. He lives in North Houston on Pennington Street, out there between Berry and Tidwell roads. He had read in the paper that there's no such serpent as a hoop snake. He wrote me and said he knew better, and that's why I went to see him.

But first, maybe you've not heard of a hoop snake before. Many people of age and experience in the rural regions of this state will tell you a hoop snake has no fangs or teeth, that it's equipped with a deadly stinger, that it often travels by grabbing its tail in its mouth, and rolling along like a hoop.

"I grew up," Childress began, "on the Sabine, mostly in Shelby County. I've been all up and down that river, and one time I killed two hoop snakes when I was squirrel hunting. Now I've never seen a hoop snake roll, but my mother and father did, and told me about it, and I believe them. My father was W. H. Childress, and my mother was a Spivey. Emma Spivey, before she married. When they were just young people, and courting, they were riding in the Sabine Bottom one night with some others. Riding horseback. Six or eight people in a bunch. It was a bright moonlight night, and two hoop snakes came rolling along right near those horses. Both my mother and my father could see the backs of the snakes glistening in the moonlight.

"Then later on, the two hoop snakes I killed, that was when I was squirrel hunting in the Attoyac Bottom one time. I came up on the pair of 'em together. Both about six feet long, and the way they were layin' I judged they were mating. I shot both of 'em.

Then I got me two short sticks and pried their mouths open. They didn't have a fang or a tooth in their heads. Their backs were jet black and they didn't have any scales except on their bellies. Well, I took one of the sticks and pressed down on one of those snakes, just a little ways back from the end of his blunt tail. When I did, his old stinger pooched out, maybe an inch long and sharp-pointed on the end. When I took the stick away, the stinger went back in. I just wish I'd saved one of those snakes.

"Then, in about 1914 or '15, we were living at Stockman and I went down near Kirbyville as a relief section foreman on the Santa Fe. I boarded a while with a family, a man and his wife and three boys. They lived in a house facing a creek, and right out here to the side they had a horse lot. One moonlight night—they told me about this—one night they were all out on the gallery and they saw something go through that horse-lot fence. It was glistening in the moonlight. There was a mule and a mare and a year-old colt in the lot, and they commenced pitchin' and snortin', and then the colt jumped up in the air and fell down and kicked a couple of times, and that was his last kick.

"They didn't find a mark on that colt. No fang marks, no blood, no nothing. He was just dead, and those people judged a hoop snake had stung him.

"I've even heard people go so far as to say they've seen a hoop snake go rolling through the bottom and run into a sweet gum tree and the tree will begin to wilt, and die. But I want you to know I haven't seen that. Now, people wonder why nobody ever sees a hoop snake. Well, I say it's because they're a night-prowling snake, and don't go around in the daylight."

Frank Krampitz, Jr., wrote me from Sealy that B'Lonzo Davis has a madstone he keeps in a safety deposit box at the bank. I never had seen a madstone, or met anybody named B'Lonzo either, so when I got to Sealy I went with Frank for a visit with Davis. He had checked the madstone out of the bank and had it at home to show us. It was in a little cubical box no bigger than one a wedding ring might come in. I was expecting a larger stone.

You'll find madstone in the thicker dictionaries. They'll tell you a madstone is "supposed" to counteract the effect of the bite of an animal, such as one with rabies. In folk medicine, the madstone was applied to the wound, and this was thought to draw out the rabies virus.

B'Lonzo Davis was born in 1896. He can remember people being bitten by mad animals before injections to prevent rabies were known, and he believes the madstone works. He remembers seeing the stone used in his own home in the early 1900s when he was a boy.

"Dr. Schmoeller came to our house and used the stone on a girl who had been bitten by a mad calf," Davis told us. He did not recall the doctor's first name or the girl's name either, but he remembers the procedure the doctor used. Directions for using the stone, in fact, are penciled dimly on a slip of paper that's been folded in the little box ever since Davis has known about it, which is all his life. The stone belonged either to his great-grandfather or great-great-grandfather. He isn't certain which. But it came to Sealy with Davis' father, John W., when he moved to Texas from Missouri. "Put stone in milk," the instructions say, "warm sweet milk. Let stay until warm as milk. Then apply stone to bite. If bite is not sufficient scarified, scarify a place anywhere on body and apply stone."

Why the milk? Davis said he figures the milk caused some sort of chemical event to occur in the rock that made it "draw the poison out." The idea was, you put the stone on the bite and it would stick. When it came loose, you put it back in the milk a while, then put it on the wound again. You kept this up until the stone wouldn't stick any longer. That meant all the virus was out of the blood. "It's an old Indian remedy," Davis said.

The madstone is maybe half the size of an average chicken egg and light tan in color and made me think of a petrified wasp nest, with deep indentations. Some say it looks like a solidified sponge. Some say a piece of lava.

The reason that doctor came to the Davis home to use the stone, that's where it was kept, in John Davis' possession, and likely it was the only madstone around. The elder Davis was a barber, which gave him a close association with physicians. Barbers in early times often helped doctors, especially with surgery.

The story that has stuck with Davis about the madstone is that it came out of the stomach of a white deer. Dictionaries and books I've checked do mention deer as a madstone source, but not white ones. The latest Webster's we have at the *Post* suggests that the madstone is a solidified hair ball that might be found in a deer's stomach.

For all I know, Davis may be right about the madstone's effectiveness. Still, I think if anything foaming at the mouth bites me, I'll just go ahead and take the shots.

And Other Natural Wonders

In Fred Kasper's store at Warda a small bunch of us was gathered around the domino table, talking about spirits and ghosts and wispy apparitions. Warda is the little town you whizzed right on through the last time you drove U.S. 77 between La Grange and Giddings. In places like Warda you sometimes run into some good conversation, ranging in topic from the price of syrup to the general style and makeup of spirits seen on country roads at night.

"Now a lot of white folks," Willie Donovan was saying, "will tell you they don't believe in spirits, because they don't ever see one. Well, to see one, you've got to have a dark and misty night."

Tyree Pendergrass agreed. "And you got to be born to it," he said. "Some can see 'em and some can't."

If you haven't ever seen a spirit, you naturally wish to know what one looks like. "Just a natural man," Pendergrass said. "But Willie there, sometimes he sees 'em without any heads." And Donovan said that's true.

I asked for a specific example of an encounter with a spirit. Pendergrass took us briefly back to 1930, when he was about twenty-three years old. Said he was walking along a dirt road there near Warda one dark and wet night. "Just as I turned onto that road leads down to Rocky Creek, I seen somethin' standin' in the road up ahead. When I got closer I picked me up some rocks and commenced chunkin'. I'd chunk, and I'd get closer, and I got as close as from here to the door (not twenty feet) and I *know* I had to be hittin' whatever it was, but it just kept astandin' there, and them rocks apassin' right through it."

"You can't hurt one," Willie Donovan said, shaking his head. "You can't hurt a spirit."

"Well, when I come out on the highway," Pendergrass went on, "I seen another somethin'. Don't know if it was the same somethin' or not. I was walkin' by it and all of a sudden my cap commenced raisin' up off my head. Just kept raisin', and raisin', and I couldn't keep it on. So then I told myself, 'Tyree, it's time for you to hook up.' So I hooked up. I was young then, and I could run." Then he threw his head back and laughed long and loud.

Will a spirit harm a person? "No, they won't hurt you," Donovan said. "But they'll make you hurt yourself." Then he told about the night he was obliged to go to a vacant old farm house that belonged to a man he was working for. He had a little dog with him. While he was in the house he heard this noise. "Went like this," he said. "Plump-de-plump. Plump-de-plump. Well, I looked down at that dog and I said, 'Pup, let's me and you go.'

Well, that white man had four new bob wires in his fence and I went through 'em and tore up a brand new pair of overalls. Next day Mister Fred there told me what was makin that noise."

Kasper said he figures it was a cow that had wandered into the old house. But my sympathy lies with Willie Donovan. If I were alone in an old house in the country at night and heard something go plump-de-plump, I'm not at all sure I'd go skally-hootin' about from room to room, trying to meet up with whatever was making the racket.

Both Donovan and Pendergrass told me they have had visits from their dead fathers-in-law. And Pendergrass has seen his mother since she died. "Everybody, you know," he said, "leaves a spirit behind when they die."

He told about a man he knew at Granger. Said this gent was asleep in a seedhouse one night, bedded down in cottonseed. And "a somethin' " came and peered in at him. "He grabbed a handful of cottonseed and hit that somethin' in the face. It didn't leave. He threw another handful of seed, and then that somethin' hopped in there on top of him and put its thumbs on his face, like this, and pulled his eyes down and after that he couldn't see for half an hour."

Fred Kasper and I wanted Pendergrass and Donovan to take us out that night and show us a spirit. They said the night wasn't dark enough. And Pendergrass grinned and said anyway he isn't so young now, and can't "hook up" the way he used to.

Maybe the custom survives in some form or other. I hope it does. Long ago we called it Telling Ghost Stories. It was popular in all seasons, even the deeps of summer. But it was best at Halloween. We would gather in great semi-circles, two or three tiers deep, and the Teller would sit before us like some kind of guru and talk low and whispery, drawing out the words for effect.

The Teller sometimes was one of the older girls whose imagination had ripened, but on special nights such as Halloween the Teller would be an adult, and that was best. It gave more weight to the stories. This wasn't just a children's amusement anyhow. The grownups sat with us always, not in the front tiers but back a little way, where they silently judged the performance.

The stories we liked best were not the classic ones out of books. Instead, the favorites were local tales, about people who lived nearby, or used to, and about things that crept and floated by night over territory that was friendly and familiar in sunlight.

There was the Light. Or the Devil's Lantern, some called it, or Hell's Fire. It was known of fifty years ago, and even still it showed up sometimes, bobbing and flickering in the darkness down yonder over the low field next to the road, where we had the corn this year.

Uncle John was the one that saw it last—close to midnight, about this season a year ago. Wasn't that right, Uncle John? He'd been to Bently's to help, when Tom Bently had the bone felon that time and liked to died. He was walking home late at night, through the stubble there along those woods of Harley Jennings, and came out on the road at the old stock pens. And there it was, the Light, waiting for him in the road ahead.

It wasn't but about a hundred yards in front of him, hanging there, all wicked and shimmery, hovering about twenty feet over the wagon ruts. No, it didn't make any noise. Well, wait, it did, too, in a way. It kind of swished, seemed like, and hissed. Somehow or other Uncle John couldn't get closer to it, or farther away from it, either. If he turned back it followed him, and if he went ahead in the road it drifted along before him, like it was watching. Well, finally, it zipped on off to the east, and when it went out of sight over those clay knolls in the back pasture, why there was this ghost call, faint and far away: *Who-o-o-o-o-o.*

All right, some of y'all remember Billy Joe Conway. You know that white streak in his hair, here in front? The Light, is how he got that streak. Hadn't anybody ever been as close to the Light as Billy Joe Conway was. He was coming along the road there on that red mule his daddy had. Been to a play party at Jim Grover's, out the other side of Newby. It was about this same time of night, late, and black as smut. He struck the Light about the same place Uncle John did. Except it was behind him, and following along, and gaining. Billy Joe put that old mule into high gear, a pretty good running old mule, too, and still the Light came on, right on up to where Billy Joe could feel its heat on his back and see his shadow in its gleam.

Then it commenced to swish flaming circles around his head, and the mule went into a fright and planted his forelegs and throwed Billy Joe I don't guess any less than fifteen feet, and he lighted on his stomach in the deep sand. And the last thing he remembered was the sound, dim and distant: *Who-o-o-o-o-o.*

Billy Joe's Mama said the next morning he had that white streak in his hair, and for a long time he kept off to himself a lot, and didn't talk much.

All right, look, it's getting on pretty late now, and a black night this way is when the Light shows sometimes. Let's face down yonder toward the road, and see what we can see.

So we would all turn, taking shallow breaths and huddling shoulder to shoulder, to watch into the blackness. After a little bit somebody would complain that he couldn't see anything and the Teller would say, "Wait now. Just you wait, and watch." Then somebody would see it. "Yonder it is! Off to the east some, left of the windmill here!" Yes indeed, there would be the Light. Or at least a light. It would be dim and red-orange, but a light on the road, sure enough.

And it would do those same things that the stories said it did. It would hover, and shimmer, and go up and down, and dart along the road a way as if it was chasing something. It would even do the flaming circles that Billy Joe Conway saw. I tell you this, it was pretty effective, even after you got up big enough to know that it was Cousin Thomas down there on the road, riding a plow horse and carrying a coal oil lantern.

There were weaknesses, sure. Sometimes Cousin Thomas would get excessive when doing his flaming circles and the lantern would go out and you'd have this delay, until the Light appeared again. And maybe the prearranged timing between Cousin Thomas and the Teller would get faulty, and the Light would perform ahead or behind schedule. But overall, I can't fault the performance. I always considered Cousin Thomas was a real winner at doing the eerie call at the close of the show: *Who-o-o-o-o-o*. I'm surprised he didn't frighten his own self, out there in the darkness.

7

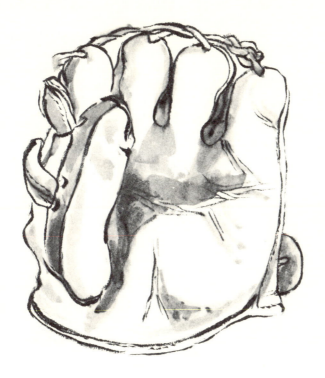

*"You gotta knock it
in the creek,
Orville."*

In Fort Worth I went back to Bewick Street on the South Side and found the house where we used to gather on the front porch and listen to the ball games. The Fort Worth Cats of the Texas League. All their games were broadcast on WBAP.

This was in about 1930, and not many houses on that street had radios. Our house did not. We had a portable Victrola that you wound up. The music that came out of the Victrola would be called country and western now. Then it was just music, just Victrola records. Guys singing through their noses. Singing "When the Work's All Done This Fall." Singing "The Big Rock Candy Mountain."

> In the Big Rock Candy Mountain
> All the cops have wooden legs.
> The bulldogs all have rubber teeth
> And the hens lay soft-boiled eggs.

We had one scratchy record of hymns, and my father would have my sister and me learn the words and sing along. We sang "Living for Jesus" and about a fellow named Andy. The chorus went:

> Andy walks with me.
> Andy talks with me . . .

But about the ball games. The radio those people had at the house with the long front porch would be turned to face out the window, and we would all get in the yard and listen, and sometimes we would act out the play as the announcer told us about it.

We were all members of the Knothole Gang at LaGrave Field. That meant we got in the games free and sat in the bleachers in right field. You could go see nine innings of baseball without a dime in your pants pocket. Not a penny. You didn't drink soda pop or eat peanuts. You drank water and you watched the game and you felt highly privileged to be there in that exciting, beautiful place.

When the Cats were on the road, between innings we would sit on the grass at the house with the radio and talk about what we would do when we were older and went out and got work. We would buy a car and follow the Fort Worth Cats all around the Texas League. We would go to Wichita Falls. Even to Beaumont.

The announcers on those broadcasts had a peculiar custom that we loved. But baseball fans now would never put up with it. To tell the audience what a batter did, the announcers tapped on a little set of chimes. I suppose it was an instrument similar to the NBC chimes we still hear on the air. If a batter knocked a single, the announcer sounded one of the chimes. Two notes for a double, three for a triple, four for a homer. You didn't know what the batter did until the chimes sounded. There was a torment of suspense in that. Holding the breath. Gasping as the chimes tolled the message. One note. Two! *Three!* If the fourth note came we entered into delirium and had running fits and joyful spasms.

Today's announcers tell us so much that we don't need to use the imagination. If a hot-dog wrapper blows across the pitcher's mound, that intelligence is broadcast. It's broadcast even on television when we are sitting there watching the wrapper tumble and we know what it is and still we are told.

On those old Texas League broadcasts we got only essentials. We didn't need details. We were there, in our minds. We were inside the players. We were on the field, playing. We would draw names from the lineup. Say you drew the third baseman's name. For that game, you *became* that man. You played third, and batted cleanup. If the announcer sounded two notes on the chimes, that was you, getting that double, and you were given credit for it by your associates. Of course you had to take the blame for his boners, as well.

The sound of those notes and what they mean are so deep in me that now, after half a century, I can't hear the NBC chimes without thinking that some old boy somewhere has belted a three-bagger.

Got this young friend I see three, maybe four times a year. Long as I've known him he's been a wheel of a football player. He's a senior in high school now. Asked him about school and he shrugged. Said school was fun as long as football was going on. Said he was pretty much of a top dog around there during the season, but sure didn't amount to much when it was over.

I thought he was kidding me. I asked, and he said he wasn't. So I wonder if things have changed all that much, around high schools. So much that being a football hero is a seasonal proposition? The way I remember it where I came from, man, once you got to be a football hero you were a hero twelve months a year. And the adoration of the home folks lasted for years after your final game.

The high school football teams I knew from the thirties always formed exclusive clubs, socially as well as on the field. They ran in packs, keeping together in winter and summer both, and retaining identity that way as a group to be admired and respected and smiled upon.

If a traveling tent show came to town in the depths of July, the two front rows would be filled by football players, identified by their polo shirts and their pants legs, which were rolled up a couple of turns to show white sweat socks. They would make a lot of racket, and say funny things so that the entire audience could hear. We would smile and say, "That's the football team down front there."

There was no member of it who wasn't known by every daughter's mother and father in town. Yes, and by bankers and lawyers and doctors and feed-store owners and all the important people like that.

Even if he was ugly enough to sour milk, a football player who made outstanding runs or catches could have his choice of several pretty girls. I always thought that must have been one of the principal benefits of playing football—that you received fringe rewards you could get in no other activity. If you were the best debater in the state and destined to become a statesman, if you could play the violin with sufficient beauty to make the very flowers weep, still you weren't a knothole in a barn door compared to a second-string fullback.

In some small towns I used to know, the football team formed a sort of public-school vigilante corps, and sometimes the players actually took part in police actions. Or backed up the authority of local police just by standing around in their sweat socks, looking interested and eager and physical. Like maybe mischief-makers from a neighboring town would come over and begin spreading trouble just for the exercise and cause local peace officers to escort them out of town. The next day at school we would nod in study hall and say: "The whole football team was down there. Hadn't been for them, those vandals would have wrecked the courthouse."

Being heroes of that brand, then, the players were naturally not leaned on too heavily when they got themselves out of line. We always used to say, "Don't get caught stealing buns at the bakery unless you're a starter on the football team." Also, if you had made two touchdowns the week before, you didn't have to worry much about chemistry tests and book reports and things like that of secondary importance. I can't remember bristling about the injustice in the system. I did not see any. I wanted to win next Friday the same as everybody else.

At heavily attended functions such as high school plays and variety shows featuring local talent, the football team would sit in the front the same as at tent shows, and provide entertainment between acts. An example is, they would give these short yells in unison, and the message would be directed at some well-known member of the audience. Say the first act is over and we're waiting for the second. The audience is hushed. There is a popular teacher, a bachelor, who has escorted an attractive lady to the play. Nobody knows who she is, and everybody is having kittens from curiosity. So the football team makes up this yell, and delivers it thirty voices strong, with deliberation and great volume: "We *see* you, Mister Jack-*son!*" Mr. Jackson would turn forty shades of red, and folks in the audience would clap and scream and whistle and beam, the same as they did at the last football game. The play itself would not get half the ovation.

Monday night I watched a baseball game on television for a while. The New York Yankees against the Boston Red Sox. I kept watching until I saw what I wanted to see—Reggie Jackson striking out. I don't mean that I get a perverted pleasure from seeing Jackson make an out. I simply think that watching him swing at a third strike and miss is one of the worthwhile shows in professional sports.

It is certainly more spectacular and ten times more of an entertainment than the majority of pro football plays, where twenty-two giants bump each other on signal and fall to the ground and nothing happens. Or at least nothing that the spectator is able to see. But Reggie Jackson taking that magnificent swing, and missing, I love that. Since I don't much care whether the Yankees win or not, I had rather see Jackson miss than make contact. Because when he hits, I don't really see his swing. Instead I watch where the ball goes, which as you may know is quite often out of the park.

Jackson swinging a bat is the most artistic demonstration of manpower I've ever watched. Yet it's a natural-born, old-fashioned, vacant-lot kind of a hardball swing. He goes at it with all his might. That's the way the big old boys did it long ago, before there was any such thing as a batting coach, and baseball was played in pastures.

The big boys didn't just have to knock the ball over the fence. There was no fence. Home runs had to be legged out the same as singles, so the heavy hitters needed to knock the ball so far that the outfielders would need five minutes to chase it down. You gotta knock it in the creek, Orville. When an old-fashioned long-ball hitter swung and missed, the force affected the pattern of air currents for fifty feet around. And like as not the swinger ended up on the seat of his pants.

Reggie Jackson almost did that Monday night, on the strike-out I mentioned at the beginning. To keep from falling when he missed the ball, he was obliged to back-pedal furiously, at the same time turning to see if the catcher had dropped the pitch, and it seemed to me he was ten feet from the plate before he recovered from the awesome force of his own swing. And yet, even in that struggle for balance, there was infinite grace.

I admire a batter who can strike out, and look good at it. Maybe that's an acceptable definition of a pro, in any field. One who can fail, and do so with grace. It's not any strain to look good when you knock it out of the park, or when the verdict goes your way in a courtroom, or when they open the envelope and announce that you've won the little statue. The test, on grace, comes when you lose.

This Jackson fellow, I've read a lot about him that was unfavorable but never mind that, he's a fine performer and a showman. My vote for the greatest piece of pro sports showmanship in recent times came in that World Series game—was it last year?—when Jackson knocked one a mile and a quarter and didn't run. Just stood there and watched it go out before he trotted around the bases. It was like saying to us, "Well, folks, there she goes. That's what you pay your money to see. Not any point in me getting in a hurry to run, because all the outfielders in the league couldn't catch that one in a wagon sheet."

If you were not rooting for the Yankees you probably hated him for doing that, but you got to admit it was tremendous theater. Maybe it didn't beat that old story they tell about Babe Ruth, when he pointed to center field with his bat and then put the ball where he pointed. But that's just a story. I mean I didn't see it and I don't know if it happened quite the way they tell it. I'm a little surprised Jackson hasn't tried that. I'd like to see him try, just to hear the wind whistle if he missed.

A little bunch of us was sitting around sipping soda pop, talking about games we used to play and describing the ones we loved the most. When my turn came, I told about the scrub baseball we played on the schoolground back in the middle thirties. I took part in a good deal of competitive activity after that time, but I never found a game I loved as much, or learned more from.

Actually, it wasn't baseball. It wasn't played with the kind of ball used in the Astrodome. This was what we called an indoor ball. It was bigger than a softball and had leather seams sticking out all around, and you didn't use a glove to catch it. All the same, it was hard as wood, at least when it was new.

Scrub baseball was the same game that later came to be known as workup. There was no team involved. It was every man for himself. The way it worked was this. Say you walked up on a scrub game in progress on a vacant lot. You didn't join a side, because there wasn't one. You took the lowest position, and then worked up toward being a batter. That's where the name came from, that working up to the privilege of being at bat. The lowest position was always right field. When a batter made an out, the right fielder moved to center field. On the next out he moved to left field. Then to third base. Next to shortstop, to second base, to first base, to pitcher, to catcher and, at last, to batter.

For a standard game, then, you would need a dozen players, nine in the field and three at bat. However, as far as I know, no scrub baseball game was ever standard. You always had too few or too many.

The games played at school were unique because the entire student body from the sixth grade to the eleventh was somehow involved, either as participants or spectators. A few of the girls would play, but the ones who didn't watched, which is why this activity was so important to boys. You might have seventy-five to a hundred players, all in one baseball game. It was played during the noon hour, the lunch period. I used to run home, water the milk cow, stake her out to graze on a fresh vacant lot, wolf down my lunch and run back to school so I would have thirty minutes left to play in that exquisite game before the bell rang at one o'clock.

The great thing about the game was, even if you were a skinny kid in the sixth or seventh grade, you still had a chance to achieve something in competition with extraordinary citizens and important people such as juniors and seniors in high school. In that way you could get recognition when you didn't amount to anything in any other endeavor.

You understand this was not a supervised playground game. It was just play. A teacher might take part, but he or she would be playing the same as the others of us and not supervising. About twelve-thirty, the field would be so full of players it was impossible to hit a ground ball that failed at least to ricochet off somebody's shins. The outfield would be wall-to-wall players watching for fly balls, because if you caught a fly, you went directly to bat without having to work up.

I used to sit in class and study about how I could attain immortality in that game. I decided working up was a weak investment. You might spend half an hour working around from right field to the bat and then pop out on your first swing and there you'd be— a failure. It was better to roam the outfield and hope for a fly ball.

My study showed me there were ways for a smaller and younger and inferior player to overcome the enormous handicap he faced. He would be out there trying to snag a fly, and his competition would include half the high school football team and all the basketball players who were seventeen feet tall. Those big guys tended to defeat each other, though. When a tall fly ball descended, a dozen of them would jam up beneath it and leap for it at once. Often as not, the ball would tip up, off all those fingers and fists.

If you were standing to the side a little, alert, the ball might come your way and you could just reach out and get it before it hit the ground and go trotting on in to bat and leave those jocks out there looking around to see who made the catch.

That game wasn't just fun. It taught me things of value, in surviving in a competitive society. It showed me that sometimes it's better not to go bulging into the middle of the conflict, but to keep apart, and watch for what comes glancing out of the fight.

At Buckholts, a little country town on U.S. 190 a few miles west of Cameron, I watched the first football game I've attended in almost ten years. It was six-man football, and I liked it pretty well. I am afraid six-man football is fixing to disappear from the earth, and I never had seen one game. It bothers me for almost anything to disappear before I have even sampled it.

All right, the Buckholts Badgers against the Abbot Panthers. Abbot is up on Interstate 35 between Waco and Hillsboro. I drove to the stadium lights and found a parking place within fifty steps of the front gate. That was the *first* thing I liked about six-man football. A friendly, athletic-looking gent was selling tickets out of a cigar box. I figured he was a former coach who had become principal of the high school. "No," said Jim Hauk, from behind his cigar box, "I'm the superintendent." But I was right about him being a former coach. Coached this very Buckholts team several years.

Actually, to see most of a football game at Buckholts you don't have to buy a ticket. The field is fenced, but only with hog wire. So you can stay outside the gate and see all the action except when the stands get in the way, and the stands aren't long. "We have a few who do that," Hauk said, "but most of them go ahead and pay and support the program." Tickets cost two dollars for adults, one dollar for students.

I missed the kickoff. Buckholts had the ball on the first play I watched. A peculiar looking lineup. A center and two ends on the line, a quarterback and two halfbacks in the backfield. Here comes the snap, to one of the short backs. He flips behind him to a tailback. Abbot rushes only one man on the play. The runner sidesteps him and skips around left end for eighteen yards. I expected that to cause excitement in the home crowd, but it didn't. In fact a big fellow in a cowboy hat who was standing near me spit into the grass and said, "Dang. He ought to have scored."

Pretty quick I found out that in six-man football the spectators expect something large to happen on every play. None of this old three yards and a cloud of dust stuff. A little while later a Buckholts back danced and dodged for thirty-five or forty yards and went on in for a touchdown, and the big fellow beside me grunted, "That's more like it."

I drifted back to the front gate. "It's a wide open and high-scoring game," Jim Hauk said. "It takes fifteen yards to make a first down, the field is eighty yards long and forty-five wide, and everybody is eligible for a pass. And the quarterback can't carry the ball across the line of scrimmage." That is, he must either pass it or give it to another back. Makes for a lot of ball handling. Good for the spectators.

Before the first quarter was over, it was plain enough to me that six-man football is a far better spectator sport than eleven-man. When twenty-two players are on a field and keeping most of the time in a grunting pile, there is really not much to see. Especially not for the paying customer with a low-altitude seat and a fat man in front of him. But eleven-man football is worshipped in this state, and six-man is fading, along with small schools. "I think thirty or thirty-five schools in Texas still play six-man," Hauk said. They are places with names like Paint Rock, Cranfills Gap, Priddy, Mullin, Marathon, Cherokee. Most six-man schools are in thinly-populated West Texas. In fact, Buckholts is the state's eastern-most team.

Buckholts' coach is Lawrence Hanke. I looked at his bench and counted six substitutes. He has a squad of twelve, then. "Yes, it's common to have twelve or thirteen on a squad," Hauk said. "This year we have thirty-four students in high school and nineteen are boys, so twelve out of nineteen play football. Some years, all of them play." Abbot had about the same size squad. I counted seventeen supporters who had made the trip to Buckholts to watch the Panthers play. That included four cheerleaders.

Buckholts' backs were too fast for Abbot, and the Badgers moved the ball easily. In the second quarter when they were leading 18-0, Hauk commented that it wasn't a very high-scoring game. "Last year this team beat us in the fading moments 39-38. One time Mullins beat us 83-38. They had one kid who scored ten touchdowns against us." Scores soaring as high as 136-0 brought a change in six-man rules. In the second half, if one team gets ahead 45 points, the game is over.

There was no half-time show. Buckholts doesn't have a band. How you gonna have a band with thirty-four students in school and twelve of 'em playing football? There's a pep squad that has a brass drum, though, and makes a satisfactory racket.

The smallest man on Buckholts' team is Curtis Morgan, a 130-pound end. The biggest is Bobo Kuzel, 185. He plays center. My favorite play of the game was when Kuzel snapped the ball and trotted into the end zone and caught a touchdown pass. I expect that's the last time I'll see a center catch a pass. The play of the center is something else I like about six-man. I mean you can see him. In eleven-man an All-American center in college can play an entire season and nobody will know he's out there except his mother. But in six-man, the center is really somebody. The spread formation is popular, and when both ends split to the sidelines, there is the center making up the entire line all alone. When he makes his block, you can see him do it, and see it when he misses, too. But six-man is not really a big boy's game. Hauk told me the boys who do best are the small and well-coordinated ones. A big kid who might make an excellent tackle in eleven-man may not make it at all in six-man.

With a minute left to play, Buckholts was leading 42-12. I left, which is bad journalism, but I am fairly certain the Buckholts Badgers emerged victorious and avenged that bitter one-point defeat of last year.

The fiercest and most exciting and satisfying sports competition I ever saw or took part in were games played on vacant lots and bald prairies and city streets and corn-patch turnrows. I can't remember defeats more bitter or victories any sweeter than we used to taste on a city park softball field here in Houston in the late 1940s. Every weekend the *Post* would get up a team to play the *Chronicle*. You think it didn't make any difference who won? Hoo boy.

The late Harry Johnston, *Post* city editor in those days, was the manager of our team. If the *Chronicle* beat us on Sunday, Harry survived it with very little grace. In all the years he ran the city desk he said an ugly word to me only once, and that didn't have anything to do with putting out the paper. It came on Sunday, when I was running between second and third and got my feet tangled up and fell down and was tagged out, and the *Chronicle* won the game. You'd have thought Harry had lost the seventh game in the World Series.

But what I love most about intramural or sandlot games is that they can provide beautiful moments for individuals who really need such moments, and can't get them any other way. I think about a pudgy kid named Carl something, from my days in school out at Lubbock. He was a history major and wore thick glasses and corduroy pants and thick-soled canvas shoes. He couldn't run from here to the bathroom, and he had the coordination of a bale of hay. But he was always hanging out around the softball fields where the intramural games were played.

Nearly every student enrolled played in that league. You wanted to play, you got nine other guys and you played. You'd find a piccolo player out of the band on shortstop, and a fullback off the varsity football team on third. It was a fine setup. I mean there was no fooling around. Everybody played to win. We celebrated when we did, and I do still. There's not anything wrong with wanting to win.

One afternoon our team came up a man short, and we had to recruit that Carl something to fill in. He was forever around, hoping he'd be asked. We put him in right field because that's where you always put your weakest fielder. You didn't have as many lefthanded pull hitters then as you do now, and the right fielder could sleep a lot. We stayed lucky. Nothing but a few lazy grounders went out to Carl, and he managed to lay down in front of 'em and hike back to the infield with the ball. The only damage he did was striking out all the time.

Then in the last inning, he became a hero. He caught a fly ball, and it wrapped up the game for us. If he'd missed it, two runs would have scored and we would have lost. You have to understand it was an impossible catch, for the reason that this guy did not know how to catch. He couldn't have caught a fly ball if you'd given him a shrimp net and four major league outfielders to hold it. But this one he caught. I still think he was running from it, trying to escape. It hit his fist some way, and careened along the inside of his arm, and bounced off his head and shoulder, and shot up straight, and he grabbed it, I expect, to keep it from hitting his glasses.

So he was a hero, and we mobbed him. The piccolo player

whammed him between the shoulder blades, and so did the full-back from the varsity, and we lifted him over our heads, and the girls passing by stopped to see who it was, and I would not take a silver dollar for the memory of that old boy's eyes, glistening in triumph behind those thick glasses. I feel certain that, from that day, life for him was better.

Less than two blocks from where I live there's a park with a softball field, and when the wind is right I can sit by an open window and hear the shouts of the players. I enjoy those sounds. To me they represent long-lost summers. I once loved the game of softball so much.

The players who shout over there in the park are not children. They are men in their twenties. Some well into their thirties. And a few who may be past forty. Old softball players are slow about retiring.

That game would be no fun without the shouting. The chatter, as they call it. The purpose of it is to keep spirit up, to encourage one another, to pass along tips and reminders. I can sit here and reconstruct what is happening, over yonder in the park, just by listening to the chatter. A high percentage of chatter is aimed at encouraging and boosting the ego of the pitcher. The pitcher is a special person and must be constantly bragged on and defended. Even if he has a perfectly awful day and gives up fourteen hits and ten runs, still he must be bragged on and told that the other players let him down so the bad performance was not really his fault.

"Come on, Hugh, come on boy! . . . Be tough, Big Hugh, be tough! . . . Way to *chunk*, Hugh baby! . . . Good *pitch!* Aw, ump, come *on*, man. You got to call the *corners*, ump. Good pitch, Hugh . . . OK, baby, way ahead now . . . Throw strikes, Hugh. Throw pills, baby. They can't hit what they can't see."

This must go on the entire game. The pitcher expects it from every player, and if you do not chatter to him that way you are not very nice.

The fellow who receives the next most chatter is the one who is at bat. He gets it from his teammates at the bench. He is not really expected to listen to it, because it doesn't mean much, at least not literally. But he would be a sad batter if the bench remained quiet.

"OK, Billy, be a hitter now. Pick you a fat one and rap it out . . . Just a base hit, Billy, don't try to kill it . . . Need a runner! Need a runner! . . . (Billy swings and misses.) Good *cut*, Billy! Way to swing that stick . . . Be tough now . . . (Billy takes a second strike.) Just takes one to hit it, Billy . . . (He swings and fouls one off.) Way to *hang*, Billy! Way to hang in there! . . . Come on, Billy, come on *boy!*"

The reason people play this game, and keep on until their hair gets gray, there are so many things about it that make you feel good. For instance, it feels so good to have this kind of confidence. Say you are out in center field, and the batter swings and the ball soars and you know, immediately, that you are going to catch it. You can tell it's going to be an easy catch, but the best thing is, it's going to look very difficult. Because you must turn your back on it and run hard for ten or twelve steps toward the fence. Still, you know that when you turn to look again, there the ball will be, descending in just about the place you knew it would be. You must reach out, arm's length, and get it one-handed, but there is no way you could drop it. That sort of confidence, it feels just beautiful.

Another thing that feels wonderful is catching, just by reflex action, a sizzling line drive that comes at you from close range. I mean like if you're a third baseman and playing close for the bunt and the batter explodes a line drive into your glove and it hits there and sticks and makes that dreadful, lovely *whack* sound. Something else I loved was playing catcher (hind catcher, we used to say) and catching a really fast pitch that has been swung at and missed, so that it seems to have passed through the bat and landed in your mitt.

Then the really exquisite experience is hitting a good pitch solid, out there on the meat part of the bat, and knowing from the feel that the ball can't stop before it goes over the fence. I did not experience that many times, descended as I am from a long line of weak hitters. But it happens now and then even to weak hitters. I can still get a good feeling out of this game, when spring comes and the chatter from the park floats in the open window.

A norther had blown in. It wasn't so cold. Mainly it was noise and bluster. The sliding front doors of the neighborhood ice house were pulled shut. On the side windows, which are barred but have no screens or glass, they use an old tarpaulin as a kind of shutter, and it works all right except in really severe weather.

The tarp was down and tied but one corner had worked loose

and it was pop-pop-popping in the wind. The popping made the world seem colder. Canvas popping even in a warm breeze is a cold sound. So the norther was blowing and the canvas popping and he sat there talking about baseball. Baseball, in a December norther.

He talks about baseball all twelve months, they say. I'd never heard him talk before. The others talk football now or basketball and he bothers them with his year-round baseball talk. It didn't bother me, and I listened a long while. It didn't bother me, because it wasn't your ordinary baseball talk. It wasn't about what happened to the Astros last year, or about the winter trades, or about contract negotiations, or how many days are left until spring training. He talked instead about the joy of playing.

He's around forty-five now. Not more, I'd say, than forty-eight. He played all through school, including two years of junior college, and he played one season in pro ball. In the low minors, of course. That year of getting paid for playing was the greatest happening of his life, and that's why he talks so much about it. I understand that. He was a catcher. Which is another reason he talks. Catchers are all talkers, as far as I know. Day in and day out they have the hardest job on any baseball team and they know more about what's going on out there than anybody else and I figure they are entitled to talk, even in December.

Anyhow, I liked the things he talked about. Things that don't get talked about much. About the thrill a catcher gets when a fastball blares across the inside corner of the plate and the batter swings mightily and the ball seems to pass directly through the meatiest part of the bat and never touches wood. Instead it makes that satisfying gunshot sound when it strikes the pocket of the mitt.

I wasn't working when I went there, and I had no notebook and I can't quote him directly very much. But he said, "A missed third strike that ends the inning is one of the best things that can happen to a catcher. It gives him a chance to show class." Do you know what he meant? You've seen it, time and again, but maybe you didn't really watch. Say you've got the pitcher batting. Two outs. Count goes to three and two. Here comes the pitch. Batter swings and misses. He's got to turn, to look back, to see if the catcher caught the third strike, because if the ball got away the batter can run to first if he has hit the pitch. When he turns, the catcher flips the ball to him in a high, gentle arc, and when it hits the hand of the batter the catcher has already sprung out of his crouch and is trotting to the dugout, peeling his mask.

It's the catcher's way of saying to the struck-out pitcher, "You ain't goin' nowhere, pal, except back out on the mound to pitch. Here's the ball." When it's done with class, it's pretty to watch and it's part of the game. The pitcher who has just fanned has some class to show, himself, on this play. He must catch the ball with flair, almost without looking at it. To drop such a toss, even though it would have nothing to do with the game, would be an embarrassment.

"On third strikes to end the inning," he said, "if the batter wasn't the pitcher I always rolled the ball, underhanded, out to the mound. Lot of catchers do that. I used to try to make the ball stop in the trench. There's a kind of trench on the front of the mound where the pitcher's lead food comes down and digs in. It gave me a good feeling if the ball stopped in that trench. I felt like it was a good omen, that it meant we'd score runs in our half of the inning."

He talked about private superstitions that ballplayers have. He said—I don't recall his exact words—he said the club he was with in the pros had a center fielder named Hardt, and when he ran to the dugout after the third out, he always stepped on second base. Nobody on the team had ever mentioned this habit. But one night Hardt didn't do it. He came running in and cut across the infield, and missed second by forty feet. "Everybody in the team saw it," he said there in the ice house while the tarp popped in the wind. "We all howled, and made him go back out and tag second before we'd let him in the dugout. Somehow or other we'd gotten the idea that unless Hardt stepped on second coming in from center field, we'd lose the game."

He spoke, too, of the kick a catcher gets from squatting up close under a batter, so close it seems when the batter swung, the catcher would get his head knocked off. "The thrill is in knowing exactly how close you can crouch without being hit. That's one thing that makes a catcher, knowing that by instinct. Knowing it is like being close to death and not being afraid, and it's a great feeling."

Those are the things he spoke of at the ice house, about baseball. During a December norther.

8

*"My Aunt Ruth
would hold one and rub
its feathers and talk hen-talk to it
and pretty soon that thing would begin to sing,
to produce long squawky notes
which very plainly made up a
hen's love song."*

Driving along State Highway 36 in Fort Bend County, somewhere near Wallis, I pulled off the pavement to check what felt like a low tire, and I drew a pretty good crowd of cattle to the fence. At this season, when the weather's wet and cold and cattle are accustomed to being fed, they will often come up to anything with four wheels under it. Because they are fed out of a vehicle, and a truck or even a car stopping along the road may mean something to eat.

Well, these cattle crowded up near the fence and stood around looking disappointed, and I made the acquaintance of one old brindle cow that acted like somebody's pet. She stuck her nose up and let me scratch her neck and did a good deal of talking and visiting, and you could see she was accustomed to being paid attention to that way.

Even on big ranches that don't spend any time gentling cattle, you may find one or two old cows that are extra tame. Or maybe there'll be a pet steer standing around, or an old mare that everybody loves. But overall, your real ranch people don't care anything about having extra gentle cattle.

Looking at that old brindle cow at the fence, I thought about what Shorty Kleine had said a few hours earlier about gentle cattle. Shorty is foreman on the Nash Ranch, out of West Columbia. I was there and ate dinner with Shorty and his ranch hands. Anyhow, Shorty was saying that he'd ten times rather work cattle that are just ordinary wild than real gentle ones. Because if you go to working a bunch of pet cows that have names and get scratched under the neck all the time and talked baby-talk to, they're hard to move.

"And if one steps on you," Shorty said, "you can't get her off your foot. She'll just stand there and you got to get somebody to come lift her off." I am guessing he has lately had experience at working pet cows, because he seemed pretty sincere about saying he wasn't going to do it again. Shorty may have been kidding Ruby Lee Tilley a little, about gentle cows. Ruby Lee was there at the ranch visiting her Aunt Kate Hudgins, who presides over the kitchen and cooks for the hands. Ruby Lee Tilley lives at Sweeny, and she has cattle of her own. She looks after them and feeds them the same as a man does, and when they are worked she oversees the working. She likes gentle cows. Not pets, but not wild, either. Says she's careful who she hires to help work. Because so many times you get an old boy that wants to pick up a board and bust a cow across the nose with it. Then, she says, when you need to pen your cattle again they're afraid to come in.

I do think some cattle people are rougher with their stock than they need to be. Kleine says it's true that sometimes he'll get a cowboy there on the ranch that wants to start roping steers and playing rodeo when it's not necessary.

But I bet he's right about working pet cattle. Imagine you're a ranch hand, and it's four o'clock in the afternoon, and you've been out there since dawn. And it's about 36 degrees, and wanting to sleet, and you're trying to move a bunch of cows. And you come up behind an old sister about like that pet brindle one I talked to at the fence. And you yell at her to move out and pop her on the rump with your rope, and she just stands there and looks back at you, with her feelings hurt. Now that wouldn't put you in love with pet cows, I bet.

The Chamber of Commerce bull was a central figure in a livestock improvement project sponsored by the merchants in our town. Farmers around there were using poor old bulls on poor old cows, a combination guaranteed to result in poor little calves. Owners of the cows simply couldn't afford to buy good bulls. So the Chamber of Commerce, ever eager to help farmers make more money to spend in town, bought this great bull and made his services available to all. Any livestock owner could bring his cows to visit this bull. The fee was something like a buck per cow, if it was paid at all.

The Chamber of Commerce bull was kept in a mesquite pasture out north of our little town. He was an ugly, high-headed, red-eyed creature. I don't know that he had any better breeding than our resident bulls. But he sure had them whipped for size. Driving by his pasture you would often see him standing out there on a limestone ridge, his nose to the wind. "There's the Chamber of Commerce bull," we would say. And down at the pool hall the men playing snooker would make bad jokes about that animal. "If it's ennythang that Chamber of Commerce don't need, it's more bull."

Not all the livestock owners in that territory were farmers. Some lived in town and kept milk cows in the back yard. My family was one of them, as I expect I have told you a dozen times. Never in all my growing up years did I go to a party or have a date or attend a football game that I didn't have to milk a condemned cow before I left, and get up early the next morning and do it again. At a time when I needed the worst way to impress the girls with how sophisticated I was, I was forever being seen leading a milk cow down a city street in search of a vacant lot, where she could be staked out to graze on johnson grass.

Being country then was not cool, folks. Being country even in the *country* wasn't cool. Being country in town was a dark social sin. Everybody in our town was trying to escape the country and get citified. We hadn't yet learned that in that place, getting citified wasn't possible. Having a milk cow in the back yard was a dreadful stigma to me. I wanted to play tennis and get a suntan. Instead I milked cows. To this day, if you gave me 10,000 acres of rural real estate, I would not allow a cow to pass through the front gate.

One morning my father said to me, "Pretty soon the cow's going to come in heat. When she starts bawling, I want you to take her out yonder to the Chamber of Commerce bull." Then he left town. He was a traveling salesman and he loved a milk cow. He loved to be up on Palo Duro Canyon, or on the Colorado at Marble Falls, or some such neat place, thinking of home and seeing me milking that old cow in the mud.

There's nothing in nature less subtle than a Jersey cow in season. She will not sleep, or let anybody else. She will climb fences, or anything else, and she will bawl her head off, night and day. "The cow is bawling," my mother told me. That was her way of saying the creature was in heat and needed to be taken to the bull. My mother did not speak to me of delicate matters like animals being in heat. "The cow is bawling." That said it all.

It was a Saturday. The worst time. The entire community would be out and about on the streets. The tennis players would be walking up to the park, in their white shorts and new sneakers and their smooth suntans. No way I could lead that cow across town to the mesquite pasture without meeting up with the tennis players. Half of them would be girls, and I was secretly in love with every one, needing so bad to impress them. Some impression. I'm leading a Jersey cow in an embarrassing condition. Bawling every step. Little kids following along, laughing. Dogs running with me, barking.

And the boys among the tennis players giving me a hard time, so the girls could hear. "Hey, how come 'at old cow's bawlin' like kat?" They knew very well how come. They'd just lately graduated from milking cows themselves. "Hey, whattza matter 'at old cow? Where you takin' 'at old cow?" Then, in chorus, as if they had rehearsed: *"He's takin' her to the Chamber of Commerce Bull! Haw! Haw!"* It was a long trip across town.

I began to feel better when I finally got to the depot. I had lost the little kids and most of the dogs and street traffic had thinned. All I had to do was get the cow across the railroad tracks and over the creek bridge and through the wire gap in the mesquite pasture. Then I could turn her over to the Chamber of Commerce bull, and they could go back in the mesquite and consummate their deal in private.

But this was not to be. When the cow trotted across the bridge, bawling, the bull heard her, and answered from up there on his ridge. She caught me with a loose grip on her chain and she broke free and ran ahead, toward the voice of the master, and I couldn't catch her.

She stopped, and so did I, when we saw that great red monster descending from his hill. Issuing deep, awful bellows. Trotting stiff-legged and high-headed. The Chamber of Commerce bull, advancing to answer the call. Two or three seconds before he came through it, I could see he wasn't going to stop at the fence. It was a joke of a fence anyhow, three rusty strands of barbed wire, sagging. That beast trotted through and the wires fell away like spider web and he came on out to meet our family milk cow on the shoulder of the road and things were out of my hands.

So it came to pass, there beside the highway. And I wish I may never again hear music or taste pie or see wildflowers if half the cars in the country didn't pick that very time to file by. While I seemed to be conducting a public cattle breeding demonstration. I believe now it was a funeral procession. I'm still not sure, because I didn't really look. I went back to the bridge and sat on the rail and faced downstream and pretended I didn't have anything to do with what was going on. I sat there and made a promise that if I survived the mortification of that day, I would never again have any close association with bovine creatures. And I have not.

The fruit of that roadside alliance was a useless male calf that my father sold, for two dollars, before it was weaned. It had the angry red eyes of the Chamber of Commerce bull.

All my life I have known people dedicated to teaching dumb creatures to speak. I have not seen that they've ever made much headway. One time my Cousin C. T. claimed he taught a bull calf to talk. The calf's mama died of hardware disease, which is brought on by swallowing baling wire, and nails, and rusty bolts and the like, and Cousin C. T. was assigned the job of raising the calf on a nurse bucket. When the calf was drinking out of the nurse bucket, Cousin C. T. would manipulate that bovine's mouth in such a way as to make it bawl, or try to, with that big rubber nipple in its mouth. C. T. would then shape the noise into words. Anyhow, this was his claim.

The calf would say "mama," and "bad man," and "Miller Barton." That was the extent of its vocabulary. Miller Barton was a neighbor about a mile down the road. I expect one of the noises that came out of the calf suggested the name to Cousin C. T., and he refined it some, and made it pass for "Miller Barton." I doubt Miller Barton himself would recognize his name being called by that calf, because it hadn't any notion of how to pronounce the letter T.

My own mother was a most dedicated teacher of English to creatures that weren't meant to speak it. In the evening time of her life, when the nest had long been empty, she took up with a bird, a parakeet, and tried to teach it everything she knew. She taught it to call the names of all her children, and when we came home on a visit she and this bird would have something special worked up for us to hear. She would say, "Now listen to what we've learned." She would get up close to the parakeet's cage and tell it, "Say the Golden Rule. Say the Golden Rule."

Presently the bird would say, "Chirk gawky weckle weckle chucker brr-r-r-r tschooka cawk-cawk-cawk gut."

She would turn back to us with the modest smile she used when she felt the most triumphant about an achievement. I don't entertain an ounce of doubt that she could hear that bird telling us to do unto others as we would have others do unto us. I couldn't hear him saying it, though, no more than I could hear Cousin C. T.'s calf pronouncing the letter T. But the lessons gave her pleasure, and you can bet I never disputed her claims. I wouldn't have disputed her if she'd said the bird was reciting Act II out of *Hamlet*.

She did undertake, after so much success with the Golden Rule, to teach the parakeet to quote John 3:16. Now John 3:16, as you likely know, is a mouthful. I don't have a Bible before me right now but the way she taught it to me, thirty years before that bird was hatched, is as follows: "For God so loved the world He gave His only begotten Son, and whosoever believeth in Him shall not perish, but have everlasting life." I personally doubt there will be a bird even in paradise that can deliver that verse. But I don't believe any such doubt came into her mind. And when the bird would get over in a corner of his cage, muttering inside himself, she would consider that he was making a brave stab at John 3:16.

That bird got out one day, and flew away, and never came back. It always pleased me to imagine that at another house, another sweet old woman was astonished when a strange parakeet came and sat on her kitchen window sill and looked in and took a deep breath and said, "For God so loved the world He gave His only begotten Son . . ."

Few years ago I got acquainted with a doctor who kept suggesting I'd likely live longer if I quit eating eggs so often. So I gave eggs up, except about once a week when I'd eat 'em with bacon and buttered toast and great pleasure, to reward myself for staying out of jail and similar accomplishments. But now I've struck another doctor who eats eggs like he owns shares in a chicken-feed plant and is forever making sermons on the nutritive value in eggs of all sorts. So I've returned to eating eggs, and plenty glad to be back.

I think one of the really pretty things God has given us to eat is an egg laid by a happy hen, and properly cooked. Poached is one of the nicest ways. It's also the easiest of forty known methods of ruining an egg in preparation. There's not any style of fixing eggs where quality counts more than it does in poaching. But poached, scrambled, or fried, the eggs I've eaten in this life that have been the best were laid by birds I was personally acquainted with. Birds who considered humans to be friends.

We had some ducks one time, back when I was coming up. I've heard people talk ugly about duck eggs, but I got a great satisfaction from going out in the morning and picking up a couple for breakfast. Those mama ducks loved me because I fed them. They seemed pleased for me to have what they produced, and would waddle along talking to me about it.

Then back on Grandma Hale's farm out west of Fort Worth, my Aunt Ruth had a flock of Rhode Island Red hens that loved her like a dog worships a boy. Late in the day she'd call them the way a mother calls a child, and they would come and group around and look up and make love-sounds and almost rub against her legs the way a cat does.

Not many birds like to be picked up and handled, but those red hens did. My Aunt Ruth would hold one and rub its feathers and talk hen-talk to it and pretty soon that thing would begin to sing, to produce long squawky notes which very plainly made up a hen's love song.

Those birds laid eggs with yolks the color of an October sunset. When stirred in with yellow meal they would make the cornbread pretty near orange.

Another little bunch of hens I think felt loved belonged to the great-grandmother of my offspring. She lived almost in the middle of Bryan on what was once a dairy farm. Long after the town swallowed up the farm and the cows were gone, she kept a few old hens. And she kept them, and kept them, and kept them, until I expect they were the equivalent of ninety years old. Only hens I ever saw with feathers that turned gray.

I used to watch them come out of the hen house and walk about, tottering and cautious, like nice old ladies taking a stroll.

One or two of them walked sideways. That is, they quartered the ground, like dogs in the country do sometimes. I think it was because they needed to lean into the wind to keep their balance, they were that weak.

But they were loved, and fed, and doctored, and they seemed to know about this privileged treatment. They'd try to pay the rent. That is, every once in a while each one would take a deep breath, and concentrate, and summon up the remains of the fruitfulness she had as a pullet, and by the expenditure of a mighty effort, bring forth in triumph—behold!—an egg. A big old thick-shelled, orange-yolked egg that, all by itself, could put character into a great big pan full of cornbread.

For the past hour and a half I've been sitting here at home, by the window, watching an invasion going on in the back yard. A force of about two hundred fat-bellied robins is trying to take over the big hackberry tree from a lone, scrappy mockingbird.

The mockingbird lives here the year round. He looks on the hackberry as his personal tree. Just now he is plenty jealous of it because its little berries have lately reached the right stage of ripeness. So he naturally resents the coming of this horde of empty craws. He has been guarding the tree for weeks and weeks, waiting for the berries, and he does not want to share them with a flock of strangers.

My sentiments are with the mockingbird, seeing he is outnumbered 200 to 1. Yet for the first hour of the battle it seemed to me he did not need sentiment or anything else on his side. When a robin flew in his tree, or even near it, he flogged the invader out.

The main robin force is sitting like a bunch of vultures in the trees just the other side of the fence, looking at the hackberry. Every thirty seconds or so they will send over one bird, to test. "Chirk!" yells the mockingbird, and runs the robin back across the fence. That "chirk" is his battle cry. He will not follow a robin across the fence. He is only defending his hackberries, not attacking. Nor does he mind other species of birds being in the tree. Blue jays are in it, and house sparrows, and doves on the ground below. But they aren't much of a threat to the hackberry crop. And they ignore the invasion. They don't care, and they give the mockingbird no support.

After about an hour of sending over token invaders, the robins launch the second phase of their offensive. They begin sending over two and three birds at a time, to perch in different parts of the tree. The mockingbird can handle two and three robins without straining a feather. But flogging off three birds takes more time than getting rid of one. While he is "chirking" and chasing over yonder the other side of the tree, two, three, and sometimes four more robins slip in to take the places of the ones that got chased out.

Now the mockingbird is often faced with a dozen or more invaders in his tree at once. He is fearless, though, and charges from branch to branch, hollering "chirk" and booting them out. And he will get rid of the entire dozen, too. But while he's at it, a dozen and a half will come in.

Now they have begun to eat berries. This makes the mockingbird plenty furious. He loses his composure. He flops frantically among the branches, flogging but not flogging effectively. Not even following up. Just hitting and glancing off. The result is, the robins quit running from him. They get out of his way, but he can no longer scare them off.

A while ago I called Ellen Belle to come watch the war. What was happening in the tree offended her sense of justice. She went out to give the mockingbird some support. Personally I keep out of these little conflicts that go on constantly in nature, but Ellen Belle refuses to stand by and see a mockingbird get rooked out of his hackberries. She made loud noises by slapping the soles of two old shoes together, and it scared the robins off. For a while. As quick as his support went back inside, the mockingbird was invaded again.

So she would go back out and make more noise. Then she tried squirting them with the garden hose. Scaring them with loud rock music from the portable radio. Ended up parading around the back yard beating on a tin pan with a cooking spoon. Which got anyway as interesting as birdwatching. But beating on tin pans is tiresome duty, and she gave up. At about the same time, so did the mockingbird. The robins literally stripped the tree.

All this began about noon. It is now 5 P.M., and I can't find one berry left on a twig. The robins are gone. A minute ago I saw the mockingbird, drooping on a low limb, not a "chirk" left in him, looking mighty disconsolate. I figure he mishandled his defense, and at least ought to have learned this lesson: When you see you are outnumbered 200 to 1, don't waste your breath by flogging around on the enemy. What you better do is start eating hackberries, while there are any left to eat.

9

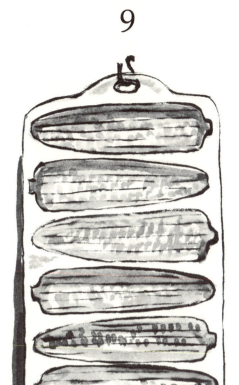

"A little more of the likker, Maude."

Down on Highway 288 in the Brazosport area I was taking on my afternoon coffee in a little cafe, and in there eating a bowl of beans and a piece of cornbread was an old gent who made me think of Uncle Billy Crockett. He had the same small frame, and was dressed all neat and starchy, the way Uncle Billy used to dress.

You talk about clean, now somebody is really taking care of that little gent. He had on khaki pants with a sharp crease and a black belt. Those khakis must have been washed a thousand times, till the color's almost bleached out. He had on a clean white shirt and a little narrow tie and black lace shoes with white socks. He kept

his straw hat on while he ate, but fine wispy white hair was showing around his ears, which were pink.

The old fellow in the cafe even ate his beans in a style similar to
the way Uncle Billy did it. His face way down low, so his mouth
was nearly at a level with the rim of the bowl. In Uncle Billy's case
that position wasn't any strain on him, because he was pre-bent,
and went around bent down all the time. I used to wonder if
that's what bent him, eating that way with his face at table level.

If the old gent in the cafe had crumbled his cornbread into his
beans, he would have made a carbon copy of Uncle Billy at the
table. The women always served Uncle Billy in a shallow bowl, so
he could mash and mix and stir. A plate wouldn't work for him.
He couldn't contain his project in a plate. We used to study him
while he worked in his bowl. He would start out by mashing
everything. Most often it was beans. Brown beans, we called 'em,
or red beans. Pintoes, is what they were, served to him with lots
of juice. He'd call it soup, or likker.

One of the women would check him every little while. She'd
bend down, and put a hand on his bony shoulder, and get right
up in his ear because his hearing wasn't so good, and she'd ask,
"How you doin', Uncle Billy?"

He would stop whatever he had going on in the bowl then, and
raise up just an inch or so and start working his mouth this way
and that, warming it up so he could talk. Finally, he'd squeak
something out. "I need a little more of the likker Maude." I thought
of his voice as pink, same as his skin. It *sounded* pink. A pink
person with a pink voice.

When he got all his beans mashed, he added in the cornbread.
Crumbled it in by hand. I remember the women reminding each
other, "Watch out you don't give it to him hot." Meaning the cornbread, because he would claw into it without testing for heat and
burn himself sometimes. After he had crushed and stirred he
would switch from a fork to a spoon and check consistency, to see
if he needed a little more of the likker to thin 'er up. Or extra
cornbread, if he wanted higher viscosity. When he got it to suit
him, he would sink a little deeper into himself and eat ever so
slow, gripping the spoon handle in his fist like somebody might
try to snatch it away.

While he ate he would make one short statement, somewhere
along in the middle. He would make it with a spoonful of his
mixture in midair, halfway between the bowl and his mouth. It
didn't have far to travel, but you knew when he stopped it en-
route, he was about to let go of his statement. Everybody would

see the signal and pipe down and let him get it out. It would be high and tinny and pink. "Well, we missed our rain agin."

The women would answer then, almost in unison, like responsive reading in church. "We sure did, Uncle Billy. We missed our rain agin, we sure did."

Those women loved that old fellow so. I marveled at it. They patted him, and waited on him, and talked baby-talk to him, and scrubbed him, and looked after him. Every one of them, just crazy about that little old pink man.

Everybody always called it the Gilbert Property. A nice piece of real estate. About four acres, and it fronts on the highway, and it's well drained, and has a stand of healthy middle-aged oak trees on it.

More than twenty years ago now, when Isabella came along and bought that piece of ground, you could almost hear the gasps from all those silk-stocking folks in that neighborhood. The Gilbert Property is surrounded by some of the grandest and most expensive homes. Houses with two stories and fish ponds and fountains and curving driveways and tennis courts and swimming pools. And there was Isabella, coming in with papers proving she'd bought the Gilbert Property. A Chicano woman, about twenty-five, without a husband.

How she got hold of that acreage is a mystery yet. The Gilbert family was early, and they faded. At one time they had a big fine home at the head of the slope among those oaks. But it burned, and then the property got involved in a law suit of some sort. You'd hear it said, when the area started building up, "That Gilbert Property is prime, but it can't be bought. It's all tied up in litigation." But it was on the proper side of town, away from the railroad tracks and the warehouses and the garbage dump, and those fancy homes sprung up around there.

What Isabella did on the Gilbert Property was open a beer joint. She moved a little shotgun house onto the property to live in. Then for the beer joint she brought in a whipped-out GI barracks from one of the army posts out west. She put a makeshift kitchen in one end of the barracks. She came in with a bunch of wobbly tables and old throwaway kitchen chairs from junk shops and trash heaps. She didn't make any improvements on the outside of the barracks. Just put up a sign: Bell's.

Not Isabella's. Bell's. She was proud of that name, Isabella, which is one of the most beautiful of names when called the correct way in Spanish. But she hated what happened to it when the cowboys and the truck drivers pronounced it. The name came out "Izz-uh-bell-uh," and that saddened her. So she'd say, "Just call me Bell." And they did.

Where exactly she came from I don't know. Somewhere down along the border. And she had a little black-eyed baby girl on her hip.

For such a long time those silk-stocking folks in the fancy homes around there kept fighting her. Tried to get an injunction to keep her out with that beer joint. No way. Wasn't any zoning, and she had the right papers. The Gilbert Property was hers, all right. You'd hear half a dozen stories about how she got her hands on it. None of them was ever proved or disproved. Those folks in the fancy homes never did get reconciled to having Isabella's beer joint in their front yard. On Saturday nights when she had a big crowd, they'd sic the sheriff on her about how loud the jukebox was. They'd file on her for creating public nuisances and eyesores. They'd try to catch her selling beer to minors. They never did hurt her, though.

She drew the working people. The carpenters, the bricklayers, the cowboys off the ranches. The electricians and house painters and wallboard men and paper hangers. She treated them right, and they learned to love her, and she prospered. Doubled the size of the place, and brought in her father and brother from down on the border to cook and help out. For almost twenty-five years, there on the highway, Isabella's was a place the working folks loved. Some nights you couldn't get a place to park anywhere near Isabella's without blocking a curving driveway in front of one of those fancy homes.

Well, the reason I bring all this up now is, last summer, Isabella quit. And the beer joint's gone now. Early in the spring she went out in the country and bought her a grand old white two-and-a-half-story plantation-style home, with gingerbread trim and a broad front porch. She hired movers, and they cut that house in half and hauled it into town and put it back together right up there where the Gilbert house stood, at the top of the slope behind the joint. Then she got all her customers together—the carpenters and painters and electricians and paper hangers—and they remodeled that house, working on weekends from what I hear, and working mainly for free, with Isabella furnishing materials and beer.

And when the house was done, she had the beer joint torn

down and hauled away, and grass planted on the place, and trees, and shrubs, to hide all the signs. I haven't gone to see it yet, but the reports I get say there's not a finer or more proper home in that neighborhood now than Isabella's big white house, there on the slope among the oak trees.

A brief note, from one of the bunch that used to hang out at the Joint, brings the news that Rudy is dead. He was sixty-six. Which means that in 1941 and 1942 when that bunch was in college and going out to the Joint to hear Rudy sing, he was thirty-seven or thirty-eight, and that surprises me. I always thought of him as older at the time. Around fifty, maybe.

He was a big, round, grinning fellow with heavy jowls and small eyes and hardly any hair, which is likely why we thought he was older. He worked there in the Joint. He swept, and washed dishes, and helped wait tables sometimes during rushes. We all liked him because he was forever smiling and full of good nature. He wasn't, as they say, quite bright.

We started calling him Rudy after the first night he sang. He was just so full of warmth and friendliness that he suddenly had to sing, and he stood up there and did a song by the juke box, which we then called a nickelodeon. His singing was funny and pathetic and ridiculous, because the fact is, he couldn't sing a note. Couldn't carry a tune in a hay wagon. Yet he was so sincere about trying, wanted so much to be a singer, that nobody could bear to tell him how bad he sounded.

So we reacted too far in the opposite direction. The first time he sang, we all got up and clapped and yelled and whistled and called for more. And somebody said, "Why, he sounds like Rudy Vallee." And from then on everybody called him Rudy. On cold wet nights we'd go out to the Joint and get him to sing. It was a joke, and yet it wasn't. He sounded so terribly bad that it was funny, but he enjoyed those little performances. I know his very soul was nourished by our applause, because he couldn't know the whole thing was a sham.

Some of us used to talk about whether we were being cruel. We decided we weren't. How could it be cruel to applaud something a man so loved to do? I can see him with that little grin on his round face, peering out the serving window in the kitchen, waiting for us to call him for a performance. Why, he even began shaving more often, and staying cleaner, and combing what hair he had.

He did, before it was all over, have some bad moments. Like on nights when we weren't in the mood to hear him and wouldn't call him out. Finally he'd come out and sing anyhow, and nobody would listen, and he'd get only scattered applause.

Then an outsider, an older guy, got into the act. I thought he'd mess the whole thing up, because he had no feeling for Rudy and couldn't see but one side of it all. He brought this home recording machine out to the Joint. Not a tape recorder, because I don't think one had been invented then. It was a machine that cut a wax record, the first I ever saw. He recorded Rudy singing a couple of his songs, and told him he was going to have it played on the radio station and that Rudy would be famous and make a lot of money.

Now that *was* cruel. It made us mad. We'd try to talk to Rudy about it, explain that it wouldn't happen like the fellow said. He'd just nod and grin.

Of course the record never was played on the radio. But we talked the fellow into putting it on the nickelodeon there in the Joint. To Rudy, that was the living end, a front seat in paradise. He was on the nickelodeon just the same as Rudy Vallee and Bing Crosby and Carmen Lombardo. I don't doubt he thought he was just as famous as any of them. It comforts me to believe that he kept on thinking it as long as he lived.

Went out to watch a baseball game the other night, and there was a guy behind home plate giving the umpire a hard time. His style reminded me a little of Mister Sloan.

Mister Sloan was a great big thin-haired, cigar-chewing, bull-voiced fellow I used to see out at Lubbock in the late 1930s and early 1940s. He came out to all the games played by the Lubbock Hubbers in the West Texas–New Mexico League. That was pretty bushy baseball, but a lot of fans were always in the stands because baseball was still our national sport then.

Mister Sloan always sat in a box just behind the screen where he could call balls and strikes and shout insults at the umpire. He had a voice that carried like a rifle ball, and he could make comments even in a casual tone and you could hear him all over the park. He called every umpire Dim-Eye. Some nights he was very funny, and he was good for the gate because if the ball game was dull, the fans could always listen to Mister Sloan.

Just before every game started, when the umpires would have their little meeting with the managers at home plate, and the crowd was quiet, Mister Sloan would pick his time when he was certain of being heard. Then he would call out, slow and distinct: "Hey, Dim-Eye. Dim-Eye? I'm here. I'm here, Dim-Eye, and I'm gonna hep you call this ball game."

The fans would then roar, and applaud, and poke one another in the ribs, and point at Mister Sloan. You would see the regular customers leaning over and explaining to newcomers about Mister Sloan. "There he is," we'd all say. "That's Mister Sloan. Watch him now. Watch Mister Sloan." And from that moment on, Mister Sloan had the crowd in his hip pocket.

During the few moments that the fans would forget him and do their own yelling, Mister Sloan would remain quiet. He would never open his mouth when others were making noise. Say there'd be a close play at home plate that Dim-Eye would have to call. It would generate a rhubarb, and the crowd would be hooting and making a big racket. Mister Sloan would lean back in his seat, all relaxed and tolerant, like he was waiting for the bush leaguers to do their yelling and get it over with, so a major leaguer could then rise and show 'em how it's done.

When the noise died, and the pitcher made ready to throw again, during the expectant hush that comes just before play resumes, Mister Sloan would lift himself about half out of his seat. He did that as a signal to all the fans, to tell them to look, and listen, because he was about to perform again. He would cup his hands and bellow out, "Dim-Eye? Dim-Eye! When you get home tonight, I want you to write on your little slate, fifty times: 'I missed that play at the plate . . . I missed that play at the plate . . . I missed that play at . . .'"

And, oh, that little stadium then would just explode, with laughter and with cheers. Men would take their hats off and slap their thighs. Little girls would jump up and down and clap their hands. Women would stand up and put their heads back and laugh and laugh and laugh. That Mister Sloan. He was our hero. And baseball was more fun to watch then.

In about the year 1934, I saw a guy in a carnival sideshow eat an eight-ounce water glass. He stood in the back of a flatbed truck rigged as a stage. The truck was parked way over in a corner of the carnival layout, where the lights were dim. A single electric cord was strung from the cab of the truck back to the tailgate. Hanging from the cord were two lightbulbs, the clear-glass kind with the filament showing.

Below those two weak bulbs this fellow had a small table draped with a dirty fringed cloth. Before the show started the man's wife came out and stood beside him. She had on these shorts that might have fit her at one time and a tight, flowery sort of top. Her costume just barely covered her principal parts. You could see purple veins in her legs. She must have been fifty years old.

The glass-eater was maybe five years older. He had a red face and wore an oriental-looking jacket that buttoned in the back. He talked about what he was going to do. His voice was all husky and hoarse and it seemed a great effort for him to talk loud. He said he was going to eat that glass. He talked some about glass-eating in a general way. He said he once ate an entire window pane in Chicago.

Then his wife picked up the glass. She held it with her thumb and index finger and turned it this way and that under the lights. Then she took the teaspoon and tapped it lightly several times against the glass. It made a ting-tong sound. Real glass, don't you see. She put the glass and spoon back on the table, taking special care to place them just so. Then she flounced—a fifty-year-old fat woman, flouncing, with purple veins showing in her legs—and she high-heeled several cute little steps around back of the table and stood there with her feet together and smiled. And she had a black tooth in front.

I thought the fellow would never begin on the glass. He held it above his head, talking about it and inspecting it as if it was the first eight-ounce water glass he ever saw. At last he stuck it between his teeth and bit a hunk out of the rim and chewed it up. Yes, you could hear the cracking and crunching as he chewed, and when he swallowed—or pretended to?—there were little groans from the small crowd, standing on the ground alongside the truck.

Maybe fifteen of us, mostly young boys, were in that audience. At a dime a head. I wonder if any of us really wanted to see it. Probably not, but we watched because here it was being done right in our town, on a vacant lot across from the city hall—a man eating glass, a man who had once eaten glass in Chicago, a tragic man who eats glass because boys will pay a dime to watch him.

He consumed the entire glass, too. When he finished he bowed and disappeared behind the curtain strung on a rope. Then his wife picked up the spoon, performed several fifty-year-old-little-girl bows and flounces, and disappeared too. I don't think I've ever seen anything sadder than that.

This was in the spring, a long time ago, when we were just little old shirttail kids. One day we were roving along the railroad tracks, messing around, chunking lizards and picking dewberries, and we met this old man. He was staying in a rickety shack back in a scrub-oak thicket. He was sitting out front of it whittling. He said, "You boys want a whistle?" Maybe he wasn't so old, but he had a beard and beards then were for old men and not for college boys like now.

Well, he took this piece of wood, just a switch. Willow, I guess. He cut a piece off between three and four inches long and took a nail and pushed out the pithy middle part to make a hollow wooden tube. Next he cut a notch near one end and whittled a plug to go in the end opposite the notch, and it made a real neat whistle, and he gave it to us.

He went back to whittling. He was carving on chunks of wood that he would make into shapes of things. One was a rooster and one was a bear and the one he was working on looked like a dog. He said it was a sheep. Said he was figuring on selling those things in Fort Worth. "People in Fort Worth pay good money for stuff like this."

When we started to go, he said, "If you come back tomorrow bring me a couple of your mama's clothespins." At supper that night we showed the whistle, and they wanted to know where we got it. We told them the old man made it. They wanted to know what kind of old man. "Just an old man," we said. They said, "Well, you better keep away from an old man like that."

The next morning we got two clothespins off the line and went back to the shack. These were wooden clothespins. Not plastic like now. He nodded and said they were nice new ones. He took the clothespins apart and inverted the wire springs and fitted them onto the parts of the clothespins so that they made little guns, little clothespin guns. You cocked them with your thumb and a part of the wire spring made a trigger and you could shoot pebbles and things with them, and they were fun to have.

He said, "Go to the filling station and see if you can find us an old inner tube." We brought one, and he cut rubber bands out of the inner tube and showed us how to make a rubber-band-powered riverboat. He took a flat plank and shaped it like a boat, and at its stern he rigged a thin paddle and fixed it on with a strip of the rubber. You wound the paddle backward and set it in the creek and let it loose, and as the rubber band untwisted, the paddle turned and made the boat go and it was pretty nice. He laughed with us and showed us how the things were put together and explained what made them work.

Once he made a small birdhouse, suitable for wrens, he said. When we took it home they asked where we got it, and we said it was given to us. They said, "Are you still fooling around with that old man? You don't know anything about a person like that. He may be a bad man." The next day we found an apple crate behind the grocery store and took it to him, and he made us two boomerangs.

Sometimes he would talk about what he had seen. He had been everywhere. He had seen where the Mississippi River begins and ends. He had seen trees in California three hundred feet tall. He had ridden across Panhandle ranches where you wouldn't see a crossfence for forty miles. He had stood on top of buildings a hundred stories high.

One day a deputy sheriff came to the shack when we were there. He said he was looking for some batteries and wrenches stolen from Western Auto. The old man said he didn't have any batteries or wrenches. The deputy looked in the shack and searched in the bushes around there. He didn't find anything. He said to us, "You boys come on with me." He put us in his car and took us home. He knew our folks.

At home he told them, about the old man, "He's a bum, off the railroad. We get 'em through here sometimes. Bad about stealin'. We'll just move him on down the road." When the deputy left they told us, "They're going to run that old man out of town. Now, for the last time, you stay away from people like that." For a good while afterward, we would go back by the shack and sit there in that place where he had been our friend.

At this minute I have a painful catch in my right shoulder, and my stomach hurts, and my left ankle is sore. I feel like Beatrice.

I do not remember her last name. Back in dim and ancient times when I was young, my mother operated a rooming and boarding house. Beatrice was one of our customers. We had the boarding house I think two years, and I can still see every one of them, even though I can't recall all their names.

I can see Beatrice sitting at the head of the table, buttering a large chunk of yellow cornbread and talking about her appendix. Something was always hurting Beatrice. When something did, she talked about it. My father used to say that Beatrice was in love with pain. He said she talked about a stomachache as if she were engaged to marry it.

In those days, appendicitis was a very popular disease, and Beatrice had a lingering case. People today do not get the mileage out of a bum appendix the way Beatrice did. I mean if you get appendicitis now, you check in with the doctor and he cuts you open and snatches out the offending organ and you have to quit talking about it. But Beatrice's bad appendix lasted for years and years. Frequently it would kick up on her and give her thirty minutes of lecture material.

My father was a traveling salesman in those times and on the road a lot. Beatrice loved for him to come home because he would always ask what had been hurting her lately. She would be delighted to answer the question. She would run down the list, describing every disorder, giving its history. For some reason my father pretended to be very interested in the state of Beatrice's health. Probably he did it out of mischief. He had a little wicked streak that way. The other boarders failed to appreciate his encouraging Beatrice to speak so much about health problems. They weren't big talkers. They seemed to prefer quiet meals, with a lot of meditating over fried liver and pinto beans.

I understood that when they did talk, they tried to steer around health topics. Because if you touched on ill health, it might give Beatrice a little daylight, and she would be off and running on her gout and how active it had been the past week. She refused to let the gout die. She would go back and pick up the first case of gout known in her line, four generations past. She would detail symptoms, speculate on causes, rank degrees of intensity. She would cover the table with gout. So I think the boarders considered that they had experienced a successful meal if they got as far as the bread pudding without ingesting a couple of Beatrice's disabilities.

You can see, then, that they weren't real thrilled when my father would arrive home from one of his selling trips to Amarillo or Fort Stockton and come in to supper full of grins and handshakes and pats on the shoulder and sit back and say to Beatrice: "Well, Beatrice, you're sure looking fine. Are you feeling as good as you look?"

Have you ever heard silent groans? Every eye at the table would turn to bore its hole in my father's face. There would be a moment or two of quietness, when no forks made their bean-scooping noise and no voice said thank you for the squash. My father would pretend he didn't notice, and wait eagerly for Beatrice's reply.

She would reply that she had, in fact, stayed awake half the night with lower back pain. Which would remind her that her mother suffered lower back pain as well, as long as she lived, and her father was obliged to wear a truss thirty years due to a rupture from pulling a yearling out of a bog.

From there she would go on to bone felons she had known and blood poisonings among distant kin. Then carbuncles, and charley horses, and shingles, and salivation, and female trouble. My father would sit there and listen in smiling amazement while Beatrice ran the scale of abnormalities experienced by herself and her loved ones, and it was plain she treasured every one.

From the boarding house we moved on to other non-profit enterprises. Long years later we got word of Beatrice's demise. She was up into her eighties somewhere.

10

*"That night they'd ask,
'What happened at
school today?'
And we'd say,
'Nothin'."*

A little gang of youngsters was in a loose huddle at the corner of the park. It was about 11 A.M. on a weekday and I wondered why they weren't in school. Then suddenly the huddle broke and they ran, around in circles, hopping over bushes, pushing one another down, yelling, laughing. So then I recognized the symptoms. The reason they weren't in school was that school is out for the summer. The time had slipped up on me.

Those children were doing the only thing they could think of to express the way they felt, about being turned loose. I see it every year at this time. I remember how it felt. It is possible to feel that way as an adult, but it is so much harder. The running and the jumping and the yelling that the children do are almost a fit, a seizure they are unable to control. The spirit of freedom has ballooned inside them and is bulging out of them and they must do something very physical to relieve the pressure. Else they might just explode.

You will see animals do exactly the same way. A pet dog that has been penned up a long time is subject to happy fits when it is freed. It will run in great circles and yelp and laugh the same as the children. It will stumble, I think probably on purpose, and roll and tumble all out of control. I like that as much as anything I ever see a dog do. It's infectious and makes the observer feel good too.

A young horse will do that. Older ones too, sometimes. But I always loved to watch a young horse turned out to pasture. Watch him fly, with his tail and his head up and his ears forward. There is something about him then that is so victorious and invincible. He'll have you thinking that if he came to a fence thirty feet high, he would just rise and fly over it.

Sometimes horse people will talk about how fine a horse looks when he is all dressed up for work, with half of him covered over with straps and buckles and blankets and leather, and a rider on him to keep everything under proper control. All right, I agree, he looks fine, but not beautiful, not with a rider on him. The only time he looks beautiful to me is when no human is near him, and he's running free and expressing how it feels to be unfettered.

On Grandma Hale's old farm there was a black mare that everybody rode, a long time ago. I always thought she looked ugly when she was saddled. She was long-nosed and mule-eared and pot-bellied. She had a way of holding herself that made you think whatever was on her back, even if it was a fifty-pound child, was just going to break her spine and let her fold up in the middle. But you keep an eye on her when you took the saddle and bridle off and turned her back in the pasture. Mister, she went through a transformation. Suddenly she was a queen. She'd straighten up and go off down through the pasture in a high lope with her head up and her flags flapping and her eyes gleaming. She looked so grand, going off that way to be free for a while.

You know, I hope, how the child feels when he runs and shouts for freedom's sake, how the released dog feels, and the freed horse. I learned it in school, as I suppose most of us did. The first great piece of knowledge I acquired in school was how great it felt to get out.

In the times before I learned to like schools, I attended one that was like a county jail. It was two-story and dirty brick and ought to have had barbed wire around it. I think in fact it did, on two sides.

It was run by a woman better suited to operating a prison. She was big and tough and kept her hair pulled straight back, so awfully tight, and done into a ball at the back. I always imagined it would have improved her disposition if she had let her hair loose. It seemed to me her hair was pulled back so tight it made her face hurt and her eyes mean.

She had a brass bell, a hand-held bell. In the morning before we took up books, as they then called it, all the pupils would stand in line in the gravel before the front door. She would put us in two lines, boys in one and girls in the other. When the lines were organized to suit her, she would ring the bell and we would march in. When school was over, we had the lines out front again. Nobody could go home until the two lines were perfect. If there was movement, or whispering, or anybody standing out of line, she would not ring the bell and set us free. If anybody dropped a speller, we were all punished by being kept there in line a while longer.

I went to that school one year. Before school was out, my family decided to move—we were always moving—and so I knew in advance that I would not return to that stack of bricks. This circumstance set up what became, for me, one of the grandest moments of my entire time.

Came the last day of school. And three o'clock, or whatever time she let us out of jail. At all other schools I attended, the final day of classes was a sort of fiesta. But not at this one. It was business as usual, the lines, the bell, everything. So there we were, on the last day, standing in the lines, waiting for the final bell. I can yet feel my heart throbbing. The weakness in my legs. The moment of release was near. Of course she made us wait longer than usual, being reluctant to set us free. Everybody tried so hard to keep still, but she would see us wiggling and keep her fist on the clapper. It pained the poor thing, I know, to lose control over us for three months.

When she finally let the clapper loose, to me the sound of that bell was the ring of liberty. Two or three of the boys were able to keep up with me. We ran wild, for I guess a mile, until we dropped. We threw tablets and pencils and construction paper in the air. We leaped the two-strand barbed wire fence we'd been afraid to try all the year, and cleared it by a foot, I bet. We ran through briar patches and never felt a scratch, fell sprawling on gravel and knew no pain, and ended up gasping and laughing in a sweet patch of bluebonnets in a pasture the other side of town. I can relive that experience even yet, and it makes me want to get up and turn flips.

Coming down through East Texas, somewhere near Mount Enterprise, I just happened to notice a little bunch of barefooted boys playing at a house. They went running across the yard and disappeared around the corner of the porch, chasing whatever it is that boys chase before they begin chasing girls. Anyhow, what caught my eye was one boy lagging behind the others. He was hobbling because he had something the matter with his right foot. He had a bandage that went under his foot at the heel and then around his ankle, and tied at the back.

Any adult who ever went barefooted in the summer knows what's the matter with the boy's foot. He has stepped on a nail. At least, that's the most likely thing. It's possible he has cut it by stepping on a piece of glass, or he might have stuck a thorn in his heel. But stepping on a nail is the best bet, when you see a bandage of that kind.

Keeping the feet in proper operation in the summer has been an awful maintenance problem for boys ever since the invention of shoes caused feet to get tender. Remember the stone bruise? You got stone bruises early in the summer before your feet toughened up. And I don't suppose it would be possible to gather a dozen young country boys without at least one of them will have a bandage on a stumped toe. (Stubbed toe is proper, I think, but we always called it stumped.)

Any kind of injury or illness in summer is tough on a youngster, because it keeps him from a lot of fun activities. In winter it's not so bad, because he doesn't miss anything but school.

Kids used to have what their mamas called bilious spells. When you came down with a bilious spell you had to take calomel pills. I once thought the word was "cow-mell," and I bet I took a book satchel full of the things before I learned any different. I'm not sure what this disease amounted to, but it was common as colds. You'd all gather to play ball and somebody would ask, "Where's Red?" And the answer, "He's home sick with a bilious spell."

Another thing that would put a youngster out of commission in summer was a risen. I suppose we were trying to say "rising," but it always came out "risen." Same thing as a boil, I guess. A big sore. Then a carbuncle was related to a risen, but much worse. If you could get a carbuncle you earned a little respect, because it was considered dangerous to have one.

The things we really feared were blood poisoning and bone felon and lockjaw. Almost daily we would hear about people just a few miles away dying from blood poisoning. The symptoms were red streaks running up the arms or legs when you had an infection of some kind. Bone felon we considered to mean automatic death. It was worse than getting hit by a steam locomotive. For years I had no notion of what a bone felon was, but I would use the term when I wanted to speak of something dreadful.

We would worry a lot about getting lockjaw, after we stepped on a nail. (I wonder now why more of us did not get it, in fact.) We imagined that a victim of lockjaw had no warning and that one morning he would wake up and be unable to open his mouth. Therefore he would slowly die of starvation.

I think the best disability a kid could suffer in the summer was a broken arm. On the average, a broken arm wasn't any more painful than a seriously stumped toe, but it gained you recognition. There was also an immunity from punishment when you got an arm broken. If you climbed the chinaberry tree when you'd been told not to, and fell out and broke your arm, you didn't get a whipping. In fact, as soon as you got the arm set and hung in a sling, they would give you homemade ice cream.

It used to be a great entertainment among country boys to climb a tall straight willow and keep going on up until the tree began to bend over from the weight of the climber. Then the climber just hung on, and the willow would bend all the way to the ground and give the climber a thrilling little ride. I never knew a willow given this sort of treatment to break, although I refuse to guarantee that one of these modern willows will hold up under the strain.

The best bunch of riding willows I ever knew was on the Paluxy River a little way downstream from Glen Rose, in about 1930. They grew very close together and had a lot of height in relation to trunk diameter. I want to say a boy weighing seventy-five pounds could get thirty to thirty-five feet of height, going up one of those trees, before it began bending over. But my memory may be bad about that. My copy of *Forest Trees of Texas* says willows seldom get taller than fifty feet.

A few willows get really huge. There is one up in Jasper County in the lower end of Angelina National Forest that's 104 feet tall. Of course that sort of willow wouldn't ever do to ride down. But if it would—hoo boy, what a ride.

I always liked willows because they grow around water. The sight of a clump of willows generally meant a swimming or a fishing hole. I've seen willows spring up and do well on the banks of slush pits at abandoned oil wells, and the pits so full of grease and oil and gunk you wouldn't think the least particular weed could grow there. It doesn't seem possible to dam up a creek in Texas that willows won't begin growing along the edge of the water. The seed travel everywhere. I think this is because they are produced in little capsules equipped with long wavy hairs, and the wind catches those hairs and distributes willow seeds all over creation. Birds carry them around too, I expect.

Next to that bunch on the Paluxy in Somervell County, the best stand of riding willows I ever met up with was on the Colorado River, near where Pecan Bayou runs into it out in Mills County. Close to Goldthwaite. Back in the thirties, when high school turned out for the summer, a gang of us used to go to that place and camp and spend a few days fishing and swimming and just lying around, celebrating the end of school. Man that owned the land along there had a grandson about twelve. Little bitty old kid not hardly big enough to count. He'd hang around our camp a lot and pester us. We had to put up with him because his granddaddy let us come through his land to get to the river. One thing about that kid, he could swim like a cottonmouth. We'd entertain ourselves sometimes by slinging him in the river. Couple of us get him between us and one, two, three, heave. Kid was so light you could pitch him fifteen feet out. He loved it, too. We called him Shorty.

We got to riding willows one day, and we had this idea that we could ride down a big stiff willow, and attach Shorty to the end of it some way, and aim it at the river and let it go, and it would catapult him maybe forty-five or fifty feet out. I look back on that day and I can say we seriously planned that event, right down to choosing the tree and arguing whether Shorty might fly off at an angle and hit a big cottonwood downstream, or whether he might get more distance than we estimated and go clean across the river. In which case his granddaddy would surely have been offended and might not ever have let us come through his place again. So we didn't catapult Shorty, after all. I can't remember, though, that Shorty himself was opposed to it.

Of course I'm glad we didn't do it. But one of the most satisfactory mental scenes I carry from my early times shows me Shorty whipping off the top of that willow and doing a dozen somersaults before hitting the Colorado in twenty-five feet of water.

You used to hear jokes made about a town being so small that meeting the train was the high point of the day. I have to confess those jokes weren't ever very funny to me, because we lived in a town where the train coming in really was the big event of most days.

Small armies of young boys in our town could spend about two hours meeting the train. You'd go down to the depot long before the train was due and walk the tracks and put your ear down on the rail and have arguments about whether you could feel anything coming yet or not. You put pins and pieces of wire on the rail and crossed them so when the train came they'd be smashed into patterns of scissors and crosses and stars.

Even now I can retrieve a little of the excitement when I see a train coming around a bend. The only thing lacking is the smoke. I always thought the smoke boiling and belching out of the stack had a fearsome beauty about it. I love smoke. Always have. And I grieve that there is no longer a place for it in our environment.

The moment the train pulled in was really grand. It made an actual physical event. The shuddering of the earth beneath that great weight set your heart to tremoring in your breast, and the racket was so loud that all other sounds were shut out and nothing else in creation could make a noise except that train. Look at the freight agent pulling that steel-tired wagon, which normally makes so much noise on the brick ramp. But as the train comes in, that wagon goes silent, unable to compete. Dogs ran and jumped and barked without making a sound. Chickens flapped and scattered. Women came out on porches, wiping hands on aprons, looking at the train as if they hadn't seen it a thousand times before.

You walked beside the man in blue overalls while he poked the spout of that ridiculous oil can at the innards of the engine, and you stood close, to see if you had grown as tall as the drive wheels. Then you ran down the length of the train, past the baggage and the mail car to the coaches, with their windows open and human heads and shoulders protruding.

Sometimes they would talk to you. Ask you questions. "What's the name of this town?" And you would shout it out, in a proud way, just as if knowing the name of your town showed you were smart.

You learned to look for special faces framed in those train windows. Some faces were dull and unseeing, and some belonged to brat types which stuck their tongues out at you. But sometimes you came to a face which seemed to hold you with its eyes, and you could stand there a little while, and communicate with a pure stranger. "I don't know your name," you said to each other, "and I'll never see you again, but I like you." There was a warmth in knowing a stranger that way. But there was a sadness in it too. When the train left and you stood between the tracks and watched it grow smaller, you felt a personal loss.

To most who grew up in our town, the day came when money was drawn out from where it was kept, and a ticket bought, and you, at last, became one of the passengers. For purposes of experience. When my time came, I rode the train to visit kin. A throbbing adventure. I marvel now, looking at the map, that the trip covered only thirty miles.

January was the month when we looked for snow. We always watched the skies for prospects and listened to the old folks who would talk about conditions necessary to bring snow down. But we never did really get ready for it. The reason was that in this state most of your snow departs at about the same time it arrives, and it's a fairly rare snow that stays around long enough for the public to get any benefit out of it.

So when a good snow did come, it would catch us all unprepared, and there would be a huge scramble for materials to build home-made sleds. They would be mostly crude jobs, with tapered two-by-fours for runners and one-inch decking, and nothing whatever to hold onto. With the result that the passengers were forever getting spilled and scattered everywhere, which of course was part of the game.

When I was the most interested in sleds, I never once saw a store-bought sled being used. We would see them in mail-order catalogues and discuss how slick they looked and even talk about saving up to order one. But nothing would ever come of it, and when the snow surprised us, here we would go after the hammer and the nails and the saw, and then to the scrap heap for materials.

We were mighty short in the matter of hills to slide down, and so most of the sledding was done on the streets, with the sleds being towed along by cars. That interests me now. Because those were bitter times, economically, when the heads of so many families were out of work and holding a tight line on spending of all kinds. And a sad percentage of adults were going about with faces drawn from worry. Still, when the snow came, you would look out and here were all the old cars out on the street, pulling sleds full of laughing kids, and the old man at the wheel looking back and grinning.

Some of those men-faces looked unfamiliar to me, and it was a long while afterward that I understood why. It was because they were grinning. They grinned so seldom, when they did it they looked like somebody else. That was the principal benefit that I ever saw in a snow. It improved humors that needed improving. Even the worst old scrooge in town would emerge from his counting house, all overcoated and mittened and mufflered, and slip and slide around right there at the corner of Main and Sycamore, and look at him—by john, he's laughing. Something about snow did that to us, and it was good.

I hear people who have lately moved into our state from colder places up north expressing surprise that we have freezes and ice storms and sleet. They may have even greater surprises.

From those sled times I am talking about, I remember stretches of cold weather when a snow man wouldn't melt for ten days. A spell like that would start with a fluffy snowfall that covered us over pretty well. Then we'd get a temporary thaw the next day. It would melt just enough of the snow to make everything wet. Then that night, hoo boy, here'd come a tight freeze, down about 12 or 15 degrees. It would put a glaze over the snow and preserve it, just like somebody was trying to save it for next summer.

Those were the best times for the sleds, but you'd always have some who'd overdo, try to stretch the snow past its usefulness. They'd just wear it out. You'd see guys riding a sled behind a Model A chugging along a gravel street that didn't have much more snow than the equator did. Two more days and they'd have been kicking up dust.

It would be on a day just about like this, bright and calm and glistening with spring. Me and old Dude, and sometimes Riley if we couldn't slip away from him, we just wouldn't quite make it to school. Somewhere along the crooked mile to that old stack of red bricks that looked like Huntsville's prison walls, we would take a wrong turn, and end up on the river. It wasn't a turn we planned. All of a sudden we would just be walking toward the river instead of the school. It was mysterious. We would have laid a hand on any Bible in church and sworn we couldn't help it.

We would push through the bloodweeds and the willow sprouts on the sand bars and look for turtles to chunk. It was too early in the morning for turtles to sun, and anybody knew that, but we looked anyhow, and the dew from the weeds and the willows soaked our britches and our tennis shoes.

That bitter, skunky smell would be hanging over the river. We used to say, to believe, that cottonmouth moccasins gave off that smell, that when you smelled it you better watch out because a cottonmouth was close. I wonder how long we believed that. We used it even after we quit believing it. Wasn't any use discarding a good belief like that just because it wasn't true. So we'd go in-junin' along the bank, dividing the jungle of green things growing there, and the smell would boil up, and we'd say, "Cottonmouth." There was a satisfaction in it.

First thing we knew, the eight o'clock whistle at the tailor shop in town would be blowing, far away and hoarse, with a mournful seagoing quality, and we'd be surprised, and say the same thing, every time. "That's not eight o'clock, is it?" Well, sure it was eight o'clock. If old Jimmy at the tailor shop pulled that whistle string at any other hour of the morning, it would have wrecked the schedule of every enterprise in town. Listen, clocks inside a two-mile radius of the tailor shop were set and checked and judged by that steam whistle, just like it was coming out of the Naval Observatory. Years later, when I went back and saw old Jimmy, white-headed and retired, I asked him. "Where did you get *your* time? How did you know exactly when to pull the string?" And he said, "I always pulled it when Old Man John Pitcock drove by the shop on his way to the office." Which was probably a lie, but it's such a lovely one.

That whistle meant more things. One thing, if you were on the river when you heard it, it meant you couldn't get to school on time. And you'd have to go through the principal's office and explain why you were late. How could you explain the reason for a wrong turn that you didn't even understand yourself? So the best thing to do was just not go. If you were going to have to run that obstacle course of explaining why and getting written excuses and seeing principals, you might as well get something of value for your trouble.

We would wade across the river at the rock-bottomed shallows. Books and maps say it's a creek. You would call it a river as we did if ever you saw it on a ramble, after a cloudburst upstream. I've seen it put water into the low end of town deep enough to swim a horse off the dock at the gin. Sure, seen it done. We would go to the bridge and lie in sandy sunny places and watch the cliff swallows carry mud to plaster their nests. We would have rock-chunking contests. Try out cuss words we'd heard. Smoke cedar bark. Have car-guessing games. That is, somebody would crawl up the bank far enough that he could see the road and those left under the bridge would guess the kinds of cars that came over. Guess according to their racket. Then we'd climb the limestone bluff, pulling ourselves up by the stumps and saplings that poked out of its steep face. And at noon we'd be up there on the bluff, and we could see the school, and we'd eat the cold biscuits and pan-fried sausages fixed for us and put in brown paper bags before seven o'clock that morning.

That night they'd ask, "What happened at school today?" And we'd say, "Nothin'."

Crossing a little creek up in Montgomery County a couple of days ago, I noticed a short way downstream from the bridge that two young boys were standing on the bank looking at the water. Just looking. Not fishing or chunking rocks, just standing there. You could tell what they were doing by the weather, which that afternoon happened to be warm and beautiful. So there isn't any doubt those youngsters were checking that creek to see when it would be warm enough to go swimming.

Almost all towns, even little old country places, have concrete swimming pools now, and yet you find boys going into the woods to swim in creeks. It is very important for boys to do this, and maybe girls too, but I am unable to speak for the girls on this question.

I don't know if it still holds, but there used to be a great competition among country boys to see which guy in a group could stand the coldest water in early spring. You could gain respect from older boys if you were willing to torture yourself by going naked into water that had the chill of February on it. If you could stand to go in before anybody else, you became an outright hero, and they talked about you at school. I can still feel the pain of that creek water in March. There is no way you would get me into the water at this season of the year now, but it seemed necessary at the time we were doing it.

You saw various systems for getting into cold creeks in such a way as to suffer the least. The most admired way was to take a running leap and just hit it. I can remember doing that one time, and I found it a terrible experience. It was a little the same as cutting yourself with a pocketknife. It didn't hurt much the second it was done, but then here would come the pain swelling up in a great surge and engulfing and defeating you.

As a general thing, boys took the gradual approach. Which

means you first worked up whatever it took to stand ankle-deep in the shallows. Then you dipped water with your hands and rubbed your legs until you thought you could stand to take a step on out toward the middle of the creek. When you got knee-deep, you dipped and rubbed again, higher up. Then another step or two, and rub higher up still. I think this had a kind of anesthetic effect and prevented at least part of the shock that resulted if you took the bolder route and just jumped in. Of course you always had some smart alec who would destroy your schedule by splashing that frigid water onto your backside while you were still working down about your calves. This sometimes caused fist fights, the discomfort of which was even greater than that of going into the water. Because two boys fighting naked on a creek bank in March are exposed to all manner of hazards.

I reflect on those times and I find now that I understand them only partly. I can remember knowing at the time I was doing it that it was just plain stupid to go into a body of water that wasn't yet meant to be gone into. And yet, knowing that, I had to go, anyhow. It was a thing we did, and it had to be done. It was best to do it in the hairy-chested, running-leap style, but if you couldn't manage to do it that way, you did it other ways that you could stand. I don't think it ever occurred to any of us not to do it at all. That's the part I can't understand now.

The bunch I ran with back home was bad about standing around on the street corner Saturday night and speaking of what a crummy town we lived in. When the fact was, we didn't believe any such thing. We only said so because we had heard the older bunch say it, and thought it was the best thing to say. We can now get together and talk about those times until daybreak, as if they were golden years, and they were.

We did a thing then that I now think of as Staying in Town on Saturday Night. I loved it. We had a little money in our pants pockets, and we spent it and got every penny's worth and more. The way we got money was by working after school and all day Saturday, at various little jobs available for people with our skills. Sacking and carrying out groceries. Setting pins at the bowling alley. Washing bottles at the creamery. When we got off work Saturday night, we had a buck or two, and we went forth to vitalize the local economy and put that cash into circulation. I expect our employers had most of those dollars back in their cash boxes before Tuesday.

Along about then I learned some remarkable things about the world of finance. One was this—that it was possible to get money for work you hadn't even done yet. It was called drawing. Say you got paid two bucks at closing time Saturday. But maybe you were in bad need of $2.50 for some special purchase. You could stand respectfully, with your head bowed just a little, and your hands behind you, and say to the boss, "Mr. Walters, you reckon I could draw fifty cents?" If you had a good record, if you were always on time and worked all right and didn't say the wrong things to customers and had shown you wouldn't steal, you could draw the fifty cents.

The first time I ever did it, I was plenty proud. Because it was a trust that was made in you. It said you were a sound risk, that they were depending on you to come back and work out that four bits. But the most startling thing about it to me, it was against every principle I had ever heard about earning money. The way they told me was, you worked and then you were paid. Getting paid first, now that was something special. I remember going home and telling about it.

In those times I learned some things about credit, too. If you worked, it was known all over town. And so you would sometimes get asked for a loan from one of your friends. Maybe fifty cents or less. We had guys around town who worked, and those who did not. Those who did not seemed to need the money as bad or worse than those who did, and why they didn't get jobs I could never decide, but they didn't. And so some had a hard time paying back their loans.

You want to know how much money I lost, lending out my money that way? Of course I remember. Twenty cents. All the other loans were repaid. Friend of mine borrowed that twenty cents off me to go to the show. I could take you to the place, to the very crack in the sidewalk in front of the barbershop where we stood when I dug out two nickels and a dime and forked them over. And I never got paid. If I ever see him again I will dun him, you bet. What is the interest on twenty cents over forty-two years?

Mostly what we did on Saturday night in town was feed our faces. We would first go to City Cafe and eat a bowl of stew for fifteen cents. A big deep bowl, with plenty of crackers and catsup at no extra charge. A sisterly type of waitress worked in that place, and if her name wasn't Hazel it ought to have been. She had a smooth, ageless face that needed no powder or paint, and she had a nice gold tooth in front and a friendly way about her. Sometimes one of our bunch would draw so much cash from his boss that on payday he would get very little, maybe no more than it took to go to the midnight show. When that happened, if Hazel knew and trusted him, she would let him have a bowl of stew on credit until the next Saturday night. This was a personal form of banking, as Hazel made clear. I mean if the guy didn't pay, Hazel would have to dig the fifteen cents out of her own apron pocket.

So we gradually found out that in that little town all of us were constantly being observed and judged, and these observations and judgments were then woven into our personal reputations that were important to us as long as we lived in that place, and maybe even afterward. We were observed not just by parents and teachers and bosses but by Hazel, who wanted to know who she was standing good for on a bowl of stew.

The other night I was sitting in this little refreshment parlor, sipping on a cool one and watching the customers dance to the juke-box, when I spotted a young woman who made me think of Matty Lou. Matty Lou was one of the girls we used to dance with when the bunch of tomcats I grew up with were still single and free and trying to be what we then called smooth operators.

Being a smooth operator just meant that you could walk into any place where dancing was allowed, and lead out onto the floor a girl you never had seen before, and dance with her in a reasonably graceful fashion without falling down or having embarrassing collisions.

The good thing about Matty Lou, she was a leader and not a follower. On the dance floor, I mean. She was a pretty fair looker and enjoyed twisting and wiggling this way and that before an audience, and she kept up with all the latest steps. And she would be happy to show these new steps to any guy that didn't know how to execute them. So most of the time she was leading when she was on the floor, and counting one-two-three, dip, and so on. It was a service she rendered to guys learning the boards. She was giggly, and considered forward by other girls because she would grab a boy's hand and pull him out on the floor and get him hitting on the beat. But she did a certain amount of good, Matty Lou did.

Then I remember Edna Faye. (All the girls from about that time seemed to have double names that way. Well, so did a lot of the boys, Billy Ed, Johnny Bill, Joe Lee.) Edna Faye was a pretty little girl wouldn't weigh ninety-seven pounds wrapped in wet towels, and she was sweet-natured, but she could wear out a two-hundred-pound farm hand on the dance floor. It's a mystery of physics to me yet, how she was able to do it. Something in the way she hung onto you. She would wrap her left hand around the back of your neck and just sort of suspend her weight there. At the end of about three numbers, the guy dancing with Edna Faye would be pretty near a hospital case. It was like shuffling around with a sack of oats suspended from your collar bone. Wasn't any way you could break her hold on you.

Then I recollect another one named Edith something-or-other, a blonde-haired girl with fine strong legs and a good figure all around. She was what the boys called an elbow pumper. She had a couple of big brothers two or three years older than she was. They were the kind who would spend the summer working in the oil fields out around Odessa and Monahans, and they learned their dancing in the beer joints out there and came home and taught their little sister. Those old boys for some reason thought that to keep moving on a dance floor, you had to pump the elbow, just like the pumping would force fuel into the carburetor and keep the motor going. Their sister had the same style, then, most likely out of self-defense. Anyhow, when you danced with her wasn't anything to do but pump along with her. She was stronger than most of us, so we just held on and let 'er pump. Didn't make any difference what the music was—fast or slow, loud or low—here would come old Edith elbow-pumping around the outer edge of the floor, the other dancers giving her room so they wouldn't get clipped. She was a dear sweet girl.

Then there was Velma. I think Velma Sue. She was a runner. I mean her notion of dancing was to keep backing away from you so you wouldn't ever touch her. If a boy slipped up on Velma and danced cheek to cheek, she considered it to be an attack. I remember here a few years ago, young folks danced far apart, so separated you often couldn't tell if they went together or not. So our friend Velma was born thirty years too early, as dancing twenty feet from the partner would have sure suited her general style. I often wonder if she ever got close enough to anybody to get married. We used to make the joke that Velma's idea of heavy petting would be to stand out front of the drugstore, and shake hands at arm's length.

Getting big enough for summer work was a great marker in a boy's life. Once he went to work, even for just a couple of summer months, he was never again completely free. There was fun to be had at work and satisfaction in making money, but getting that first summer job changed a youth's life forever.

As a rule, summer work was something like skeeting soda at the drugstore or sacking potatoes at the grocer's. Low pay and long hours, but that was true of all jobs summer or winter. I went through at least a dozen types of summer work, and I learned a little something from each one. The best summer work I ever did was at the Western Union office. All I did was ride around on a bicycle delivering telegrams and seeing new people and watching their faces when they opened their messages. Getting a wire was still a large event then, exciting and frightening.

Of course farm boys had ready-made summer jobs, but everybody tried to keep away from farm work. If you lived on a farm, you didn't get paid for working on it. Most of the farm boys I grew up with were trying to get to town. They came in and applied for summer work "with the city." That meant chopping broom weeds and johnson grass out of the graveyard or the city park, but you did get a little pay for it and you were in town, sometimes within sight of the swimming pool and the girls. (All of us immediately hated the guy who got summer work as a lifeguard, and circulated rumors that he wouldn't have the job if his daddy didn't have influence.)

Several places I always wanted to work in the summer but didn't get to. One was the pool hall. I thought that would be a great spot to work, walking around wearing a green eyeshade, racking the balls, collecting the money. Then I yearned for a job in the hardware store too, so I could sell fishing tackle and rope and gasoline lanterns and saddle blankets and other masculine stuff like that. Lumberyards would be a good place too, I thought, because of that great pine smell. But lumberyards and pool halls didn't hire young boys, any more than banks did. (I never went near the bank unless I was ordered to. The people who worked there seemed stern and unhappy to me, and it didn't have a smell. Every other place smelled—feed store, drugstore, printing shop—but the bank didn't. I had the idea then that you couldn't trust a place unless it had a smell to identify what sort of outfit it was.)

Substitute jobs provided a good bit of summer work. Like you would carry a paper route a couple weeks for a guy who went to see his grandmother in San Angelo. I substitute-drove a dry-cleaning delivery truck one summer. Nice work but bad pay because you worked on percentage.

Door-to-door selling was an awful tough proposition in our town. In summer we'd have these promoter types come through, needing salesmen. Like for magazines. These guys all looked the same. They drove big cars and wore suspenders and smoked cigars and told the keenest stories about how much money you could make door-to-door selling their magazines. But man, you couldn't make picture-show money selling magazines in our town.

That was another summer job—working at the picture shows. Like taking tickets. It was a pressure job, though, because your friends would all come slipping and whispering around, wanting you to let them in the show free.

A lot of story-telling went on among us about summer work and what it paid. It was common for some boy about seventeen who'd never worked a day in his life to brag about what a neat job he'd nailed down. But you'd notice it was off in another town somewhere so you couldn't check on it. Like once all of us laughed for a week when a guy claimed that soon as school was out he was going to work at the airport at Abilene, washing airplanes for three dollars a day. No way he could make us believe that. Any one of us would have worked for nothing washing airplanes just to be around an exciting place like an airport, and we couldn't conceive of getting paid three dollars a day for such a privilege. I still don't believe he got summer work that good.

Back before Christmas when I went to West Texas, I tried to locate the remains of an unpainted frame house that once stood about two miles east of my old home town in a bunch of scrub-oak timber. I couldn't find the house or any clue of where it was, so I suppose it's been torn down or burned or hauled off. It's not necessary for me to find the house. I just wanted to look at it because of the great discovery I made in it about forty years ago.

I am only guessing at how long ago it happened. But I expect we were somewhere around fourteen. This friend and I were standing out front of the barber shop one Saturday morning, and a man in a big cow-working hat stopped in an old pickup and asked if we'd like to make fifty cents apiece. We said yes, sir, without asking what the job was. Fifty cents apiece was good pay then for boys, even if the job was hard and took all day. Grown men were working for as little as a dollar a day in those times, and supporting families.

My partner and I were at the point in the lives of young males when we were feeling pretty chesty about our physical selves. We weren't going to be bull-necked football types, but we weren't weaklings either. We could run a long way and throw things well and swim and monkey up a gym rope all the way to the rafters.

But we hadn't ever done any really hard labor, at least not for very long stretches. We were fixing to get introduced to it, when we got in the pickup with that old boy. By that time I had picked a little cotton and chopped some, too, and helped bale hay, and I'd dug a few post holes in rocky ground and even shocked oats, which is long hot work. But I never had done the kind of thing we were about to do.

The old boy in the pickup was big, with heavy round cheeks and a fat stomach. I don't remember his name. He kept cattle out there in that scrub timber. He drove to his house and hooked onto a creaky four-wheeled rubber-tired trailer loaded with johnson-grass hay and about twenty sacks of oats. He pulled the trailer out into that scrub timber east of town and stopped at the old house I told you about at the beginning of this. Nobody had lived in the house for a long time, but it was fairly sound and our boss man was using it to store hay and oats for his horses. He wanted to fill the attic first. He got up in there and stood on a couple of ceiling joists to straddle the access hole. My partner and I would then wrestle the hay off the trailer and carry it in and muscle it up to the boss. He would grab it and pull it on up into the attic and stack it.

At first it wasn't so bad, handling the hay. They weren't real solid bales, and we could muscle 'em up pretty well. We took several bales and built a sort of stile concern on the floor below the hole, to cut down on the altitude to the lift. The trouble was, the old boy in the attic just didn't know when to quit. He kept rushing us. Said he needed to get this done, go get another load.

Even before we got to the oats, those johnson-grass bales were weighing forty tons apiece, and me and my partner were having to help each other handle 'em. My skinny arms began feeling like they were full of lead. When we started on the oats, the work was just torture. Every sack was a gut-wrenching test. I finally got so I couldn't lift my feet off the floor to take a step. Mouth tasted like it was full of pennies. I'd try to spit and nothing would come out. Finally I got sick and had to stop and gag. Old boy in the attic said well, I must have got hold of something bad to eat.

I was sick for two days, just from exhaustion and over-exertion, trying to make my body do something it wasn't capable of doing. While I was recovering I decided if that was what hard work was like, I was sure gonna find me something to do for a living that didn't require it. So I did, and I haven't ever to this day done another hard, weight-lifting day of labor. I expect an experience of that kind made a lot of country boys put on a white collar and come to town.

We used to walk all day, along creeks and lake banks and through scrub timber. We'd follow sandstone ledges in mesquite pastures and trace out little branches to their spring sources. We'd rest, leaning against the trunks of sycamores and cottonwoods and oaks. Trees we'd known from our earlier times, that we'd climbed and shot squirrels from and built houses in.

October was the best time for the walking. On Friday afternoon I'd hitchhike home from school out at Lubbock, and on the way in I'd watch to see if the old black Chevy was hunkered into the johnson grass beside the gray frame house west of town. If the car was there it meant Ellis was in from his job at Fort Worth and we could do the walking.

We'd leave for the lake before the sun was warm and laugh about how late it was. Because when we first began those all-day walking expeditions, we'd leave long before day, and sometimes then we'd be sitting on the lake bridge when light rose in the east. But that had been when we were very young. We'd actually say that. "When we were young." We were twenty, I guess, when we'd say that. Ellis maybe twenty-one, when he had the Fort Worth job and the Chevy and would come home October weekends. But we felt mighty adult. Grown up and wise and already looking back and grinning at the people we'd been at sixteen.

"You 'member 'at time you stood up on the bridge in your skivvies and chickened out and wouldn't dive off?" He'd had an older brother in the Navy and had learned to call underwear skivvies.

"Whatta you *mean* I chickened out? You begged me to come down. Begged me not to dive."

"Shoot."

Old men talking. Old men of twenty and twenty-one, talking about when they were young, when they were sixteen.

He was almost right about the chickening out. We would go to that bridge to fish for crappie when the mayflies were out. You could sit on the rocks and pick your bait off your shirt collar or your hat. Just reach up and grab a mayfly and stick it on your hook. Once in broad day I climbed up on one of the metal bridge trusses and said I wished I could dive off, because the water looked good and the sun was so hot. Ellis said shoot, that I'd be scared to dive off there. I knew I wouldn't. Go ahead then, he said, do it. But I couldn't right then because the lake was our town's water supply and swimming in it was against the law and might be a game warden watching. Ellis said we'd come back early next morning then, before sunup, and see if I'd dive off then. Wouldn't be no game wardens out then. I said fine.

We did go back. I skinned down to my shorts and climbed up

on that cold fog-slick railing and looked down, and in the dim gray light I couldn't even see the water. It was shrouded in mist. It had to be down there, about fifteen feet below, but to me it wasn't there at all, and diving off that bridge would have been leaping into hell's very septic tank. "Come on down," he said. "Don't dive off there. You might hit a stump." I'd never heard love songs or read poetry with prettier words than those. I came on down, and we didn't mention the incident again until we got twenty, and old, and could look behind us and laugh about what had been sensitive matters.

On those October weekends we would mosey along the lake bank and remember things from ancient times, four or five years back. Yonder off that point? That's where the boat sank with us that time. And just to the right, there, of that old snag, is where we had to rescue the dog that couldn't swim. Dog about to *drown*, man. And on a quarter of a mile is Deep Draw.

The boat, we found it in the woods. A homemade job, full of holes as a kitchen colander. We got tar and melted it and patched the holes and chopped paddles out of old planks and went out on the lake in that thing, and it sank. Had to swim to shore. An excellent adventure. And we were privileged to know the only beast in the canine family that wasn't able to swim. We'd go out wade fishing, up to our armpits, and this old dog would try to follow us and he'd get in water over his head and he'd go down. We'd have to carry him out and tend to him. Big old dog weighed eighty pounds, and couldn't swim a stroke. I swear.

Deep Draw was a finger of water deeper than it looked and we'd put throw lines there, and three or four times we hooked onto something monstrous. Big old catfish, we thought. Maybe so. We never saw it. It'd straighten a hook and get free. But I count it even today a high privilege that I got to feel that what-ever-it-was, and know the awesome strength of it. When we spoke of it at home, Ellis' father said it was probably a big old moss-back turtle. Shoot.

Those are the things we'd talk about, when we were twenty and felt old and went for the October walks.

11

*"Pete's wine wasn't
anything to a dose
of castor oil."*

Did I ever tell you about the day my Cousin C. T. stole the wine his brother Pete made and forced me to help him drink it, that time in 1933? Stop me if I did. We knew where Pete made the wine. We'd always know, from the day he picked the grapes. He kept his crocks and things in an old sway-backed, deserted farm-house that he and his father used as a hay barn. He'd build a little room for his stuff, just a small cubicle, out of johnson-grass hay bales. Pete was the only one who ever fed hay out of that old house, and he wasn't much worried that anybody would find his wine.

We'd go there often. Cousin C. T. would take away just the

right bales so we could look and see Pete's wine working, and smell it. He generally had two or three fruit jars with wine left over from previous batches, and they would be in the hay around there. Cousin C. T. liked to take the top off a jar of wine and sniff and grin and brag about how one of these times he was going to drink himself some of that stuff. I didn't think of issuing a challenge, telling him if he was going to drink wine then go ahead and drink it because nobody was there to stop him. I didn't do that because I understood such an adventure took courage, and planning, and needed to be worked up to in a gradual way.

We thought making wine in a pasture was a good and proper enterprise because Pete was doing it and whatever Pete did was the right thing. He was twenty-four and big and single and the handsomest fellow alive. He knew everything there was to know and had done everything there was to do and had done it better than anybody else. He could roll a Bull Durham cigarette with one hand and he could cuss real well and he could tell the finest lies about the girls in town. We didn't know they were lies. How could *we* know?

The reason Pete hid to make his wine, his folks wouldn't have it in the house. They were leather-laced prohibitionists the same as about 90 percent of all my and Cousin C. T.'s kin. If his father had ever found the wine in the hay house, I expect he'd have flung Pete's other pair of pants into a pasteboard suitcase and sent him on off to hell.

The day Cousin C. T. forced me to help drink the wine was a Saturday. Pete had gone into town early and wouldn't be back until after the dance, way late. We went to the hay house and Cousin C. T. picked out a fruit jar of wine and we took it to the creek. He had also snitched about half a sack of Bull Durham. There on the creek bank he sat and leaned back against an elm and grinned at his wealth—a quart of wine and a sack of smoking tobacco. He had the tobacco in his shirt pocket. The little round paper tag on the sack's drawstring's hung out of his pocket the way Pete's did. It did look really good, I thought.

I wasn't entertaining the vaguest idea of drinking any of that wine. I had learned my lessons well, on that stuff. Before I could read, I had been taught what drinking alcohol would do to a person. The first thing was, the person would lose his job and nobody would ever hire him again. Then his wife and children would leave him, and his friends would not speak to him, and he would be a bum, and he would steal things and go to jail and end up in an asylum somewhere, and his life would be ruined. So if alcohol could do that to a full-grown person, just imagine what even a taste of it could do to a kid in overalls.

But I understood Cousin C. T.'s need for a witness. He couldn't perform a courageous act like this without a witness. He took a swallow. I thought I saw him wince some, but he wiped his eye and said it was good. He waited a good long while before he took another drink. He said it was *really* good, that second time. He got out his tobacco. "Think I'll roll me a smoke," he said.

So he smoked along and sipped and talked about how good it was, and once he said I wouldn't believe how good it was, and in that way I was compelled to try it, as you can understand. I thought it would taste like grape juice. It tasted like medicine. It burned. But at that time in my life I was expert in the matter of swallowing what didn't taste good, because of all the evil medicines that had been poured down me. Pete's wine wasn't anything to a dose of castor oil. At the second swallow I examined myself for signs that my life was going into ruination. I couldn't see any, so I went ahead and sipped and took a lesson from Cousin C. T. on how to roll a smoke. I guess the last clear recollection I have of the day was Cousin C. T.'s teaching me how to inhale, the way Pete did. After that, things were hazy.

We must have spent hours on that creek bank, wallowing in wretched nausea. In that time my only comfort was in raising up to see Cousin C. T. being sick as I was. I always felt it served him right, forcing me into debauchery as he did. But that experience convinced me, and I stayed convinced for years and years, that everything they taught me about booze was true. I have acquaintances who are teetotalers and non-smokers yet, on account of similar experiences early in their lives.

Many years ago, somebody took a deep breath and quoted the father of our country as saying to his daddy, "I cannot tell a lie." Most of the biographical stuff you read now about George Washington insists that he never said any such thing. So evidently that quote, about his being unable to tell a lie, is itself a lie. Which doesn't much surprise me. My position on this matter all along has been that if Washington *had* said he couldn't tell a lie, he would have been telling one when he said it. Because any person in shoe leather is capable of lying. It doesn't take any talent whatever. I know a few folks who say that they don't ever lie, but I think that's just because their definition of a lie is different from yours and mine. I mean they can let go of a mistruth tall as a windmill and call it a kindness and not a lie at all.

But no matter what name you put on it, the smallest lie has an awful potential for making trouble. The reason is, a lie is so fertile and productive. It is also immortal. Say you tell a tiny lie, not as big as a mustard seed. You may think it'll do its job and fall to the earth and fade away and never again be heard from. It's not so. It's going to resurrect, I promise you. That one little lie has got the immortality of any angel you can name in heaven. It'll rise up and fertilize itself and produce what it needs to live, and what it needs is another lie. And after that, another still. And another and another and another, forever and ever amen, until the one who told the lie to begin with comes and gets it and confesses in public that it's his and puts it back where it came from.

I discovered all this about lies in 1932 when I told my father I had watered the cow when I had not. I was supposed to go up on the hill, behind the house where we lived then, and get the milk cow and bring her to the house and water her in the middle of the day. Several people staked out milk cows on that hill. It belonged to somebody who didn't care if cows grazed there. I would tie the cow to a mesquite sapling in the morning, and go back at noon to water her and put her in a fresh spot. Except that on this day I was playing ball and I didn't go. That night before he milked, my father said the cow came in looking awful gaunt and asked if I watered her at noon. I said I did, thinking the lie would give me less trouble than the truth. I was wrong.

You need to understand that to my father, not watering a cow was a crime ranking right in behind homicide and maybe ahead of it, depending on who the victim was. He asked me where I took the cow to water her because he couldn't see any sign that I'd done it at home. I said I had watered her on the other side of the hill. That was Lie Number 2, that Number 1 needed for support. He asked *where* on the other side of the hill, and I said I'd watered her out of a puddle left over from a rain. Number 3.

He let me try for a night's sleep before he said it hadn't rained in a month and it seemed strange that a puddle would still be up there on the hill. I said I supposed then it was a spring. Yes, that was it, it was a spring I'd discovered. Made a good place to water the cow. He said then if the spring was the other side of the hill, it must be on Mr. Pickett's place because his fence runs across the top of the hill. Did I take the cow through the fence to get to the spring? So I had to have a gate, and I put one in. I couldn't do without it. Then he had to know if I'd gotten permission, because he hoped I didn't open Mr. Pickett's pasture gate and take the cow in and water her at the spring without permission.

Well, that's when my string ran out. I wasn't able to say I'd gotten permission. I'd already created a puddle of water, and canceled it and put in its place a spring, and I'd built a gate in a good tight five-strand barbed wire fence, but even in a lie I couldn't bear to face Mr. Pickett and get his permission to take the cow in to the spring.

After I'd confessed, my father asked if I didn't think it would have been better to tell the truth in the first place. I said yes. And that was no lie.

Back in my old home town there was a squatty hotel down close to the depot, and all the boys growing up around there often talked about what a bad place it was. It seems to me now that from the time I was eight or nine years old I was aware that the hotel somehow represented evil, even though I didn't know what went on in it and in fact I can't remember that my folks ever told me it was a bad place. It was just something you knew. Knowing it was in the air you breathed around town.

All during those fine summers we were going down to the depot two or three times a week to put pins on the railroad track, when we came to the hotel we walked on the other side of the street from it. As if whatever was there might pop out and grab us. The hotel did have a suspicious look. At that time I had my notion of what an old hotel ought to look like, that it ought to be tall and white and bright and dignified. But this one seemed to crouch, and try to hide itself behind the heavy foliage of the trees out front. It was two-story, but it wasn't white. It didn't have a tall and proper roof. Its windows were dark.

Later on when I was told it was a brothel, I considered that the place looked just perfect for that purpose. And now, all this time later, when I read about a house of prostitution I always bring up a vision of that old hotel down by the depot. Peculiar thing, it lately hit me I don't really know whether the place was a brothel or not. I just accepted that it was. In high school when we hid in the rest room to smoke cigarettes, we would make jokes about the hotel and what went on there.

Then here's a stranger thing yet. The first time I ever went into that hotel, I was afraid to tell about it at home, even though the only reason I went was to deliver a telegram in the lobby. Almost all the young people I grew up with were afflicted with these deep guilt feelings, about practically any subject. I think this was because we were forever getting told by our elders that if we did bad things we would go to hell on a fast horse. That was a tough enough rule to live with, but the one that finished me off, really laid me waste, was when they insisted that if I only *thought* a thing, that was the same as really doing it. They said it was in the Bible and it was true. That rule right there scattered me all over the devil's back yard and plowed me under. Because at that time I was at least *thinking* about how it would be to commit every last blasphemy in the Handbook of Sin. So you see, then, why I didn't mention at home that I went to the hotel. Little too risky, when dealing with anything so hard to control as a flickering thought.

Anyhow, on the day I went, I expect my pulse jumped forty points when the Western Union operator handed me that telegram with the name of the hotel showing in the window of the yellow envelope. And five minutes later, when I walked in the front door, my heartbeat had spread all the way down to the bottom of my stomach. The lobby was dark. A sleepy-faced man was sprawled in a big chair. I told him I had a wire. He waved toward the desk where a big woman appeared in a doorway. She looked exactly right to me. Her hair was pinned up, but it was tousled, and she had on what we then called a bathrobe at three o'clock in the afternoon. She was sort of fat, but not too. And she looked tired.

I waited while she read the wire because we did that then, waited to see if there would be an answer to take back to the office. I tried to find in her face something to say she was an evil person. It seemed there ought to be a sign to say so, if she was one of those bad women. I was afraid of her, but she was the most interesting woman I'd ever seen because of what I imagined she was. Poor thing, she was probably just a tired lady, somebody's mother. "No answer," she said, and turned away.

Years later that encounter seemed funny to me, and when I was about thirty I told my mother about it. But she didn't see anything funny in it, even then, and I'm sorry now I told her.

Up in Waller County I stopped to watch a bulldozer operator cut through a small tank dam. It was an old tank, all silted up, and I suppose the owner wanted to drain it and dig a new one. Four or five pickups had stopped. The men out of them had climbed through the fence. There's something about a tank dam being cut that's certain to draw a crowd.

While we were waiting for the blade to cut through and release the water, I thought about the time in 1932 that my Cousin C. T.

convinced me he was going to drain the big stock tank behind his father's barn. The idea of being associated with such a crime scared the very liver out of me. But it was an exciting notion, and I believed C. T. was really going to do it. He was talented that way, at convincing others he was about to do outrageous things. He did, in fact, do a number of outrageous things, which gave substance to his threats even when they were empty.

For example, I doubted him the time he wrestled a middle-sized watermelon up the loft ladder and said he was going to bomb a horse. It was an excellent thought, but I didn't buy it, because his sister Gladys was riding the horse he was threatening to bomb. I didn't doubt he was capable of doing the bombing. I just didn't think he'd have the sand to try it. Because Gladys was a sturdy country woman, grown, with children of her own. She had a temper with a delicate balance, and when she got stirred up she was a mama tiger. But he did it, all the same. Gladys came riding in on her mare and went right along in front of the barn on the way to the horse lot, and C. T. dropped his bomb from the open hayloft door. He miscalculated his lead a little. The melon sort of grazed the mare's tail and made a spectacular landing just behind her heels, and I guess she jumped six yards. And spilled Gladys off, real abrupt.

So it was a satisfactory bombing, with the predictable result. Gladys pretty near burned out the seat of C. T.'s overalls. But you see what I mean about believing. When he'd pull off a bombing that way, knowing in advance the punishment it would earn, why, you had to believe he'd drain his father's stock tank.

A good big tank, too, maybe eight feet deep out in the middle, and plenty important. It furnished water for all the stock and poultry on the place. And in dry times we'd irrigate from it, siphon through a rusty pipe bent in the shape of the dam, and water a little patch of garden down below.

That tank was often the topic of Cousin C. T.'s lectures to me. When he'd get to feeling especially irreverent, and ordinary blasphemies failed to ease his spirit, he would talk to me about how that old stock tank was full of sins. Sure it was, because baptizings were held in it. At the finale of brush arbor revivals held nearby, entire congregations would come to the stock tank of Cousin C. T.'s father. The converts would huddle over here apart, in a kind of wrinkled bunch, dressed in raggedy clothes that wouldn't hurt to get wet. Then they'd be passed out one at a time to the preacher, and he'd get 'em in water about navel deep and put 'em under and wash their sins away.

Didn't it follow then, Cousin C. T. would say, that the tank was

infested with those shed sins? Up to a half-million was his esti-
mate. He had personally witnessed the baptizing of some mighty
wicked folks that had to be really loaded when they went in. You
take that one-eyed gent, worked for the Crocketts so long, and
they'd have to go into town every Monday to get him out of jail
and sober him up. Last summer he came wobbling along the middle aisle on the last day of the revival and made a public confession and was baptized the next afternoon, Cousin C. T. would
say, right here in these very waters. Now don't you imagine *that*
fellow left a wagonload of trespasses in the tank? Enough to sink
a goose.

C. T. made me *see* those sins, in the water. They moved, he
said. They wiggled around a lot, like tadpoles, or darted backward the way crawdads do, and if you went swimming sometimes you could feel 'em, scraping along your stomach or snap-
ping at your toes, the sins of all those baptized folks.

One time when a heavy rain filled that tank to brimming,
Cousin C. T. decided to drain it. He was able to see that all he'd
need to do was cut a trench across the top of the dam with a
shovel. Just enough that the water would start coming across.
Then it would cut its own trench and eat through the dam, and
yonder she'd go, roaring down the ravine. Bring a shovel, he
said. He was going to drain that tank and get rid of all those sins.
It wasn't healthy, having so many sins on the place. Beginning to
smell bad. Hand him the shovel.

I knew he wouldn't do it, and yet I didn't know it, either. He
bombed the mare, didn't he? So I ran. I went to the house and
stayed in the presence of adults, so they'd know I wasn't a party
to draining the only stock tank on the farm. An hour later he
came grinning in and said he'd changed his mind. Said he'd decided instead of cutting the dam to seine those sins out of the
tank and sell 'em to the devil for fifty cents a pound.

Last week I took a very wet trip up into East Texas, which I will
be telling you about a little later on. Coming home I made a coffee
stop, and I overheard a story that interested me. Two young guys
were sitting near me at the counter, and one was telling about the
time he got in trouble by shooting a rooster. He was out roaming
around the woods with a .22 rifle, shooting at snakes and turtles
the way country boys have done forever and do still. For a reason
he couldn't explain, he raised up and took a shot at this rooster.

Which is not a fair target even in normal circumstances. In this particular instance, shooting at that bird represented the worst sort of impulse because it happened to be a high-bred fighting rooster, and it belonged to the father of the shooter.

The bird was tethered to a stake, the way you will often see fighting roosters kept, so they won't get together and fight one another to a finish. The tether seemed to make the shooting of the rooster even worse. Something like killing a deer tied to a tree. Still, as the young man told the story, it wasn't anything this side of a miraculous shot. He couldn't do it again in a month. Which may have been the reason he shot in the first place. What harm could it do, when hitting the rooster was the first cousin to an impossibility?

Well, the potential harm was that the slug might pass directly through one of that proud bird's most important parts, such as his head, and that's precisely what it did. Echoes of the shot hadn't settled before that rooster was a tranquil heap of feathers, dead as Stonewall Jackson. Killing a bird like that can carry a mighty severe penalty because breeders of game chickens set a high value indeed on their top roosters.

Those two young fellows got up and departed then, so I didn't get to hear what the punishment was. They left me wondering if the incident turned out the same as a similar disaster I remember. I was mixed up in it with my Cousin C. T. that I have told you about. This one had to do with the killing of a pig, something like fifty years ago.

It was in the shimmery, sultry time of summer, a season when you sure don't want to be killing any hogs. Cousin C. T.'s father, a stern man, had assigned us that summer to keep a certain spotted pig in its place. This pig had an adventurous spirit and a talent for escaping from a rickety split-log pen. He would get out and find his adventure in the garden. When Cousin C. T. and I would get involved in some activity that interested us, which certainly wouldn't have to do with chasing pigs, that porker would show up in the garden, and we would have to go and drive him out and put him up again. Which went on for weeks. We sure got tired of that spotted pig.

On the day of the disaster, we were chasing that animal in the edge of some scrub timber, and he was dodging and refusing to cooperate, and Cousin C. T. entered into one of his little fits of temper. He picked up a big rock and flung it at that pig. This was not a standard chunking rock. It was bigger, about the size of a softball, and not even a grown man with a good arm could have pegged it more than fifty feet. Cousin C. T. got maybe fifteen feet of distance on it, and the rock caught that pig square between the eyes. It went down like a sack of oats, and stayed. We tried everything short of artificial respiration. But that porker was finished.

You want to know what's guaranteed to put a farmer in a bad humor? It's having to come out of the field in July and dress a half-grown hog that isn't due to be slaughtered until anyway December. Cousin C. T.'s father was the sort who would give a boy a strapping for spilling a bucket of horse feed. We figured he would at least skin us for killing a pig. The curious thing was, he did not speak of the matter. Just looked at us with thoughtful contempt. All the time we were eating fresh young pork, he did not mention the killing of the pig. Every day we expected his wrath to descend. But it did not. And it never did. What I always thought was, he just couldn't think up a punishment bad enough to do the crime justice.

12

*"I still believe that the fellow
who dies and goes to hell
ought to get credited down there
for the time he's spent cleaning
out chicken houses."*

Wheeled up in my driveway the other afternoon late, cut the engine and looked at the house, and noticed for the first time that the place is showing its age. It doesn't look anything at all like the new homes being built in the woods across the creek. Yet up to now I've thought of it as a new house. Built sixteen years ago, or almost.

I've never before lived in one house as long as that. When I was younger I thought I never would, because the family that raised me was mighty mobile. We would move for almost any reason, even just on the suspicion that the next landlord might not be so much of an SOB as the last one. By the time I left home, never to return except for short visits, I'd lived with my family in nine different towns and in a couple of other spots out in the country. In the one little town where I did most of my growing up, we lived in seven different houses. Just for the fun of it I've figured up that, counting temporary spots such as military bases and rented rooms, I've lived in forty-two different places.

I expect to stay the rest of my time in the house we've been in the last sixteen years, and I would hate to move again. But up until I got used to staying put, moving never bothered me. I'd done so much of it that I didn't question whether it was a good or a bad thing; I just accepted it as part of the game. There was sadness about moving because it meant leaving friends and a place you'd learned to love, but the sadness faded fast when you started making new friends and seeing new country, drinking different water, breathing new-smelling air, learning new trees, new grass, new bugs, new everything. I never could tell that getting uprooted hurt me any.

Once in a while when I see a neighbor moving, I can feel just a hint of the old itch to pull up and move on. There's an excitement about it. I can recall the feeling from back in the twenties, when the truck would be loaded out front and we'd be sleeping on pallets on bare floors and cooking in the back yard, like a band of nomads ready to ride come sunup. We had some grand adventures, moving from town to town. I see now they weren't large, but they did seem to be at the time, and that's all that counts.

The first move I remember must have been about 1925. My father had gone ahead of us to take a job in a dry goods store in some little West Texas town with white dusty streets. Hamlin, it might have been, because that's one of the places we lived for a while. Anyhow, my mother drove out there in an old beat-up touring car, with my two older sisters and me and the car bulging with a load topped by a white cat with pink eyes and a terror-stricken canary in a cage. We went up Ranger Hill in a rainstorm. You can't know what it means unless you drove the road between Fort Worth and Abilene before pavement. About halfway, east of the town of Ranger, that hill was a pretty good test for a car even after they paved it and called the route U.S. 80. In the mud, with kids screaming and rain curtains flapping and wheels spinning and lightning bouncing off those rocky ledges and zizzling through the cedar brakes—well, it didn't get funny for a good while after it was over.

Another time—the towns and the moves, those early ones, tend to run together in my memory—we were following the fellow driving the truck hauling all our stuff. People did that then. And we came round a bend and there was the truck, overturned, our belongings scattered across the pasture in a 200-foot semi-circle. Apart from the damage was the embarrassment. All our things—our mattresses, our chests of drawers, our ice box, even our old rickety cook table with the oilcloth cover—strewn out for the motoring public to see. It was like being caught naked.

The truck driver wasn't hurt seriously. He claimed the truck got away from him while he was trying to roll and light a cigarette. My mother always blamed that wreck and the damage on the nicotine habit, not the driver. She abhorred cigarettes almost as much as alcohol. For years afterward, on dark winter afternoons, she would sit at her quilting frames and deliver arguments in which she tried to prove, by simple logic, that the nicotine habit was responsible for her broken mirrors. If the driver had not been addicted, she'd say, then he wouldn't have been trying to light up and the wreck wouldn't have happened.

I think the move that I was happiest to make was when I was in the second grade. We came off the road into an old duplex in Fort Worth. It had four small rooms and a kitchen with a coal oil stove that later exploded and pretty near killed us all. For about a year I lived there with my parents and my two sisters and my grand-mother and, off and on, a couple of itinerant uncles—all of us in four rooms, and a bath we shared with still another family. Yet I liked it, because the year previous to that, we didn't live any-where. Mostly just on the road and on kinfolks' farms, dodging starvation during the depression. We took part in a couple of country moves which really weren't ours, but they were fun for me because we moved in wagons. My cousins and I would sit waving on top of the load, bouncing down rocky-sandy roads, milk cows tied onto the tailgate and dogs trotting in the shade between the steel-tired wheels.

The last time I moved with the folks was when I was eighteen. I helped with later moves but never actually moved with them again. From the time I left home until my mother died, they lived in seven other houses. My father outlived my mother five years, during which period he moved four more times. I expect he'd be surprised to hear, now, that I've lived in the same house for six-teen years.

In every one of the neighborhoods where we lived in my early times, there was a spring custom we called cleaning out from under the house. We did it around the first of April, and always on the same day that you wanted to go fishing. At the supper table you would put out little probes, to see if anything big was going to happen the next day. You would know the fishing trip was off if the answer came, "In the morning we're gonna clean out from under the house."

That meant you went under the house and pulled out the cans and boxes and boards and a great long invoice of general junk that collected under there during the winter. I felt in those times that junk was able to multiply in some way, under a house. The same way old neckties do now, in dark closets. And ragged socks, in dresser drawers. There was also a general agreement among dogs and cats and large rats that if they felt like dying, they went under the house to do it. So what was left of them had to be brought out and hauled off. The principal reason, as far as I know, that human beings began building homes on solid slabs of concrete is so they wouldn't have to clean out from under the house every spring.

Cleaning out from under the house came about the same time of year as going through the potatoes did. "I've got a job for you," they would say. "What?" "I want you to go through the potatoes."

So you went to wherever the potatoes were stored—under the back porch or in the barn or in the storm cellar if you had one—and looked at every potato that was left and brought the rotten ones out. You fed 'em to the chickens or whatever you had that would eat a rotten potato. A hog was good for that purpose, but in little country towns in those years, unless folks lived way off to themselves they didn't keep hogs. They kept chickens and milk cows, but it was considered sort of rural to keep a hog in town.

Something else you had to do in April was put out the mattresses. That was when you stripped the beds and wrestled the mattresses out and draped 'em over the front porch rail to sun. I was way up big enough to smoke cedar bark before I knew a porch rail had any purpose except to sun a mattress. One day after my older sisters had gone to high school and taken something called home ec, they came home claiming it was countrified to sun mattresses on the front porch. After that their mother sunned 'em in the back yard because she was sure struggling to get us all citified as quick as she could.

Things like cleaning out from under the house and putting out the mattresses were called spring cleaning in some regions, but I never heard the term used around a house where I lived. We knew about spring cleaning, but it always sounded a little foreign to me. It seemed Yankee some way, like it was something women did up in Boston or Ohio.

A habit my folks had which seemed strange even to me was cleaning off vacant lots. I mean lots that didn't belong to them. In the spring when we got our own yard slicked up, we'd fall over on a vacant lot next door and chop out the weeds and the mesquite sprouts and rake it all up and burn it. "Sure looks a lot better," they'd say, and I guess that's why they did it. Other families did it too. Vacant lots then were sort of like public property, and people felt responsible for them.

In those times, folks who lived in little towns and thought of themselves as city people might have two cows and, by the first of April, a pile of manure in the back yard that a five-yard dump truck couldn't move in one trip. So that was another spring job, spreading manure. Mister, before I was fifteen I felt like I'd spread enough manure right out of our personal cowlot to fertilize that Nile River Bottom. These country boys who live on ranches and farms now, I hear 'em talk about spreading manure, but you know how they do it? They hook a tractor to a mechanical spreader and go third-gearing over the pasture at three-quarters throttle and don't even smell bad when they get finished.

I see barnyard manure advertised now, for sale. That seems funny. We used to look for folks who'd take the stuff because it was covering us up. Our garden patch and flower beds were already so blamed fertile they were drawing flies. I've done this: Push a wheelbarrow-load of manure three, four blocks down the street to a woman who'd promise to take it provided it was well rotted and didn't have nutgrass in it. I suppose if she'd found it too fresh I'd have been obliged to wheel the stuff back home.

Other jobs you had to do when you ought to have been fishing were painting bedsteads, washing windows, scrubbing the porch (with the wash water), spading the garden, hauling off what trash and garbage that wouldn't burn, and what junk that wasn't useful.

About hauling off waste, I think people lost some of their sense of responsibility toward the environment when public garbage collection began. I wonder what would have happened if, all these years, every family had been responsible for disposing of its own waste. I doubt we'd have become so wasteful.

But what I wanted to say before I quit, I think the worst spring job I remember was cleaning out the chicken house. It just wasn't possible for a person to keep his dignity while he was at it. I still believe that the fellow who dies and goes to hell ought to get credited down there for the time he's spent cleaning out chicken houses.

At my house we've got a couple of bedrooms that nobody sleeps in, because their former occupants left home. Sounded funny to me to hear a recent visitor remark that we now have two guest rooms. I haven't ever thought of them as guest rooms. It takes training, to teach a person to use such a term. Back when I was being taught what to call things, I thought you had to be rich and live in Boston, or at least Philadelphia, before you could have a guest room. Now I hear even native Texans saying guest room, and it sounds funny to me yet.

Also I hear about visitors who come from out of own to spend the night, and they go and check into a motel because their host doesn't have enough guest rooms. Where I came from, that would have been considered bad manners. When you went to see a family you just got by on what they had. If they didn't have enough beds, you slept on the floor.

Long about this time of year we used to have some overnight gatherings of kinfolks out in the country at a two-bedroom farmhouse, and I bet you we'd sleep thirty people, not counting babies under eighteen months. You take about a three-year-old child, the way you knew he was finally all tuckered out, he'd come dragging up to his mama and ask, "Where'm I gonna sleep?" Going to bed was a fresh experience every night because you never knew where you'd end up.

Used to be a big racket among the smaller kids to sleep with Grandma. When a boy got up big enough he didn't want to sleep with Grandma any longer, it was a sign he was taking on maturity and he was sent outside to sleep on the porch. Some farmhouses had a bunch of old folding army cots for nights when a lot of company came. You had to be pretty close to grown before you got a cot. A boy of fifteen or sixteen would feel pretty chesty the night they told him to take a cot by himself. Younger boys slept on pallets.

The men would have to pull their little jokes on a young fellow who was going out in the yard to sleep on a cot. Like one would say, "You know, the first time I slept out yonder in that yard, I woke up about midnight and stretched out on the cot right alongside me was an old bull snake musta been six feet long." And the young man was supposed to say, "Don't matter to me. Bull snake's got no poison." But all night he'd wonder whether the story was true or not. Or he might get directed by one of the men to set up his cot "just right out yonder under the chinaberry tree, be a good place," and the chinaberry tree would turn out to be a roost for about half a dozen big old Rhode Island Red hens.

The women and the girls would sleep inside. You didn't dare go back indoors after the lamps were blown out because you might step square into the stomach of somebody you hadn't even met yet. They'd be sleeping in there wall to wall. You know why farm people get up so early? They'd have you think it's because they need to start work before dawn, but the real reason is they learned when they were children that if they slept late they might get walked on.

This system of scattering folks all over the homestead to sleep worked all right as long as it didn't rain during the night. But if a thunderstorm came up, man, when the lightning would flash you'd see 'em heading for the porch from all directions, dragging quilts and lugging cots and hopping one-footed through grass burr patches. Then as long as the wind blew and the lightning flashed and the rain fell, everybody would stand on the porch and make guesses about how long it would last.

Of course even now some big families still have such gatherings, but they seem able to get everybody indoors at night. However, I do expect some of those guest rooms are sleeping anywhere from six to eight cousins.

It's against my raising, as they say, to roll out of the quilts in winter to a warm house. At six o'clock in the morning in January, a house is *supposed* to be cold. At least it is according to the conditions under which I got accustomed to living in houses.

My line of folks were branded deep with the notion that a man gets up in the blackness that precedes a winter dawn, and he goes around making fires. I do it yet. It doesn't satisfy the tradition just to crank up a thermostat. The only things around here I can make a fire in are a couple of bathroom heaters. So I light them, and stand around holding my hands out to the flames, to see if they are going to be hot again this morning. All the men from my early times did that with fires. My father, my uncles, everybody. Some would build fires an hour before daylight and sit there nodding, waiting for light so they could see to go outside.

No, I don't have any yearning to go back to that. I don't mind a cold house when I get up, but I sure do like for my feet to hit carpet. I had a little experience one time that made me want rugs in the house. Up until that time, and I was about twenty when it happened, I can't remember ever sleeping in a bedroom that had a rug on the floor. So I just accepted that in winter when I got up, my feet would hit a cold bare floor. Either planks or linoleum.

In the forties, when I was going to school out at Lubbock, I got to know an old boy named Sid something, lived at Post. I want to say his name was Slaughter, but that may be because there's a lot of Slaughters out in that country. Just call him Sid. His father had died a couple of years before, and his mother worked at the dry goods store at Post. They had a little ranch near there, up under that Caprock. When Sid went to Lubbock to school, his mother moved to town, so the ranch house where Sid grew up was empty out there in the country. Every Friday when he got through with classes, Sid would go to Post and feed his and his mother's cattle, and check on things, and do what needed to be done. Sometimes in winter, when he was feeding, he would go down there two or three times a week. I used to go with him some.

I liked it, because I hadn't entirely given up the idea that I might become a rancher. I already knew I didn't want to be a farmer, because that seemed like too much sugar for a dime to me. But a rancher, that sounded better. I would see ranchers, and they looked solvent, and wore boots, and when they had post holes to dig they generally had somebody hired to do it. That appealed to me.

On Fridays, I would hitchhike with Sid down to Post, about forty-five miles southeast of Lubbock. We would go by the store and get the old pickup that Sid's mother drove. That was all the car they had. We'd drive to the ranch, ten or twelve miles, and spend the night in the old house. It was all right. Sid was good company, and we'd take cans of beans, and chili, and a .22 to shoot, and we had good times. The work wasn't much that I could see. Just bouncing around breaking up hay and flinging it to a bunch of old cows that were always glad to see us. Wasn't a horse on that place, even then. The neighbors came in with horses and helped when it was time to work cattle, but Sid and I just rode around in that old truck. Sometimes we would stay two nights.

One Saturday we got up to a really cold morning. Water in the pitcher was frozen. Sid said it looked to him like it was going to snow. We went around breaking the ice on the troughs at the windmills so the cattle could drink. I stayed cold the whole day. Seemed to me that every time I thought we were going to knock off and hole up in the house, Sid would find something else to do. Patch a fence. Find a calf. Chop wood. Roll up "'at old bob wire there, 'fore a cow gets tangled in it." Middle of the afternoon I stepped with both feet in a mud hole where one of the water troughs had leaked. Got wet half to my knees. Feet about to freeze. How about let's go to the house, Sid, you ready? Pretty soon, he'd say.

That night it did snow, and got colder. That old house was like sleeping in the ice plant. Sid went to bed talking about a little bunch of heifers we hadn't found. Need to get up early and locate 'em. Put some feed into 'em. I was beginning to have doubts about ranching. In bad weather it wasn't any fun. My feet ached all night from the cold. There was a crack in the floor by that bed. To keep the wind out, Sid had found an old stove pad to lay over it. Just a thin square of metal once used to stand wood stoves on so the coals that got loose wouldn't burn the floor. It seemed to me I was almost beginning to get warm, after hours of shivering in that old bed, when Sid said, "We better git at it. Find them heifers." I put my bare feet out, and they hit that metal pad on the floor.

After that weekend, I stopped wanting to be a rancher. And right up to now, I don't care how cold the house gets, I feel like I am living in luxury if I can roll out and put my feet down on a carpet.

The payment on it was five dollars a month. I remember that. I'm not sure about the year. Maybe it was 1935. Might have been a year earlier. An exciting day. They brought that thing in the house, all white and gleaming, and plugged it into a light socket that hung from the ceiling of the kitchen.

Then the next morning I was assigned to go out in the yard and wait for the ice man and tell him about it. I caught him four doors down the block. His old dull-orange truck stood vibrating, idling in neutral gear, dripping cold water into the red gravel of the street. His name was Pete. He was in the back of the truck, chipping away with his pick. I had to speak to his back, covered with that heavy black pad. I told him we wouldn't be needing any more ice, not today or ever. "How come?" he said. He turned to look at me, and there was a big drop of sweat hanging from the end of his nose. I always wondered how he could sweat so much, working all day around ice. "Because we've got a new Frigidaire," I told him.

"All right." He turned back around and said nothing more. I

suppose by then he was accustomed to such news. At the time we canceled out on him, he wasn't stopping at but two other houses on our block. It wasn't long until he took another job. It might have been as late as 1936—the year the ice man quit coming.

That thing wasn't really a Frigidaire. But that's what everybody called an electric ice box, just as many still say Deep Freeze for all brands of home freezers. I think it was a Crosley. The entire family gathered around that refrigerator when the men set it up and plugged it in. We filled the ice trays and put them in the freezing compartment and sat—and waited for our first ice.

It took an almighty long time, because we'd open the door every five minutes and stick our fingers in the water and talk about how you could tell, already, it was getting colder, it sure was. And look here, now—little bits of ice are forming in there, and hey, how about this one, way in the back, it's already frozen over and you can't even break it with your finger. So we had iced tea for supper, chilled with cubes of ice made right there in the house by our own electric ice box. My mother wrote a letter about it to the kinfolks out in the country.

We'd have family conferences about that ice box. We'd discuss the best ways to get the cubes out of the trays without melting them so much. We made rules about how many cubes ought to go into a glass of tea. We'd talk about the five dollar payment and try to figure out whether the refrigerator was practical, considering the cost of ice off the truck and the electricity the box used and all the other factors.

There was one big deep ice tray, and on Sundays when the preacher came we'd have ice cream, yellow as country butter, made in that electric ice box. Yessiree, ice cream for dinner without buying any ice or any salt and without one turn of a freezer crank. Wasn't that something? The truth is, it was all icy and crunchy and didn't taste much like the real article. But we made that stuff for ten years before we decided it wasn't any good.

You know what I do now? Sometimes in hot weather I go to the ice house and buy a twenty-five-pound block and keep it in the garage in the fish box. And chip it off to use in iced tea, because that's the only way to make tea taste the way it tasted before the ice man quit coming.

Mrs. Mitchell, I feel certain, long ago passed on to her reward in paradise, because she was well advanced in the matter of birthdays when I last saw her, and that was forty-odd years ago. She was our neighbor for a while, lived two doors and a vacant lot down the street.

I think of her sometimes because she was the only person I ever saw get butted by a goat in the classic style that goats always butt people in movie comedies and comic strips. You know what style I mean. A person bends over for one reason or another and makes a target of his or her stern. Then here comes the goat with a running start and plants his skull in the person's rear. The result is always plenty spectacular. At least in movies and comic strips it is.

One of the reasons the butting of Mrs. Mitchell made such an impression on me, the goat that butted her belonged to my family. Furthermore, I was supposed to be looking after it to see it didn't butt anything it wasn't supposed to. So the fact that Mrs. Mitchell was the buttee was a potential hazard to my health.

I think that on other days I have mentioned to you why it was my family kept goats. We had two. They were female, and gave milk. My father was a great fan of anything that would give milk. These two milk goats were supposed to stay in a hog-wire lot out back of our house, but it wouldn't hold them. I don't doubt those animals could have picked the lock on a bank vault, so a simple gate latch was a lead-pipe cinch for them. They did a lot of visiting around town, and it was my job to fetch them up when they got loose.

You would be surprised, or maybe you wouldn't, at the language an ordinarily sedate housewife can use when she goes out on the front porch and finds two milk goats browsing around in her flower beds. These goats were run out of some of the best yards in our town, and always by housewives, so I suppose they felt persecuted by humans in house dresses and checkered aprons. Mrs. Mitchell owned that vacant lot I mentioned earlier, and made a garden there every spring. She worked in it mornings and afternoons, wearing a house dress and a checkered apron and a big sunbonnet.

On this day I am thinking about, the goats got out pretty well on schedule. I caught and tied the spotted one, but the white one was feeling contrary. On Whitey's contrary days she had a trick of hustling out to the end of her chain and turning around and pulling her collar over her head. This gave her freedom, but it punished her too, with a severe neck jerk. So she would get mad, and sometimes butt whatever was handy. She would butt trees, wheelbarrows, even entire barns and houses, and once the rear end of a '27-model Chevy.

Well, we were in the road in front of the vacant lot when Whitey got free. She went trotting away from me all stiff-legged and ill-tempered and into that garden where Mrs. Mitchell was messing with some pole beans. That good lady was bent over, fooling with a stake where it went into the ground, and had her back side facing Whitey, and I could see what was going to happen two or three seconds before it really did. But I couldn't do anything about it, so I hit the dirt out in the borrow ditch and raised my head to watch. It was going to be bad, but I figured I might as well watch it. Because for just an instant it was that classic scene so popular then in films and funny papers—a goat charging a bent-over person from behind.

The actual contact was a disappointment to me. The approach was beautiful, but the impact was anti-climactic. I had pictured something fairly stupendous, such as Mrs. Mitchell leaving the earth to make a low-level flight of maybe ten or twelve feet. That's the way the buttees did in the funny papers. But Whitey evidently hit a little low and to the right, and sort of glanced off. The blow extracted a great grunt of surprise out of Mrs. Mitchell, and caused her to sit down there among the pole beans, and pretty hard. I remember feeling a mixture of disappointment and gratitude. Old Whitey could hurt a person when she hit a target dead center, and that would have meant huge trouble for me. Still, I was a little disappointed that the only classic case of goat butting I ever saw was something less than a total success.

If the butt did much damage to Mrs. Mitchell, I never knew it. I kept hidden in the ditch until she limped into the house. She saw what hit her, you don't need to think she didn't, and knew whose goat it was, but she didn't ever mention it or me to my folks. I always guessed she just didn't want to tell anybody where she was butted.

One of the most interesting things that ever happened back when I was growing up was a man and a woman who moved into a little house out on the west side, and lived there together several months, and they weren't married. That was of deep concern to everybody in our town old enough to know it was customary for a couple to get married before they set up housekeeping.

Along about this same time we had one or two genuine shootings on the courthouse square and several serious fist fights between prominent citizens, but these didn't draw an ounce more notice than the man and the woman living in the little house out on the west side. Nobody called that pair by name. We called 'em That Man and That Woman. Or we called 'em That Couple, or Those People.

I thought about Those People the other night when I was in a crowd at a kind of polite to-do, where everybody was shaking hands and introducing one another. A woman said to me about the smiling gent standing behind her, "This is my roommate." Some of them do that now, make a public announcement that way when they are not married but only sharing rent and grocery money. What I figure is, it's their own personal affair, and they are entitled to bunk in with anybody they want to. But it tickled me to imagine Those People, back in the old home town, going into a store on the square and making the statement that they were only rooming together. You would have heard the eyebrows jumping and the false teeth rattling all the way from the drugstore to the pool hall. Even so, the announcement would have stirred up a torrent of interest. It always seemed to me the people in that town were the most interested in things that they disapproved of.

Looking behind me now, when unmarried parties are living together left and right, I see that the most curious thing about That Couple was that we didn't really know whether they were married or not. We kept hearing that they weren't, and we let it go as the truth because we *needed* a pair like that in the community, to upgrade the overall interest in what was going on.

Mostly we were a dull bunch. An ankle getting sprained on the loading dock at the feed store would be talked about at supper tables all over town. We were that short of material. So we made it a sort of unofficial city ordinance that Those People were a-livin' in sin, hot dawg. They were fair game because they were transients. You could always tell when temporary people moved in by the kind of work they did, or the sort of place they rented. They didn't come to church and they didn't join the PTA, so you knew. You could say whatever you wanted to about transients. They didn't associate much and they were soon gone on down the road, after they had served their purpose.

In the case of That Couple, their role was to be a curiosity that other nearby towns didn't have, and we were proud of them. We already had a woman with a wooden leg, and a fellow who'd been in the penitentiary, and another who'd served a term in Congress. So a man and a woman a-livin' in unwedded bliss was just what we wanted to top us off as the most spectacular place in the district. We'd say to friends, "Well, I saw Those People walkin' along the road a while ago." You'd hear, "I was in the grocery store and That Woman was in there, buying flour and salt pork." Just as if we expected her to be cooking over a campfire, spit-roasting a coyote that That Man had killed on the prairie with his lance.

We wanted them even to *look* different from the standard run of folks. We'd study their faces, their general beings, the way they walked and carried sacks. And we'd be disappointed that they didn't seem trodden down, didn't have sores, didn't have holes in their clothes. When we'd hell around after dark, we'd go by that little house where they lived, and study it. Any of its detail was mysterious to us, and strangely exciting. The smoke out of their flue. Their woodstack. Their dim orange light against the drawn window shade. What are they *doing* in there? All that, and we didn't know for certain that those two were anything but brother and sister, going around scraping out a living the best they could. We lived then in such a dark age.

Just a while ago one of my co-workers passed by here and handed me a little bunch of peanuts, the small Spanish kind that sometimes look about half dried up but have a real stout flavor. This is the sort of peanuts they used to raise out in the West Cross Timbers country where I grew up. The peanuts I get from out there now are bigger and have thick spongy hulls and their flavor is pretty much blah. Everybody brags on them, though, so I suppose they are what people want in peanuts.

I remember a winter long ago when I ate more peanuts than any other food, except maybe sweet potatoes. It was either the winter of 1930 or 1931, I forget which. All the farmers made a lot of peanuts and a lot of sweet potatoes, and many families survived as a result.

I am not able to tell any depression stories of starvation, because my bunch always had plenty to eat. We ate a mighty lot of the same thing all the time, but it was filling. Maybe not so healthy, though. I read now that peanuts are such a fine health food, but the winter I lived on the things I had diphtheria and some awful kind of skin rash that gave me unshirted agony. Probably a vitamin deficiency.

It would interest me to know how much cash it took that winter to buy a bushel of peanuts or sweet potatoes. I can't recall hearing a price, because we didn't pay cash. My father traded for them. He would go out in the country and peddle magazines and swap for food, and we always had peanuts and sweet potatoes stacked up around the premises.

I would go off to school with both pockets stuffed with peanuts. I wasn't the only one that did. Teachers had to establish rules against eating peanuts in class and tossing the hulls on the floor. If I brought somebody home from school to play ball with, first thing we did was go on the back porch and refill our pockets with peanuts. I have no memory of ever getting tired eating them.

Then on the sweet potatoes, we would have them for supper several times a week. First baked. Then mashed. Then fried. I grew to love fried yams if they were sliced thin enough and cooked a little too long, so they got almost black on one side. We would also eat yams raw, such as in salads. Or between meals, peeled and sliced with a pocketknife. On Sundays we'd have a special kind of sweet potato dish with melted marshmallows on top. I considered it a dessert. Anything with marshmallows was a treat.

Peanuts would show up in surprising places—in bread, in cookies, certainly in homemade candies. Sugar was a cash item and wasn't sprinkled around in just anything, so we had a peanut-brittle-type proposition made with syrup. I wonder now that we didn't look in one another's eyes and see peanuts staring out. We often ate them parched as an after-supper family snack. Maybe I'd been eating the things all day, and before bedtime we'd parch a bunch of 'em and go at it again.

You'd get invited to a house party, and there you'd find out what other people were eating. Same thing. Peanuts. Maybe they'd have candy balls that were white inside and gooey and covered all over with shelled peanuts. It was a way of making a cheap confection look expensive. You could have covered a barn with shelled peanuts that winter without ending up any broker than when you started.

So far as I know, I was never served sweet potatoes at a party, but they were used sometimes as party decorations. Little sweet potato men, with kitchen matches for legs and arms. Then most homes had at least one sweet potato rooted in a fruit jar of water, and sprouting a vine. My mother was a dedicated sweet-potato-vine grower. She might have half a dozen jars going at once, and vines snaking clear across the kitchen. I wonder now why women didn't discover how to sprout peanuts in a similar way.

One of the best things that ever happens to a small boy is seeing his father become a hero. He won't ever forget the first time.

Doesn't matter how small an accomplishment the father makes, if people talk about it and consider it a fine or even just an interesting thing, the father is then a hero to a small boy.

I was sitting at the breakfast table earlier this week, studying a piece of toast I'd burned, and I got to remembering how my father once became a hero by taking a dozen loaves of sliced bread to a family reunion. That was when we were living in town and thought we were city folks. We thought so because that town had nearly 3,000 people in it, and was thirty miles away from the farm, and because we had an indoor toilet. About once every month or six weeks we would get in the old Chevy on Sunday and drive down to the farm for the get-together. Nobody called it a reunion. But it was, because thirty-five or forty folks would be there, and they sat around and talked and ate. The custom was for everybody to bring something. Something to eat, mostly. There was a sort of competition in the bringing of the food. Nobody wanted to bring ordinary stuff. They liked to come in with something that would make the women exclaim.

Like one time my father took an entire stalk of bananas. It was the first time I ever saw a stalk of bananas outside a grocery store. It made a great hit. The women yelled and the men were jealous. My father loved that. He liked to do flashy things, and would spend more money doing them than he could afford. I didn't consider that a weakness in him, though. I thought it was great at the time. It wasn't until years later that my mother told me he never had any sense about money, that he would go out and buy her a twenty-dollar dress every time he got his hands on as much as forty dollars cash.

The day he took the dozen loaves of sliced bread to the reunion, I don't think we'd ever had any bakery-sliced bread in our house. The bakeries had just begun to slice it for you. Of course that's why he wanted to take it to the farm. Because nobody down there had ever seen any. I can remember him carrying all twelve loaves into the house at once, stacked up higher than his head, and the women standing on the porch, throwing up their hands and saying, "Law me," and all my cousins hopping around and yelling to look what Uncle Fred brought. He took the loaves into the kitchen, which was big and square and served as a dining room as well, and dumped those dozen loaves onto the table, and everybody came and admired the sliced bread.

Think of that, bread in a package, and already sliced. What will they think of next? And just look, how even the slices are, each one just the same thickness. How on earth did they do it? My father ripped open a loaf and started handing out a slice to everybody, with a flourish, you know, like a millionaire giving dollar bills to the poor. And they all stood around there in the kitchen eating bread, taking small bites and chewing slow and experimental, as if they never had tasted bread before and needed to judge it. One of the men said it was cut too thin to suit him, and what was the point in ready-sliced bread as long as folks all had a bread knife in the kitchen drawer. I tried to make out it wasn't anything to get excited about, as if we had bakery-sliced bread all the time, there at home in that big city of 3,000 people.

Texas men who grew up in the country, or just had an outdoor-type life as boys, seem to have a great liking for guns and sport shooting. It's common to hear a Texan tell how his father took him out when he was a boy and gave him a .410 shotgun and passed on a bunch of wisdom about shooting things in a sporting way and about gun safety and all that sort of stuff. "My old daddy," you'll hear one say, "taught me the greatest sin was shooting a bird off a limb. He'd say the least you can do is give it a fair chance and let it fly before you shoot."

Not every Texan, though, gets this heritage. I sure didn't. The men I was around long ago when I was growing up didn't use guns for sport. They kept guns, for shooting things they thought needed shooting, but I don't remember that any of a great flock of my uncles and older cousins were hunters in the sporting sense, and my father certainly wasn't.

The other night I was in a little crowd talking about hunting, and a few of that bunch didn't believe me when I said I was up in high school, sixteen years old I suppose, before I ever saw a bird shot in flight. But that's sure true. It was a duck. I marveled, because it looked so hard to do and the risk of failure was so great. All the men I remember from boyhood were what we now call meat hunters, every one. I was taken on a quail hunt one time, and I can see an older cousin of mine blasting away in a little clearing, shooting into the ground, and then four or five of us ran to pick up the birds. When we got back to the house the cousin was a hero. He got eight, maybe ten birds with one shot by firing into a covey on the ground. I expect if a hunter did that now he would be asked to leave the state.

The only lecture about hunting that I ever got from one of my elders had to do with killing doves. It was during the first dove hunt I ever went on, and it dealt with the economics and not the sport of shooting. It came when we were sitting on a tank dam, waiting for doves to fly to the water hole. A bird came sailing in and lighted in the top of a post oak, on a dead limb the way they do. My uncle was beside me with the shotgun—all the hunts I remember seemed to have one shooter and four or five watchers—but he made no move to kill the bird. So I nudged him, thinking maybe he hadn't seen it. He shook his head. "Got to wait till we can get more'n one bird with a shell. It costs money to shoot this gun."

So he would hold off until the doves flew down to the edge of the water, and then he'd slip around and line up in such a way that he could kill two or three at a shot. Sure, on the ground. I don't remember that any of the men who took me hunting considered a flying bird to be a reasonable target. Too hard to hit, and they might waste an entire shotgun shell. They taught me to hunt ducks that way, and it's the only way I ever killed a duck—slip up and shoot 'em on the water and try to get as many as possible per shot.

Twelve or thirteen years after that first dove hunt, I got sent to Yuma, Arizona, where the old Army Air Corps taught people to be aerial gunners. One of the ways they taught, they put you in a turret just like one you would have in a bomber except it had 12-gauge shotguns mounted in it instead of .50-caliber machine guns. Then they would fire clay pigeons out of a high tower and you would track 'em with the turret and try to shoot them down, as if they were enemy airplanes. You would shoot hundreds and hundreds of times, and every day I'd remember what my uncle said at the water hole about how it costs money to shoot a gun. That was when it began hitting me, that even if you don't count the loss of lives and the human suffering, fighting wars is an awful expensive proposition, and it ought to be avoided.

All the men I was associated with before I left home had this same attitude about shooting, that it was expensive. In horse opera movies, cowboys are always whipping out pistols and shooting the heads off rattlesnakes, and that bothers me. I guess the reason goes back to a rule I remember, that you ought never to shoot a snake. Shoot a hawk, yes, but not a snake, because you shouldn't burn ammunition on anything you could kill with a stick.

Bunch of us sitting in a barbecue place, waiting on a sandwich order. A young woman was among us, and she had her son with her. He looked eight to me, maybe nine. He came to his mama and asked, "Can I have a dollar?" She didn't let him have it. She said if she did he'd "buy a lot of mess" with it, meaning candy and cookies and so forth. To me, the significant thing about that scene is that a boy nine years old will come floating up to his mama and try to lean on her for a buck, just as casual as if he's asking for a drink of water.

Everybody else seems able to smile and let that proposition slide by as an ordinary happening, which in these times it is. But I'll start remembering all the reasons it's extraordinary to me that a little boy will ask for a dollar. I'll see a big man coming to our front door in about the year 1931. He is my uncle, and he has come to ask his sister, who is my mother, for a nickel to buy smoking tobacco. He is big and strong and broad-shouldered, but on that day, at least, he does not know where to go to earn a nickel.

Then I see a friend of mine in those times. His name is O. E. Owens, and we pull some weeds out of a garden for a woman, and she gives us two cents. I can still see those coppers glowing in the palm of O. E.'s grimy hand, and we go to the little grocery store and buy a lot of mess.

Then I see the coal oil stove. It sits stinking in our kitchen, and it burns about a gallon of coal oil every day. Each afternoon a dime is fished out of the coin purse which holds the family wealth. I take the dime and the empty coal oil can and walk over the hill and down to the highway to the filling station. There the man fills the can from a drum of kerosene. I hand him the dime and he gives me a penny change, and I clod back over the hill and home. I am allowed to keep the penny change, and I am encouraged to save. A pint fruit jar with a slot cut in the lid is provided, and every sundown when I get back from the filling station, I drop the penny in the slot. The fruit jar smells as much like kerosene as the stove and the oil can.

At night I get out the fruit jar and dump the pennies out and count them. I already know exactly how many pennies are there, but I count them anyhow, and announce the total to anybody who will listen. Also I shine the pennies, with a rag dipped in the coal oil. Everything around the house smells of coal oil. Even the hot cakes have a coal oil flavor. Then at last I have the magic number. They talk about it at supper. "He's got a hundred pennies. He's got a dollar." After supper they watch while I count, and it is true.

They make a lesson of it. "This is how people get money," they say. "A penny every day, a nickel every day, a dime every day. This is how it's done." A long time after that old cookstove was junked, I kept the connection between coal oil and saving money. Do you know how much $100 is? It's 10,000 trips over the hill and down to the highway and back. Benjamin Franklin had it wrong. He should have said, "A penny saved is a gallon of coal oil."

Then I think of my late friend Cayce Moore of Hearne and the story he used to tell about the basketball. He is a boy up in Leon County, going to a little country school. The school's basketball wears thin, and it is decided that every boy in school will bring a dime from home and chip in, to buy a new ball. Cayce goes home and presents the proposal to his folks. They sit around the table and discuss it. To have the new ball will be a good thing, but the dime, that is another matter. At last they judge, and the answer is no. So Cayce must go to school the next day and say the words, that his folks cannot give the dime. As long as he lives, which is sixty-three years, when Cayce sees a boy bouncing a basketball on a driveway he thinks of how much money a dime once was. So do I, when I hear a boy ask for a dollar.

To people who've never lived out there, moving to the country often seems in advance that it would be the cure for all the headaches of this life. They get the feeling that as quick as they escape, and they are out there in the stillness, everything will be good at last. Maybe it will, too, but I have watched people almost wither and die of loneliness in the country. People who thought that moving into a country place would be like living just across the fence from paradise.

I never have personally hankered to live in a really isolated spot in the country, because I lived in a few of them in my early times, and I can remember some painfully lonesome days in the country. Days when the stillness and the birds and the dogs and the wind weren't enough company. It wasn't talked about, among those of us who were in those isolated places together. But I know all of us felt it.

We used to sit on the front porch and keep quiet and listen for sounds of other human beings. Of neighbors a mile away, calling cows. The sound of a car on the road, growing stronger, coming our way. The jingle of trace chains and the bump of heavy wooden wheels that meant a wagon and team were on the road. Maybe they would turn into our lane. From the front porch to the road was, I guess, a quarter of a mile. We couldn't see what was coming along the road, because a car or a wagon was hidden by the mesquite and the scrub oak until it got almost to our mailbox.

Just in front of the house the road curved sharply. That curve was significant in our lives. Because a car coming would need to slow down in order to get around it safely. It was about a ninety-degree bend and always rough. We would sit on the steps and try to guess whether the car was slowing down for the curve, or to turn into our lane. I always felt the slowing down came a little earlier if the car meant to turn in than if it were going on around the curve. I mean that's how important it was to us, for people to come, for us to have contact with others. We sometimes sat on the steps every evening for a week, listening to the road sounds, and nobody would ever turn in.

Directly across the road from the house was a cultivated field, and beyond that woods again, and then the land swept gently upward to the horizon about two miles away. Below the horizon was another cultivated field. If anybody was in that field hoeing or fixing fence, we could sit on our steps and see them, tiny figures more than a mile distant. We knew who the figures were, yes. Knew them every one. The father who was bossing the work. The boys who helped. The daughter who came along the fence row when the sun was overhead, bringing iced tea in fruit jars and cold biscuits and sausage.

In the deeps of winter when the timber was bare and the crops gathered and gone, that was when we could see the farthest and when the smallest movement out there was easy to detect. The two fields we could see from the porch we called the near field and the far field. "Somebody's comin' across the far field." The lookout, on the porch, would make that announcement. We would all come then and hold a hand up to shield our eyes and look at the small, overalled figure, its hatted head bobbing, bobbing with its stride, so far away.

So then we had all that time to guess who it was, and whether he was coming to our house or going on beyond to somebody else's place. But in any case he would stop and visit, and so that was an event, that man coming our way. Oh, of course, we would know him. No one who was a stranger to us ever walked across those fields.

Then the postman, the rural mail carrier would come. The only daily contact with the outside that we depended on. Even if he didn't stop, we wanted to know when he passed, and to see him wave, and wave back.

I'm sure all of us had days when we enjoyed being in the country in the way people talk about enjoying it now. Being close to trees and hills and streams and wild creatures, and loving the serenity and the quietness. Yet I can't remember those things with half the clarity that I recall the times when the routine of country living was broken, and *people* came, and the loneliness was swept away.

Harvest time, for instance. The neighbors would come with their teams and wagons and there would be a thresher big as a depot in our own oat patch, and dozens of men and boys working and shouting and joking. What great times, all so exciting. Women would come to help with the cooking, and their daughters, too, and strange dogs would be under the house, and there would be games, and new words to learn. But those were special events, and came along seldom.

Some people just aren't suited to a life of near-solitude. At one dreary place we lived, my mother used to walk with me a mile to a little hill that had a mott of scrub oaks at the crest. We would go up and sit there a while because from that hill we could see the tip of the church steeple in town, and on calm days we could see the smoke from our nearest neighbor's chimney off to the east.

13

"I've never known a fox-hunting preacher
who didn't put hound music on a par
with the harps of heaven's angels."

Thanksgiving, as I remember it from back when I wasn't any bigger than a pair of deuces, meant going to the farm and eating with about fifty kinfolks. We had a lot of praying men in our clan in those days, and it was of special interest to the children, waiting outside for Thanksgiving dinner, to know who would be called on to say the blessing before the meal.

We generally favored a certain uncle who was younger than all the others qualified to return thanks. We liked him because he said a short blessing, and nobody could understand it. If he got called on he'd bow and begin before the women could get the children quieted down, and he'd say, "Gray-shevenly-father-blessis-footha-nurshmenata-bodies-uhfagiva-sinz-amen." I always used to wonder why he began by addressing the Lord as a gray shevenly father. But we never questioned him, because naturally a brief blessing was a popular thing among little kids about to eat. That particular uncle wasn't apt to get called on at Thanksgiving, because it was a special time for praying, and the blessing was generally long.

One year we had a sort of ringer who came in. He was kinfolks, but I think just a great-uncle, or a step-cousin. Somebody distant like that. He was white-headed and had on a nice suit, and so he got tagged to return thanks. He stood up to do it, and stepped back from the table a little way, and put his hands behind him and closed his eyes, and waited a good while for everything to quiet down. He'd open up to start, and if somebody rattled a fork, he'd stall, and wait a while longer.

He was one of these gents that doesn't know the difference between praying and preaching. He started out on the weather, and mentioned how pretty it was that day. From there he went to the crops, and told the Lord the corn cribs and the oat bins were full of grain and the lofts in the barn were bulging with hay and cane tops, just like the Lord hadn't heard it'd been a good growing season. Next he started inviting a blessing on everybody that didn't make it to the dinner that year. They were scattered all the way from Odessa to Waco, but he called 'em every one by name and gave their locations, as if the Lord might not be able to protect 'em if He didn't know where they were. He went over the sick list, too, and asked speedy recovery for relatives who were down with every ailment from arthritis to common colds.

Finally he got around to the food, and we figured he was anyway in the home stretch. But he got off on motherhood and housewifery, and informed the Lord that the women there in the kitchen deserved a lot of credit for laying out such a fine feed, and whatever in this world would we do if it wasn't for the ladies. In the finale he cautioned the Lord not to forget that we were all sinners. Said there wasn't a one of us present and about to partake of heaven's bounty that deserved as much as a bite of biscuit. Then he leveled off and went back to the weather, forgetting, I guess, that he'd already covered it at the start. At last he shut down by telling the Lord to forgive our sins amen, and opened his eyes and looked around like he was expecting us all to give him a hand for the performance.

Driving home late that afternoon, my father got in trouble by commenting that he'd never heard a blessing that covered everything from Genesis to Revelation. Said if it'd lasted another five minutes, the bread would have molded on the table. My mother said he ought to ask forgiveness for saying a thing like that, especially in front of the children. And she didn't speak another word to him all the way home.

My friend Mel was riding with me down to the river, where we hoped to buy some fresh catfish from a fellow we know. Along the way we passed a country church and got to talking about church things, and Mel said:

"When I was a little kid, the thing I hated to do the most was pray. It was always a strain on me. My earliest memory has me kneeling by the side of the bed with my palms together like this, the way they made you do, with the tips of the fingers under your chin. Why did they make you do that? My Aunt Edna would always be there, standing beside me big as a house, listening to make sure I didn't forget anything. It was called Hearing Prayers. She'd say, 'All right now, let's hear your prayers, and then it's into the hay for you.' That always bothered me, her hearing my prayers . . ."

Aunt Edna was Mel's foster mama. He claims he was born a total orphan, and raised by this aunt. I don't know if she was a real aunt or an adopted one.

"She'd correct me," Mel went on about the praying, "if she thought I fouled up, or make me put something in if I left it out. I'd get all the way down to my amen and make a dive for the covers, and she'd say, 'Now hold up, you forgot to ask God to help you be a good boy.' And I'd say, 'Yes I did, I did it right at first, when you were still in the bathroom.' And she'd say, 'Well, I didn't hear it.' It was like God didn't hear anything unless it went through Aunt Edna's ears. So I'd have to get out of the covers, and hit the floor again, and assume the position, and open up and ask help about being good, and then close it down again. If I did it too fast, she'd make me do it over. It got so I wasn't praying to God but to Aunt Edna.

"There was a list of people I had to ask a blessing on every night. That was toward the end, and my feet would be cold, and if I could get away with leaving some of 'em out I'd do it. Aunt Edna would say, 'You left out Albert.' Albert was a big old baldheaded guy that came around every once in a while and ate with us. I don't know, I think he was Aunt Edna's boy friend. She was a widow then.

"I didn't like Albert, because he smelled bad and he was always rubbing my head. He'd reach out and rub my head and say, 'How's your conduct, boy?' And then laugh, like he'd said something funny, or dirty. I hated that. He'd say it every time he came. So I'd leave him off the bless list every time I saw an opening. My argument was that Albert didn't live with us, wasn't kin to us, didn't even live in the same town, and it didn't make any sense to bless a person staying all the way over in Winfield, but Aunt Edna would win.

"The truth was she had me about half convinced that if I left somebody out and didn't bless him, something bad might happen to him, like he'd get run over by a truck or bitten by a mad dog. I thought if I could leave Albert off enough times to get run over just slightly, maybe he wouldn't be coming around for a while wanting to know how my conduct was.

"The worst part was confessing sins. Aunt Edna was interested in hearing details on all my sinning. I learned a good time to tell her about it was during prayers. I'll say this for the old girl, she never once jerked me up and whipped me for anything I confessed while she was hearing my prayers. She'd get excited sometimes, though.

"I'd be praying along and decide it was a good time to throw in a sin, and I'd say, 'Forgive me for hitting Royce Quitman with a rock.' And Aunt Edna would grab me by the neck of my pajamas and pretty near lift me off the floor and say, 'You did *what* to Royce Quitman?' I'd say, 'I hit him with a rock.' And she'd say, 'Where?' And I'd say, 'Behind the garage.' And she'd say, 'No, I mean like in his stomach? His arm?' I'd say, 'His ear.' And she'd say, 'Did it bleed?' And I'd say, 'Some.'

"Then she'd haul off to the telephone to call Mrs. Quitman about Royce's ear, but maybe she'd stick her head back in the door and say, 'Now you get down there and finish your prayers, and don't you forget Albert, you hear?' Like I said, praying was always a strain on me that way. Even now, if I pray, I feel like Aunt Edna is listening."

The last time I went back to my old home town, I was astonished to see so many churches. When I was growing up, most of us considered that we had only three kinds of church folks—Baptists, Methodists, and Campbellites. Campbellites is what we called Church of Christ people. I don't think it's proper to call them that, but I didn't know 'em by any other name until I grew up and left home.

We had other churches in town, but I didn't pay them much attention. There was a Christian Church, which I thought was a branch of the Church of Christ for fifteen years. Then we had a little Catholic Church, with a priest who scared the liver out of the Baptist and Methodist children when he'd walk on the street because there was a story around town that he could look at you, like God, and see all the sins you'd committed. So far as I know we didn't have a synagogue, and I didn't find out what a rabbi is until I got to be a senior in high school, and even then they taught me he's a preacher in a Jewish church.

For a couple of years we lived in a house across the street from a white frame church that had a bell tower. I don't remember what denomination it was. That preacher had two boys about my age. They were pretty good baseball players and "full of the dickens," as the women always said about preachers' kids. On Halloween those boys would swipe the key to their church, and we would all go in there at midnight and ring the bell until lights came on in the pastorate. And then we'd run hide. Big deal.

I think we had some Episcopalians in town, but they must have been a minority group because I remember very little about them. Anyhow, the bunch I grew up with had a policy that we didn't concern ourselves with anything we couldn't spell.

The Baptists and the Methodists and the Campbellites didn't exactly fight each other, but each one considered that the other two were sort of peculiar. The Baptists had a reputation of holding long services, and never letting out until close to one o'clock. The Baptists never did go home, completely. Always something going on at that church. In our town, Baptists as a breed were considered to be contentious. But they always had the best church softball team, and they had good hayrides. I was coming up as a Methodist, but it was fun to get invited on a Baptist hayride.

The Church of Christ people were thought of as mighty serious-minded. I mean we didn't make jokes about them to their faces the way we did the Baptists and the Methodists. We considered it strange that the Campbellites wouldn't have musical instruments in their church and that some of 'em believed all the Baptists and Methodists were going to hell. They were mighty faithful worshippers. We used to say on a cold Sunday that a Campbellite would be at church when a Methodist would sleep in, and maybe even a Baptist.

Methodists in our community were thought to be a little snooty.

If you braced one of the church leaders with that charge he'd say, "Why no. It just happens that the better class of people in town belong to this church." Methodists had the best banquets and the prettiest music. Some thought they were a little loose, having those parties in the basement for the young people and playing spin-the-bottle and winkum. However, there wasn't a Methodist boy in town who wouldn't skip a play party in the church basement to go on one of those Baptist hayrides.

A custom that I remember from my early years of church going was the public giving of thanks. At such a service, anybody that felt the urge could rise up out of the congregation and state what he was most thankful for. As a general rule these services were held on Wednesday night before Thanksgiving on Thursday, and took the place of regular Wednesday prayer meeting. I liked them pretty well. At least there were no long sermons and not nearly so much praying as at your usual prayer meetings.

A good thing I heard at one of those thanksgiving services was said by a red-faced farmer named Mr. Murphy. I expect he had a first name and a set of initials, but I never learned them. I had no need to. He was the only Mr. Murphy I knew or ever heard of, and I supposed at that time he was the only one on the planet.

Anyhow, about a month before Mr. Murphy made his statement at the thanksgiving service, he had been mentioned a time or two by name at Wednesday night prayer meeting, after he'd got hurt building fence. I am not sure how Wednesday night prayer meetings are operated now, but in those days you didn't get prayed for by name unless you had something bad the matter with you. You could be in a purely desperate need of prayer, but if you were walking around healthy, it was no go. You had to come down with something that was mentionable, such as a ruptured appendix or a kidney stone or a bone felon or blood poisoning. If you were not sick, you could get prayed for at prayer meeting only in a general way. You had to listen, and try to recognize that your personal need was being covered.

It always seemed to me you had a better chance to be included in a general prayer if you showed up early for the service. Because before he started, the preacher would circulate among the pews, and visit, and shake hands, and ask what is new, looking for material that way, and you might have a chance to mention something you thought ought to be prayed about.

But Mr. Murphy was a clear case. He had big trouble, and everybody knew about it. He was out in the pasture stretching wire, and a strand popped, and one end of it hit him in the face. He ended up in the hospital, threatening to lose the sight in one of his eyes. So he got prayed for at church, and I think practically anybody will agree that a nice old gent about to lose an eye is a legitimate subject for praying. As it turned out, he went ahead and lost the eye anyhow, which saddened and disappointed the congregation, a bad thing like that happening to Mr. Murphy. But once the eye was lost, nothing more was said about it at prayer meeting.

Well, then up comes the annual thanksgiving service, and Mr. Murphy returned to church, with a big bandage over his bad eye, and took his normal place two-thirds of the way back on the north side. Mr. Murphy was always a quiet gent in church, but we had plenty of others with a lot to say, at Thanksgiving or any other time. They started out on things like food, and said they were thankful that the Lord provided plenty of it. They went on to shelter, and warm clothes, and all this rain that's put a season in the ground. They were thankful for friends, for good wives, for faithful husbands, for dutiful children, for the beautiful day we'd just had, and they were getting around to details like the new piano for the church.

Then Mr. Murphy got up, I think to most everybody's surprise. What's an old gent who's just had one of his lights put out gonna be thankful for? "Preacher," he said, "I want to say I'm thankful I've got one eye." Of all the thanksgiving testimonials I heard in those services, I class that one the best.

My dear old Methodist mother—and other women who looked after me in my early times and saw I went to church—used to fuss because I wasn't too good about listening to the preacher. I guess I wasn't, at that. But I was pretty good at *watching* preachers, studying their styles. From watching them that way for so long, I learned a few rules that are good to remember, even if you never in this life have anything whatever to do with preaching sermons. One such rule is, the most effective shout is preceded by a whisper.

The earliest preachers I watched were mostly all constant shouters. It was a marvel to me that men could sleep in church with all that yelling going on. I remember one old gent we had, he shouted everything from the text to the invitation. In summer when the church windows were open, you could stand six blocks away on the loading dock of the express office and hear every word that preacher let fly. So it was sure a big contrast when we changed preachers and got one that whispered.

Switching off on a siding just a minute, I have to say in favor of the Methodists in those times that they gave you variety in preachers. After a congregation kept one for a couple of seasons and he got to wearing thin, why the old boys who dropped the most money in the collection plate would put a bug in the bishop's ear. "How about let's move this fellow on a little way west," they'd say. "Give us something younger that doesn't shout so much." And zingo, next pop out of the box, you had a new preacher. It was an effective system, and while I have lost touch and can't say, for all I know the Methodists may still operate that way.

Anyhow, to move on, we had this whispering gent come in behind the shouter, and his first Sunday when he got up and started preaching so low and slow the way he did, I thought shoot, this guy's gonna have sleepers as far down as the second pew.

But he fooled us. What he was doing with his whispers, he was setting us up for his shout. He'd be coasting along, smooth and calm and sleepy, and after he got you nice and relaxed, all of a sudden without any warning whatever, he'd *bust loose with about a dozen words of hell's fire and brimstone shouting!* Mister, you think that didn't draw everybody's attention? The first few times he pulled that stunt, the congregation jerked like they'd had an electric shock in the seat of their britches.

I studied that man's style as long as the money boys let him stay, and I never did learn to predict when he would produce one of his explosions. That was his secret, his way of keeping everybody listening, and I have to say it worked, too.

Later on I studied preachers who cried, preachers who grinned all the time (even during their saddest examples), preachers who pointed. I remember one pointer who would name a sin and fire an index finger at the crowd, and hit me square between the eyes every shot, no matter where I sat. Then once we had a singer. Understand, these weren't all Methodist. I shopped around. Lutheran. Episcopal. Presbyterian. Brush Arbor. Street Corner.

That singer? Well, he tried it twice that I know of. Square in the middle of his sermon he'd tune up and begin singing, solo and a cappella. He'd pick something like "Amazing Grace," that everybody knew. He'd stand up there and tough it through two full stanzas. I believe what he hoped was that we'd all join in and sing too, and maybe rise up and step out and come ghosting down the aisle to the altar, all beaming and fervent, sending up hosannas and hallelujahs and having a Great Spiritual Experience there at his feet.

It didn't work. At least not when I was present. I confess I hoped it would, for that sincere gent's sake. I might even have got up and sung with him, if everybody else had done it ahead of me. But don't you agree it took courage for a preacher to try that? The second time, especially.

During long drives at night I listen a lot to religious programs on the car radio. And I recommend it. You can hear some really remarkable stuff on those shows. Must be hundreds of radio preachers on the air, representing a great range of denominations and styles. Some radio stations often run continuous strings of preachers, one after the other as long as you want to keep tuned. You will hear crying preachers, and drawling preachers, and singing preachers, and shouting preachers, and pleading preachers, and gasping preachers.

When I say gasping, I am speaking of the style of delivery. A gasper will let go of a phrase, and then take a great gasp, and let another phrase out, and gasp again, and so on. The result is something like this: "Now the Lord is up there (gasp), looking down from on high (gasp), and knowing your every pain (gasp), and your every sorrow (gasp), and even if your brother doesn't love you (gasp), even if your *mother* doesn't love you (gasp), the *Lord* loves you (gasp)."

Some radio preachers have the habit of putting stock religious expressions into everything they say. Expressions like "Praise the Lord," and "Lord love you," and "Amen," and "Glory to God." I get the feeling this habit is so strong on some of them that they don't really know they're putting all those expressions in. Probably it's the same as the speech habits you or I have, such as saying "you know" all the time. A radio preacher with this habit will never say "Good evening" to his audience. Instead he will say, "Good evening praise the Lord," and he won't put a comma between the "evening" and the "praise." He'll say it as if it's all one expression.

Once in a while I hear one preacher who gives the two expressions "Amen" and "Praise the Lord" a thorough working over in his every sentence. I have to admit I'm fascinated by this style, and I look for this gent on the dial when I'm traveling. He will even put in the "amen" and the "Praise the Lord" when he's reading scripture, and it gives an exceptional sound to Bible verses you've been familiar with all your life. On the 23rd Psalm, for instance, I think he would sound like this: "The Lord is my shepherd amen; I shall not want praise the Lord. He maketh me to lie down in green pastures praise the Lord. He leadeth me beside the still waters amen. He restoreth my soul praise the Lord . . ."

Of course a radio preacher, the same as anybody else who works on a mike, must keep an eye on the studio clock, to make certain he keeps within his time allotment. Last Saturday I heard one conclude his sermon with, "Well I see my time is running out praise the Lord."

I have become a big fan of Sunday morning radio too. You get a good deal of music, and a lot of it is gospel singing and spirituals, and I like those. You are most apt to hear the spirituals early, around eight o'clock. On the early programs you get some interesting announcements, too. Here's one I heard: "And now, our prayers go out to Maples Car Wash." Now what's wrong with that? If a person's gonna pray on the radio, why not for a car wash? Or anyway for the folks who work there, which I guess is what the announcement meant.

One of the principal things I like about Sunday morning religious programs, on the country stations especially, is that I hear so many sounds that remind me of my early churchgoing experiences. For instance, I heard a song leader last Sunday that reminded me of Mr. Weatherly. I am just calling him Mr. Weatherly. I do not remember his name. It might have been Weatherly, but I doubt it.

Anyhow, he was a song leader in the church I was taken to back in my green years. I was fascinated by the style he practiced in leading hymns. Like many song leaders, at the start of a verse or a chorus, he would pipe up ahead of the crowd and do a couple of notes solo, to sort of lead off and show the way. Any place in a song that looked like it might need leadership, Mr. Weatherly would let fly his solo notes that way.

The distinction in his style was that on those solo notes he would inject a jerky sort of *ha* or *he* or *heh* sound into the middle of whatever word he was singing. As an example, say he was leading us into the familiar words, "Praise God from whom all blessings flow." He would get out ahead of us with, "Pray-*haise!* God from whom . . ." You understand, everybody would join him on the "God," but he would be solo on the "pray-*haise.*" Imagine we were about to sing the line, "Rock of Ages, cleft for me." He would lead away with "Ruh-*hock!* of ages . . ." You see how he did? I studied him all the time.

One Christmas he came up to the school to lead carols in a chapel meeting. The first song he chose was that happy one that starts, "Deck the halls with boughs of holly." Of course most of the students had never been to our church. Mr. Weatherly startled them by bulling out ahead with, "Duh-*heck!* the halls with . . ." Everybody roared with laughter. Mr. Weatherly never did understand why. I felt sorry for him.

On the radio I heard a song leader with a similar style. On that lovely old hymn, "Sweet Hour of Prayer," he led off with "Swuh-*heet!* hour of prayer . . ."

It's Sunday morning at eight-thirty, and I am in Washington County near the south shore of Lake Somerville. I'm sitting beneath a big post oak tree and getting ready to go to church. There is no church house nearby, but never mind that, this post oak will do as well.

I have got a little choir of crows over yonder, sending up fervent hosannas. A steady breeze is playing hymns among the boughs of this old oak. A pair of doves is mourning the sins of mortals everywhere. So I will have church here, without any parking problems and without any thieves to steal my wheelcovers before the benediction is said.

Of course I am lacking a preacher. If I had my choice of all those I've known, I would ask them to send down my sweet old friend Brother Bob Day. Brother Bob once thundered hellfire and damnation and the promise of salvation from a pulpit about thirty miles northeast of this tree, in Brazos County, where I knew him well.

Even then, when I had under my roof little children who needed examples set, even in those days I was apt to stray off into woods and fields on Sunday morning. Brother Bob didn't mind mentioning that habit, and I would tell him I had church under a tree somewhere, like this. He nodded and understood, but he wouldn't endorse the idea without reservation. On Sunday morning he needed the sinners in the pews, sitting straight and still, so he could take careful aim, and fire direct shots.

But he knew about church outdoors, don't worry. On Saturday nights when the earth was moist and the foxes were fragrant, I've seen Brother Bob have private church at a campfire out on Turkey Creek Road. While the hounds mouthed their symphony on the damp night. To a fox hunter there's no sound lovelier. I've never known a fox-hunting preacher who didn't put hound music on a par with the harps of heaven's angels.

Sometimes the music would come in surges, on wind gusts, and the harmony would be more beautiful than Brother Bob could endure and he would leap up, and raise clenched fists, and let go a long and soulful cry. Talking to the dogs, is what it passed for. What it really was, was praise. Shouting up praise and thanks to God. For the damp night. For beauty. For campfire smoke. For love and friends and the goodness of life. All this, and paradise yet to come. Something to shout about. So you mustn't think he didn't understand church under a tree.

When I'd tell him that I'd been meditating on a sandhill some-where while he was blasting away from the pulpit, he'd nod and say, "Well, that's all right. But did it make you feel as good as going to church?" And he had me there. I've spent a lot of time in church and wishing I was somewhere else. But I can't remember ever coming out of a church that I didn't feel better than when I went in. I don't know if that has anything to do with religion. But I do think it's among the more valuable functions of the church—simply to make people feel better. It's one of the world's greatest needs, for people to feel better inside.

Being here beneath the tree while church is going on, this makes me think of Mrs. Matthews. And her husband Mr. Mat-thews, and that is the only way I ever knew them, just Mr. and Mrs. They were our neighbors one time, and Mr. Matthews was a great fisherman and Mrs. Matthews was a great church person. They used to say about Mrs. Matthews that the church wouldn't take up if she wasn't there. Mr. Matthews was a kind of scoutmas-ter type, and he used to gather up a little bunch of boys and we'd go to the river and camp out and fish. One time Mrs. Matthews went with us, which was strange because we were going to stay Saturday night and miss church.

These people were jolly, and happy, and laughed a lot as a rule. But that Sunday morning on the river, Mrs. Matthews was not. She was short-tempered, and nervous. She paced along the bank all morning and seemed worried. About eleven o'clock she spoke to Mr. Matthews, and he called us together and told us to sit in a bunch on the ground. We did, and then for a few minutes under a big pecan tree she held church. She read a little, out of Psalms, I think, where God is praised so. Then she gave a little talk about God's forgiveness, and she said a prayer and let us go. I remem-ber the look of relief on her face. "I feel better now," she said. She just couldn't stand it, not having church on Sunday. After she had it she was all right.

Last weekend I went to dinner in the home of some friends in Victoria. Before we ate, I was back in the kitchen visiting with the maid, who is Hazel Johnson, and we got to talking about preaching and hymn singing and she invited me to her church. The next morning, which was Sunday, I attended services at Palestine Baptist Church, which is on Victoria's Convent Street. I didn't get to sit with Hazel, because she sings in the choir, but I went anyhow and I had a good time.

I'm not certain it's proper to say you had a good time in church. But I did, and the reason was that everybody else, all the regular members, seemed to have a good time too, so I assume it's customary. I won't say I never had a good time in church before, but I haven't very often. Most times I was sitting there waiting for the benediction.

Palestine Baptist doesn't look like any kind of a poor-folks church, if that's what you're thinking. It's a handsome, red-brick building with a tall bell tower and beautiful stained-glass cathedral windows and about a dozen and a half concrete steps leading up to the front door. Rev. Z. Broaddus, pastor. The ushers are women, and every one dressed the same in soft tan uniforms. Palestine Baptist has not gone mod on dress. Hazel told me, for example, that the women members there don't come to church wearing pant suits.

I loved the music, the singing. The congregation sings together, and yet not together so much that individuals can't sing the way they feel. When the service began the deacons sat down front and led us in "Near the Cross." But you didn't need to follow along exactly. If you felt like singing between the lines, or peeling off a sort of solo countermelody, why just proceed. I think that's part of the good time I was talking about.

Here came the choir, single-filing from the back of the church, singing the happiest song I've heard in ten years, "The Lord Is Blessing Me." Everybody marching in and smiling, almost laughing with good feelings.

He woke me up this morning,
   And started me on my way.
   The Lord is blessing me, right now.

Now by john, I think that's the way it ought to be, happy singing in church. Church was always too much like a funeral to suit
me. Most religious music sounds like somebody standing on a
dark corner trying to call up a hearse. Those songs at Palestine
Baptist had a lilt and a bouncy beat, and it was fun to sing along.
The choir did a song called "Jesus Is My Everything," and it too
had the little shuffly beat. Every now and then between the lines
you could hear feet patting all through the congregation, and see
heads and shoulders swaying. You tell me what's the matter with
that. I liked it.

Back when I was going to church every Sunday, or almost, I
would marvel that choir members can stand still as hills and yet
sing. It must be hard. It didn't look natural. That's another reason
I liked the singing in that church at Victoria. If those singers feel
like swaying, they sway. I watched one woman in the choir who
even did a little directing, waving her hands, showing how she
felt about singing. And obviously how she felt was *good*. In most
of the churches where I've gone, a person gyrating that way in
the choir would have been an awful distraction, and frowned on.
Nobody in Hazel's church paid the slightest mind to it, that I
noticed.

But I don't mean to say there's no leadership. You better believe
Rev. Z. Broaddus leads. After the choir sang he stepped to the
pulpit—white hair, a sharp gray suit, black and white shoes—and
he commanded, "Let's all say amen!" "*Amen!*" we shouted, and
the roar that came out of us must have flushed the very pigeons
off the roof.

Participation. Maybe there's your key word that makes this
kind of church different from what I've known. Everybody par-
ticipates if they wish. If you want to shout amen, let it fly. If you
feel like thanking the Lord for feeling good, do it loud as you
want to. If the preacher says from the pulpit, "I'm fixing to tell
you something," and if you want to respond, go ahead, say,
"Come on, *tell* me!" And nobody will turn around and stare or
frown at you. Even the offering becomes a ceremony with all
hands taking part. No passing of collection plates by a few ushers. Everybody in the congregation files down the aisles and puts
his money on the altar. Did I go? I sure did, and tried to look
happy as I could because Rev. Broaddus was standing down
there reminding me that the Lord loves a cheerful giver.

He preached out of the 42nd Psalm, and did a fine thundering
job, and afterward a tall young man came forward to join the
church, and they were going to baptize him Sunday night. Before
we broke up, the sick list was given to us. It included Sister Ho-

merzell Poindexter and Brother Elbert Smith III, who were in the hospital. And a paragraph of sympathy was read off the church bulletin. The sympathy went to "Brother Edwin Lewis, whose father Raymond Lewis will be funeralized Monday at 1 P.M. from Mt. Calvary Baptist Church, Bloomington, Texas."

Hazel was in the front row of the choir. She sure looked nice.

Up until I was about forty years old, I probably spent more time in church than most choir directors and Sunday-school superintendents. I am almost certain that by the time I was twelve I had attended more different *kinds* of churches than any other country boy in this state. So they just about wore me out on church. I had the feeling it was sort of like going to school. Nobody goes to school forever. Sooner or later they quit and go out and see if they can use what they've been taught. Maybe church isn't the same, but I felt it was. I mean if they hadn't got it pounded into me in forty years, it never was going to get in.

When I was coming up long ago, I attended more church than I did school. That's no exaggeration. At least I went to church meetings more often than I went to school. You went to school five days a week, and that was it. On Sundays, we went to church four times. You got up and went to Sunday school, and when that was over, you hardly had time to go outside and get in a wrestling match and tear your shirt before you had to go back in and sit through the preaching.

I'm not counting it a time, but at our house, Sunday dinner and Sunday afternoon were very often the same as being in church. We fed the preacher a lot at Sunday dinner, and so the talk was about church while we ate and it was about church when we got through. But I can't say I ever objected to preachers eating with us. Some of them were pretty good old boys, and besides, when they came to dinner we always had homemade ice cream. I was nearly grown before I shed the belief that in order to keep him going, you had to put homemade ice cream into a Methodist preacher, the way you put gas in a car or oats in a horse.

About six o'clock on Sunday evening we went back to church for what they called League. The Baptists called it BYPU. I believe the Baptists went to church even more than the Methodists. I remember once in our town the Baptists put up a sign saying that the doors of their church were never locked, and somebody went in and stole all their song books and they took the sign down and locked the doors. It was not true, as the rumor indicated, that the song books were hooked by Methodist boys, as a prank. At least I am pretty sure it was not true. After League, you stayed for Sunday night church, which made four services for the day. Then on Wednesday night we had prayer meeting, which made five, and a tie with school for frequency.

Then during the week there was always at least one trip to church, for a special event. My mother was always volunteering me to go to church and do something that needed doing. Until I was six feet tall, I don't believe she was ever pleased to see me leaving the house unless I was going either to church or to school, and preferably church.

During the Great Depression, my family was cut loose from home and we drifted, for two or three years. From town to town, farm to farm, dodging those hard times. We did best in the country because there was enough to eat in the country. Beans and cornbread and buttermilk. But there weren't any Methodist churches, and that was a frustration for my mother. Methodists weren't too keen on building country churches in this state, and from what I see now they aren't yet. The rural churches you ran across in our part of Texas were mostly Baptist and Church of Christ. My mother soon learned she could darken the door of a Baptist Church and no timbers would split. "It's the same Lord," she would say when we walked out, but I never did think she said it with much enthusiasm.

Sometimes in those strange, strange years we would just wander, ride along with my father who was an itchy-footed traveling salesman. I always suspected he sort of liked not having a home, not being tied down with possessions. I never knew him to be anything but in a good humor as long as he was on the road, putting miles behind him, meeting people and seeing things. But being on the drift that way was a problem for my mother, about getting us to church. We ended up going to church just *anywhere*, as long as it looked more like a church than a saloon. We'd be going along back roads and come to a country town and there'd be a little crowd around a small church and in we'd go, and we wouldn't even know what branch of church it was. We'd sit half through the sermon before we'd know whether it was Baptist or Afghanistan.

The church problem was aggravated by one of my sisters, who was going for a record on Sunday-school attendance. When we hit the road, running from the mess that Hoover fellow had got us into, my sister had gone to Sunday school I think it was four solid years without as much as being tardy. But she sure had some near misses when we were on the road. She was aiming for ten years. I just now tried to call her to refresh my memory on whether she made it or not. She is out of town attending a bowling tournament and I can't find her, but I think she made the ten years, and I wonder if the record still stands.

A time or two we simply couldn't locate anything that would pass for Sunday school, and we'd pull over and have it ourselves under a tree somewhere. My mother would get out her Bible—you don't need to think she wouldn't have a Bible—and read the 20th verse out of the 18th chapter of Matthew, where Jesus Christ guaranteed her, "Where two or three are gathered together in my name, there am I in the midst of them." There'd be five of us, plenty for a quorum, and on my 105th birthday, if I have it, I will still be able to see our little bunch (as I know my mother saw us) sitting under a mesquite tree six miles south of Marble Falls, with the Saviour sitting there in the midst of us. Oh, I have been to church, don't worry about that.

14

"Peter Gray, 1853–1928.
Weep not, he is at rest."

When I was visiting friends in Victoria last week, a man in their neighborhood was found dead in his home. We sat on the front porch at sundown and looked down the street and watched the people come and stand in the yard and talk. When the ambulance came to take away the body, I thought about Old Mr. Boyd, who died alone in his house in my home town long ago. I was able to see the sheriff carrying Old Mr. Boyd along the path, while all of us stood silently and watched.

He lived in a small unpainted house that sat way at the back of its lot. It seemed to apologize for being there, to say that it was not meant to be the main house on that property, that a bigger house was planned but never built. Old Mr. Boyd lived there alone. He had not lived among us long when he died. He did not have a car or a dog or a cat or a friend who came to see him. He moved into the little house and built a chicken pen. The house sat so near the back of the lot he had to build the chicken pen in the front yard.

Two chinaberry trees were there, and in the heat of the day Old Mr. Boyd would sit under the chinaberry trees and watch his chickens. They were Rhode Island Reds. Every day he would go up to the grocery store and bring back scraps of produce they would give him and pitch the scraps to his chickens. People in the neighborhood would sometimes save their potato peelings and pieces of bread left over and let Old Mr. Boyd have them for his Rhode Island Reds. "Save those scraps for Old Mr. Boyd," we would say.

He was not especially friendly, and he did not make neat things the way so many old men did. He did not tell stories. Sometimes we would sit with him a while beneath the chinaberry trees when we took the scraps to the chickens. And he would peel pecans with his pocketknife. He was a very small man, which is why the sheriff carried him without any help. He had this heavy pocket-knife that looked huge in his little hands. He would peel pecans with the knife and hand us the halves of the meat, but we would not talk much. Next to his little house was a big vacant lot where we played ball. He would sit under the trees and watch us play, and when a foul fell in his chicken pen he would get up and pitch the ball back. So he was not the enemy. But not a close friend, either. None of us ever went into his house.

Then one day he died. The women noticed that he had not passed on the way to the grocery store, and that they had not seen him sitting under the trees. So after work a couple of the men went to check, and he was dead on the floor. We went around the neighborhood, passing the word that Old Mr. Boyd was dead in his house.

People began to come out, and look along the street toward the little house. They drew up into clumps of three and four and five, and faced the house, and spoke quietly. Some sat on their front steps. Some in their yards. A group formed around first base on the vacant lot. But nobody went in the yard until the sheriff came. He came alone in his black car. A tall spare man with a long sad face. He spoke a minute to the men who had found Old Mr. Boyd. He walked up the path and went in the little house.

Then the people closed in, and stood in the yard, and formed

larger groups, and some even sat under ~~~ ~~~
wait for the sheriff to come out. Strangers ~~~
would stop when they saw the crowd, and a~~~
was. "An old man is dead in that house," we wou~~~
strangers would join us, and wait. So there was q~~~
when the sheriff came out carrying Old Mr. Boyd in h~~~
he would have carried a sleeping child. For that tall ma~~~
body seemed a slight burden. He walked slow and easy, and ~~~
Old Mr. Boyd in the back seat of his black car and drove away.

That night at supper my father made a strange little talk, about the awful sadness of a life coming to an end and nobody knows how the life was, or where it was spent, or what it meant. Then he told us to save the scraps for Old Mr. Boyd's chickens until we found out what was to be done with them.

Up in Deep East Texas I heard a fellow talking about how sleepy he'd been all day. The reason was, he had served the 3 to 6 A.M. shift at a wake party. Wake party is what he called it. Sometimes you hear it called a wake, without the party. Or a watch. Back home it was just called sitting up with the body.

A person passes, and friends of the person come and sit up all night in the funeral parlor. This custom is fading, but it's still observed in the rural areas of Texas, and from what I hear, some areas that are not so rural. It traces back to times when it was a good idea to guard a corpse to keep wild animals away, and to prevent thieves from coming around to carry off valuables prepared for burial along with the body. What's left of the custom takes the form of an honor, a paying of respects to the deceased person's memory, and an act of sympathy extended his survivors. I class it a really weird practice.

Back in the fifties and sixties when I was a lot better about going to church than I am now, I was a member of a large men's Sunday-school class. A good many of the members were retirement age and in general weak health. One of our routine Sunday rituals was to review the sick list and hear reports on how serious an illness everybody had. One thing I enjoyed about that class was, I was thought of as a youngster in it. Even a guy nudging up near fifty wasn't anything but a pup in that elderly bunch. I liked that because I have never been one of these birds who looks forward to being old.

Well, we had a wealth of funerals for the members of that class.

227

A disadvantage of being junior grade, in point of years, was that you were called on frequently to take the 3 to 6 A.M. shift and sit up with the body. Whoever made up the duty roster—I never did know who it was—naturally would not assign any eighty-six-year-old gents to roll out of the quilts at 2 A.M. and report to the undertaker's.

I did a good deal of duty dodging, I confess it. My traveling helped me do it. I would have to be in Nacogdoches on Thursday, or Yoakum, and couldn't serve. Nacogdoches has always been a help to me in that way. Yoakum, too. But I earned my stripes, I think, on sitting up with dead people, and I had some little experiences at it that seemed so strange to me then. Now they seem even stranger.

We were assigned to sit up in pairs. That right there is recognition that if a guy is given a choice on where to go and sit around in the middle of the night, he will not pick a funeral parlor. The rules of the custom accommodate that truth, and provide you a partner. Sitting alone through a silent night with nobody for company but a corpse is just not much entertainment. I had a talent for drawing a partner.who felt obliged, during our tour, to call on the body. To pay it a visit and stand over it and study it. If he wanted to do that it was all right with me, except that he didn't want to do it alone. He would want his partner to go along and stand there and look too. You notice, hardly anybody wants to do anything alone around a funeral parlor.

The procedure was, at the first of the tour, you and your partner didn't speak of dying or funerals. You pretended you had met there at 3 A.M. in a funeral parlor just by chance, and had decided to sit around and make a social event of the meeting. Talk about football, politics, the weather, the price of steers. I figured out you could deal with any topic there at the undertaker's that was permissible on the lawn of the church between Sunday school and the general worship service. You did not, for instance, talk about booze or sex or indulge in gossip. For those, you went on down to the drugstore. About forty-five minutes into the tour, my partner would pause, and look grave, and ask me, "Have you seen old Henry?" Meaning our departed brother in the coffin. I would say I had not. Then my partner would rise, and hitch up his pants, and button his coat, and clear his throat—just as if by john he was going in to carry on a dialogue with old Henry and needed to look and sound proper.

I always went on in, to provide accompaniment according to the rules. But I never did study old Henry. I just looked a minute at his necktie. My feeling was, and is still, that when I get in the same condition as Henry, I don't want anybody peering down at me like a buzzard from a dead limb. I say if Henry has got to be studied, he has a right to get it when he's up and around and able to defend himself. I used to wonder how many of my partners were only looking at neckties, the same as I did.

It's about six-thirty on a chilly morning and the house hasn't warmed up yet, and I am sitting here thinking about my brother-in-law Pete. He was one of the best men I ever knew. Been dead thirteen years. The reason I think of him now is, I am wearing his old green, fur-lined jacket. It's meant to be worn outdoors, but I put it on a lot of times inside when the house is cold. I like the way it feels.

Not many cold days pass that I don't have the jacket on for at least a little while. Old Pete used to wear it to the power plant where he worked. When he died my sister gave it to me. It must be twenty years old now.

I have friends who don't like to use personal items that belonged to relatives who have died. It doesn't bother me. I love this jacket. And I know it would please old Pete, to know that something of his has been of so much practical use. That man was a great respecter of quality. He wouldn't buy anything second-rate. And then he took care of what he spent his money for. Everything just exactly the way it ought to be. Even the engines of his cars were always clean, not coated in grease and dirt the way most are.

But having a thing that belonged to a person that's gone is nice, I think, because it tends to keep that person close to you. Like the time I had a flat way down on U.S. 59 close to Freer, right there where the road to Seven Sisters comes in. Cold? Hoo wee. You know, I guess, what changing a tire can be like down in that Brush Country when the temperature's thirty-eight and the wind gusting out of the north. I dug in the back of the car and got old Pete's jacket out, and all the time I was grunting around there changing that tire I couldn't keep from seeing him, grinning at me.

Same way a few years ago down on the beach, at Christmas. I think I told you about it. Went down there just one time the way I've always wanted to, and escaped all the glitter and the commercialism and the crowds of Christmas and stayed at San Luis Pass. And got stuck in the sand on the beach. In a screaming norther.

229

Listen, I don't know if there's a colder place than a beach during a wet norther. Funny place to think about old Pete, but I did, when I put on his jacket and told myself he wouldn't have done a dumb thing like that, driving off into that sand.

After my friend Mel's father died, Mel took all his clothes and gave them to a charity organization. Even things like raincoats, and rubber boots, and mackinaws, that Mel could have kept and used even if the fit wasn't quite precise. But he didn't want to keep one thing in the way of his dad's clothes. Now some people are just the other way, and won't get rid of *anything* that belonged to a loved one. And won't use it, either. Just let it sit. That never has made any sense to me, but then that's their affair and not mine.

Not long before my father died he bought a couple of spiffy new suits. We buried him in one, and I took the other and had it altered some and wore it for nice, two or three years. Shoot. It was the best suit I had. Every time I put it on I could hear my father tell me to stand up straight and button my coat. I had a pair of his gloves that I kept and used for several seasons, until they wore out. I liked wearing them. Made me feel in touch with him, putting my hands in there where his own had been.

Isn't there an old superstition that it's bad luck to wear a dead man's boots? I wore a pair of dead man's boots out one time. Belonged to a friend of mine, and we had this in common: We both wore a size 12B shoe. Big-footed guys like that are not too common. His wife remembered the day he had borrowed a pair of black shoes from me to wear to some festive event. When he died, she gave me his boots. She didn't know anybody else that they'd fit. I wore their very heels off and was glad to have them. But I don't think now that I've got anything to wear that belonged to a dead person. Except old Pete's jacket, and I believe it's good for at least another ten years. I hope so.

There's this little cemetery by the side of a state highway that I drive frequently. It's what people used to call a country graveyard. A small church stood near it at one time. You can see the scars on the ground where it was. Last spring I remember passing by there and seeing a lot of people with rakes and hoes, chopping weeds and cutting grass and cleaning the place up. A graveyard working.

When I passed there again a few days ago, a burial service was going on. The weather was cold and wet. A drizzle was coming down. It had been falling for almost two days and the ground was soaked. The cars were left out on the highway because the cemetery grounds were too muddy to drive on. A small group was huddled under the mortician's canopy. Not more than twenty people. Graveside services on rainy days in country cemeteries aren't very often well attended. I saw one small boy, maybe eight years old, standing among those dark-dressed adults under the canopy. He stood a little hunched over, like he was cold. He was probably bewildered, too. A youngster that age takes deep memories away from a funeral, and they never leave him.

Seeing that boy reminded me of all the funerals my parents took me to when I was about his age. My folks were great funeral goers. I used to have the feeling that somebody must have been keeping count on how many funerals we attended, and gave us a credit when we went to one. I noticed that some of the people who came to funerals at church didn't join the procession on out to the cemetery. My mother believed that wasn't right. If she didn't consider it a sin, she put it mighty close to one. Sort of like going to Sunday school and not staying for church.

So I stood around in a lot of cemeteries at graveside services, among grown folks with their faces all dark and somber. What I dreaded most was the graveside service of a relative, because then even the children had to sit in those wooden folding chairs, set in rows on that false carpet of grass spread near the grave. It was like you were on exhibit and the spectators were looking at you to see if you were grieving or not. My kinfolks then were buried in red clay. Clay so hard it came up in big old chunks, which I thought were the ugliest of all things. It didn't seem right to have a solemn service like that with everybody standing around a big old mound of clay clods. Nowadays they cover the dirt up with flowers, but there weren't all that many flowers at the funerals I went to.

I never did dream of mentioning it to anybody, but I used to think it was a terrible custom to make the departed one's family sit there in those chairs and watch the coffin get lowered in the grave. Worse than that, then came two or three wooden-faced men who took up shovels and began dumping those heavy old clay clods down on top of the coffin. The clods made a dreadful, desperate sound when they landed. Why, it was like the loved one was going to his doom instead of his reward.

And while that awful clod-dumping and shovel-scraping went on, and with the family of the departed in the very deeps of its grief, here came the crowd. Everybody in the community paraded through, shaking hands with the bereaved and trying to say comforting words. They were always embarrassed, and awkward. It's not natural to come around spouting hollow phrases at somebody who's suffering grief pains. I always thought they ought to leave the bereaved alone at that, of all times, and I still do.

My old fishing buddy Freddy Smith died up at Huntsville a couple of weeks ago. He was gone and buried before I heard about it, but that's all right. I wouldn't have gone to the funeral anyhow, and he knew that. We talked about it one time.

It was a warm afternoon, just about this time of year. We slipped off and borrowed Bosco Monzingo's little old john boat and took it to the river. Paddled a little way up a creek and tied to brush tops and tried for white perch. The river was up and the water almost red, so we didn't catch much. But it was good to be out there.

We talked about funerals, I think, because of Tex Hardy. Tex was sick then, and dying, and we knew it. Everybody knew it. Marion Hardy, was his name. Freddy called him Tex to kid him about that cowboy hat he wore. Tex would have been there on the creek with us if he hadn't been sick. Freddy and Tex fought that fishing so hard. It was important to them.

That afternoon, when we talked about Tex, something came up about his funeral and I told Freddy I wasn't going to come. Because I don't like funerals, especially those of good friends. Then we got to horsing around, about funerals and dying. People reach a point where they do that a lot, discussing death in a light and joking way, and yet saying things they need to get said. I told Freddy that if he died before I did I sure wasn't coming to *his* funeral, either. Instead, as quick as I heard he was gone, I was going to get me a jug and go fishing. He gave a kind of snort-laugh and said, "You do that. That's fine with me."

A good many months afterward I was back in Huntsville and looked Freddy up and we went for coffee. I asked about Tex and he said, "Tex is dead." He didn't say another word about it.

Anyhow, when I was through Huntsville recently I saw Ferol Robinson on the Sam Houston campus and he told me about Freddy dying. I thought about the afternoon on the creek and what I said I was going to do. And Freddy's snort-laugh, and his words, "You do that." Later that day, I drove on up to Lufkin and turned toward San Augustine. When I was crossing the bridges that take Highway 103 over those upper fingers of Sam Rayburn Lake, I got to imagining that Freddy was close somewhere. Just like any minute I might see him in his old orange coveralls, sitting on a bridge railing, grinning at me and saying, "You do that."

I used to carry fishing tackle in the car, everywhere. Tex and Freddy taught me to love white perch fishing, the way they did it. I got so I'd ten times rather feel a three-quarter-pound crappie on a fly rod than a three-pound black bass on one of those broomsticks they use now for casting rods. For a few years there I was really hung on that perch fishing. But not now. I quit, somewhere along there, and now I don't even own a fish hook.

Still, by the time I got to San Augustine I could tell I wasn't going to get much rest till I did *something* about old Freddy leaving out of this world. So I got the jug and drove back down to Shirley Creek. They've got a marina there and a fishing pier and I figured I could rent or buy me something to make up a perch rig, even if it was just a cane pole.

The pier was open. It was getting late and people were walking out there to fish. Nice old guys with grandchildren. Ladies with poodle dogs and dainty little tackle boxes to match. All of a sudden I didn't want to do it. That kind of fishing, on a lighted pier, is all right for some, but Freddy wouldn't want me celebrating his departure in a place like that. His kind of fishing, Tex's too, was a hunt. No sitting around waiting. Move on, find where they are.

So instead of the pier I just went over the other side of the point and found me a lonesome place, and sat down where the water had washed out the roots of a big old black-jack oak. I sat there till almost dark, and had a little funeral service for old Freddy. The lake went plop-plop-plop at the shore. The sun went down dark red behind thin clouds, and silhouetted the dead trees where Tex and Freddy used to hunt those fish, out there in the flooded timber.

On a blacktop road just north of Dodge, I was looking for a shady spot to sit down and eat the sandwich I'd bought a few miles back west in Huntsville. Turned into a stone gateway concern, and ended up having lunch under a post-oak tree in Dodge Cemetery. I wouldn't want to eat lunch in some cemeteries I know, but this one seemed about as pleasant as graveyards can be. Full of trees, and chirping birds, and sunshine and shadows, and a ground cover of grass and sweetgum balls and pine cones.

Sat there chewing ham and cheese and stale bread and got to

233

reading, the way you'll do in cemeteries, the names on the stones. Beck. Winters. Daniel. Green. Maxwell. Gillaspie. Then Priscilla Morton, right there near the oak where I sat. She was born in 1868 and died in 1949, and on her stone is that old poem I've read so often, but never really saw before on a grave marker:

Stop, dear children, as you pass by,
As you are now so once was I,
As I am now you soon will be,
Prepare for death and eternity.

I finished the sandwich and walked around in the sun, reading more names. Wells. Osborn. Watts. Roark. Blackburn. James M. Blackburn, 1900–1946. His stone stands out because it seems homemade. A cross dug into the top, in a labored style. Then, below his name and dates, the inscription: "He upheld the things of Jesus Christ our Lord and Saviour." All right, I think I've known men that died with less than James J. Blackburn, who was loved enough that somebody would hand-carve a marker for him.

Bluebirds called in their soft, sad way from a dead nesting tree outside the fence. A breeze moved through the pine tops, and made them whisper. Riley. Dixon. Anderson. Kelley. Webb. Hopper. Cobbs. Jimmy Wayne Cobbs. Born August 31, 1953. Died April 24, 1971. A photograph of Jimmy Wayne is set into the face of his stone. One of those glass-encased pictures that defy weather. They must have been mighty proud of that young fellow, looking so handsome and intelligent in his high school graduation cap and gown. He'd be, as they say, twenty-two next August. Somebody must be wondering still—why? why?

Benge. Poe. Hartt. Knight. Stokes. Wooten. Price. E. B. Price, 1888–1932, Company K, 143rd Infantry. Do you find it at all strange, that men are born and live and work and love and die, and it's carved into their stones—what, that they loved? Why no, that they were soldiers. Here's another. Compton Lively, corporal, U.S. Army, WWI. And another, a Civil War vet: Ezram Josey, Company K, 35th Texas Cavalry, Confederate States of America. Then another: Ralph McGlathery, 4th Marine Division, Died July 5, 1944. The wind in the pine tops. Why? Why?

More homemade-looking stones, bearing the name Crabb. J. L., G. A., R. J., L. E., and L. F. Crabb, and all five died between 1931 and 1937. Then Peter Gray, 1853–1928. "Weep not," reads the stone, "he is at rest." So many gravestones say that. Why, then, do we weep? Morgan. Ashworth. Cooksey, Wilkerson. Dailey. Smith. Smith, Peter B. and Margaret E. He died in 1946, she in

1947. Another photograph set in stone,   a
high, stiff collar and Margaret E. in an os   i
they're sitting in an automobile you'd consider e   /25
or 1926 model. It has iron spokes in the steering w.   ɡaret
E. is in the driver's seat.

Houck. Ralston. Sparks. Webb. May. Jeffries. A fat-breasted robin made an awkward landing on the tombstone of James W. Jeffries, who died in 1927. And whose survivors caused to be carved in his monument: "Although he sleeps, his memory doth live." The robin let me get very close before he flew. Robins do that.

I had made a circle through the grounds, and come back to the live oak and Priscilla Morton's poem. A nest of sticks is high in that oak. A big nest, about sixteen inches across. While I watched, a crow flew out of it and flapped across a meadow and sat in a sweetgum and watched me until I left. The breeze came back through the pine tops. Ferguson. Norton. Matheson. Perry. Burros. Schultz. Farris. Watlington. Adams . . .

15

"Maude?
Whyn't you git Uncle Billy
to tell his story
about Gilbert sleepin'
with the
snake?"

Rowdy Pate looked up at me, from out of his black beard, and grinned and said, "Speaking of dogs." Nobody at all within ear-shot had spoken of dogs, but Pate needed to get the conversation steered toward a subject he loves. When I say Pate looked up at me, that was because he was squatting at a camp fire, and I was standing, and even then his head wasn't much below mine. Rowdy Pate is a mighty long and lean citizen.

I met him in the northwest part of Frio County last weekend, maybe sixty miles southwest of San Antonio. He lives and works in that brushy country. He has to do with cattle, as almost everybody in that region does. He is also a windmill mechanic. That strikes me as fitting work for a man built as tall as Pate. It's almost as if he could stand flat-footed and grease every mill in Frio County. He is also a fine cowboy. Down there in the Brush Country they laugh a little about the sight of Rowdy Pate on a horse, with his boots pretty near skimming the dirt. In pants—I expect he'll wonder where I got these numbers—he wears a thirty-two-inch waist and a forty-inch leg length.

"Let me tell you about my dog," he said, maybe five minutes after I'd met him. He has owned a couple of dogs so remarkable that what Pate says about them may challenge your belief.

"He was a pretty good old dog. I called him Birdsong. One time there was a mean Braymer bull in the river bottom and we wanted him out so we put old Birdsong on his trail. There was some wets (wetbacks) cuttin' mesquite in that bottom and they'd left a double-bit ax stickin' in a stump. Old Birdsong came arunnin' through there on the trail, and he hit that ax, and split himself right half in two.

"Well, I come along and found him there, in halves that way, and I gathered him up, and put him back together the best I could, and wrapped him up in a croaker sack and took him home. I sprinkled a little turpentine on him, and some tequila, and laid him down by the stove where he'd keep warm, and in two or three weeks he commenced to whine, and wiggle, and show signs of life.

"Then one day my wife hollered at me about a snake in the haystack, and I unwrapped old Birdsong to put him after that snake, and damn if I hadn't stuck him back together wrong, with half of him upside down. Two of his legs stuck up all the time, and the other two down. So for the rest of his life old Birdsong had to run on just two legs, but still he could hunt longer than any dog I ever owned because when the two legs he was runnin' on got tired, he'd just flip over, and run on the other two, and . . ."

Then there was another dog belonged to Pate, and his name was Rufus, who turned out to be too smart for his own good. "I had that Rufus dog not long after I got married," Pate said. "We were livin' then in the Hill Country, and times were close. I was doin' a lot of coon huntin' then, and sellin' furs. Rufus was a pretty smart old dog. Finally he got so smart, when he'd see me whittlin' on a board to stretch a hide on, he'd go out and catch me a coon to fit it. Well, one day my wife decided to have a little house cleanin', and she set the ironin' board outside. Old Rufus got one look at that ironin' board, and took off—and I haven't seen him since."

A few days ago when I was in Jasper, Landon Bradshaw told me the story about how his Uncle Royal Weatherford was baptized in George Nerrin's goose pond. It happened back about 1915, when Uncle Royal was around nineteen years old and living at Remlig. Remlig is a community in the north part of Jasper County. That name is Gilmer spelled backwards. It came from Alexander Gilmer Lumber Company, which once had a big sawmill there.

Seems one of the old-style brush arbor revival meetings was going on at Remlig when Royal Weatherford and Wilburn Martin got in this little discussion about a horse. Martin had a real salty horse he thought nobody else could ride. Weatherford didn't agree, and the pair made a dollar bet about the matter. So Weatherford got on the horse and won the bet. But winning it turned out to be a great deal of trouble. The animal took Weatherford for a mighty wild ride that ended in the brush arbor where the church service was fixing to wind up.

"The congregation was singing 'Why Not Tonight?' and the preacher was standing down in front to receive converts," Bradshaw told me. "Well, he looked up and all of a sudden here came Uncle Royal riding a bucking horse right down the sawdust aisle of the brush arbor." Wasn't anything for the preacher to do but run, and the congregation had to scatter as well.

It's very bad manners, I know, but at this point I challenged Bradshaw's story. Told him I hadn't ever seen a brush arbor high enough that a man could ride underneath one even on a calm horse, and if the horse was bucking and pitching, why it would surely put the rider's head and shoulders through the brush roof and just tear the place apart. Bradshaw looked at me in great disgust. "Well, I expect that's exactly what happened." And I could tell he was greatly disappointed in me, for bringing up such an unimportant point right in the middle of a story.

Anyhow, Royal Weatherford, as you might expect, ended up in considerable difficulty. The day after the incident, Wilburn Martin came to see Weatherford and said, "Well, you won the bet, so here's your dollar. You can use it to get out of jail because they've filed charges against you for riding a horse through the brush arbor during services."

Weatherford said, "I'm gonna get 'em to drop those charges."

"I bet you another dollar you can't," Martin said.

"It's a bet," Weatherford said.

So he went straight back to the brush arbor where the revival was still going on. (And where, I assume, all the damage done by the bucking horse had been patched up, but I decided not to mention that point.) At the close of the service Weatherford walked down the aisle and offered himself as a candidate for membership. It was the custom of that church to require testimony and confession. The meat of Weatherford's confession was that even a wild horse knew more about the good life than he did and had led him, bucking and pitching, straight down the aisle to the preacher.

"The confession was accepted," Bradshaw said, "and the charges dropped. And they baptized Uncle Royal in George Nerrin's goose pond." If you have ever had much to do with a small pond where a large number of geese stay, you know that getting baptized in one would be a considerable penance. Bradshaw said he's heard Uncle Royal (younger brother of his mother) tell this story many times, and when Bradshaw challenged the sincerity of that confession, his uncle would say, "Well, an entire church congregation accepted it, so why can't you?"

Friend of mine was telling me the other night why he won't go to the class reunions at his old school. It's because his principal entertainment now that he's in his twilight time, is telling stories about what happened back when he was young and full of sap. But he can't tell such stories at class reunions, because the audience there knew him from the jump, and can challenge what he uses for facts. The worst thing, he says, is telling one of your favorite stories and finding out, from somebody who was there when it happened, that it's not even true.

I am familiar, all right, with that problem. For example, the last time I went to a reunion at the old home town I found out that Ancil Owen did not really climb the north wall of the county courthouse that time in 1938. What a disappointment and an embarrassment it was, to learn that. I had been telling the story more than thirty years, until I knew every word of it was true as the first chapter in the Book of Genesis.

When the Human Fly came to our town that day, it was a large event. Streets and sidewalks around the courthouse were jammed by people come to see him perform. I expect they came from fifteen and twenty miles away, and of course Ancil Owen was there with all the others of us. He was one of my classmates.

The Human Fly was red-faced and balding and had a fair start on a pot belly. I don't guess he was a month less than sixty. All the Human Flies and Motorcycle Daredevils and Divers off High Places into Shallow Tanks were over the hill by the time they played our town.

The Human Fly warmed up that day by scaling the front of the pool hall there on the square. And he walked teeter-totter along the brick ledge across the top of the dry goods store. Then he walked a cable strung over the street from the bank to the drugstore. His finale was, he scaled the south wall of the courthouse, from the shrubbery to the very top.

He made that ascent slow and careful. Testing toe holds and hand grips. Sometimes hanging motionless outside the district courtroom for minutes, as if he was stumped and couldn't go any higher. Being careful now and then to let a foot slip, to get the proper gasp out of the crowd. When he was near the top, lacking only ten more tortuous feet, a small, round gnome-like face and a pair of skinny shoulders appeared just above the Human Fly on the courthouse roof. It was Ancil Owen.

"Hey, looky yonder on the roof! Who's that up pare?"

"It's ol' Ancil! How'd he git up pare?"

And the answer came out of somebody there in our bunch: "Why, he *climbed* up pare! He climbed the north wall and beat that Human Fly! Hey, Ancil? Way to go, Ancil!"

What a triumph. How delicious it was. There was ol' Ancil up pare waving at the crowd, looking down at the Human Fly and motioning, as if he was saying, "Come on up. The last ten feet's the easiest!" Ol' Ancil, one of our own kind. Wouldn't weigh 110 pounds. Played in the band. Didn't even come out for football, so nobody ever paid him much attention. Yet here he was climbing the courthouse and beating the Human Fly to the top. A victory for us all.

I have told that story I bet in twenty states and I know in two foreign countries. I told it so much I got so I was able actually to see Ancil Owen climbing that building. I can see him still, going up, in his yellow shirt and brown corduroy pants and black-and-white high-topped tennis shoes. Then to return to the scene and learn it never really happened, that was awful.

The pity is, it wasn't necessary for Ancil or anybody else to deny that story. The Human Fly climbed the south side of the building. So when he was climbing, the entire population of our county was standing on that side of the courthouse square. Not one human witness could have been left on the north side to say whether Ancil climbed the courthouse or not.

He's a pretty fair storyteller, but he has one serious shortcoming, which is that he shoots sometimes at the wrong target. He assumes a story that's well received by one bunch of listeners is going to be just as great an entertainment to the next bunch. It ain't necessarily so. Recently I heard him tell a long, looping yarn about the time his grandfather fell through the floor of the hayloft and landed on the buggy seat and what the old gent had to say when they came running to see if he had survived. What the old gent said is not allowable in your morning newspaper, but don't fuss, you are not missing much. When the storyteller delivered that precious quote, it sure fell on hard times and left nobody laughing but the storyteller himself.

You could see that puzzled him. He sat the next hour sort of behind a pot plant, looking dour and thoughtful. I started to go over and explain to him why the tale failed, but he didn't appear too receptive to criticism at the moment, so I let it go. I would bet you a blackland farm that the last time he told that story his audience was all family, people who had known the grandfather and loved the old boy and who'd heard the story a hundred times. Such an audience will listen and laugh at the same family tale unto eternity, but you mustn't expect that outsiders will do the same, because they won't.

I found this out in my early times from a family by the name of Dooley. They had a boy in my room at school, and sometimes I would go out to their place in the country to spend the night. There was a great gang of those Dooleys, from little babies up to high school seniors, and they were a close bunch.

On hot summer nights they would sit out in the yard after supper and talk and slap mosquitoes and shoo gnats. One night, I was there wih them and somebody spotted an orange light across the field, the other side of the creek about three-quarters of a mile away. This was a mystery because in those times you didn't see many lights that you couldn't identify. We began to speculate about that light. Some said it was moving, slow, and some said it was still. Some saw it hovering over the trees. Some said no, it was on the ground. Some said it was a night hunter with a carbide lamp on his cap. Some said it was a one-eyed Model T on the road, stopped with a flat. Mr. Dooley said it wasn't anything but a pocket of swamp gas.

Then one of the little girls, I guess about five, sang out in a high clear voice, *"It's Aunt Audrey on her mule!"* Which seemed to me a strange statement that didn't show a lot of quality, but to that gang of Dooleys it was a triumph. Every one of them joined into an ovation over that remark. They laughed and whooped and called hogs and slapped legs and stomped feet. They grabbed that child up and passed her around and tousled her yellow curls and told her she was *something*.

Now that impressed me. It was the first time I saw that making a simple remark of half a dozen short words could bring about such a great and sudden improvement in a person's public relations, and here it was being done by a five-year-old person, and a girl at that. I could use such a secret and I resolved to get it and I did, but it turned out to be only an inside joke, an ancient family story that wasn't worth a cup of clabber except on immediate kin, and even then it had to be applied with masterful timing.

Aunt Audrey had been a salty kind of woman three or four generations back. She had inspired a good deal of lore, including the tale of how she once went to a play party on a gray mule. She made herself a long white dress. She threw a halter on the mule. She hiked up her skirt and jumped astraddle and off to the party she rode.

A bunch of the children slept on the front porch that night, the way they used to do in summer. About 1 A.M. a couple of them saw this Thing, moving along the road. In the soft starlight, it was a blurry white form, floating over a gray blob and giving off a mournful noise. When the Thing turned in at the mailbox and came toward the house, the girls yelled "Ghost!" and caused a stampede. Every kid on the porch bolted. Some went as far as the barn. Some charged through the screen doors and into the house, knocking over cane chairs and stepping on cats and upending chamber pots. One almost fell into the cistern. All that memorable action, when the Thing was only Aunt Audrey coming home on her mule, humming a party tune.

So that's all there is to the tale, but always afterward when people in that family saw a ghosty thing in the night, they would say it was Aunt Audrey on her mule. If the line was delivered with the proper timing, as the little Dooley girl did that night, it would earn an ovation. From family members only, though. You mustn't bother the general public with inside stories like that, because they just won't play.

The letter was written with a pencil on a piece of tablet paper and it sure got my attention. It was from one Arp Harper, who does a lot of floundering down around San Luis Pass with a buddy of his named Doug Roberts. "Knowing that you are more than slightly countrified," the letter said, "I am writing you in the hope that you have heard lately of anybody having a female Leopard dog and a plain old setter dog that they would sell to me and my buddy for the purpose of breeding us a litter of some of your good flounder dogs . . ."

I had not ever heard of a flounder dog before, so I got hold of Harper to get him to explain a few facts to me, which he did as follows: "Me and my good old fishing buddy Doug Roberts have been gigging flounder down around Freeport for some years and we have always had us one of the best flounder dogs that a man would ever want to see or own. But we are now without a dog because our dog is now dead."

Harper told me the sad story of how that remarkable animal met his end, and I will pass it on later, but right now here is Harper explaining how to catch flounder with a flounder dog: "First off you got to have a sturdy blind, and it happens old Doug and me have got us one of your top flounder blinds just not too far from San Luis Pass. There is where we work out of and keep our decoys. We bait this place by broadcasting with ground corn. Horse and mule feed works good, but corn-fed flounder is your top flounder. What we use for decoys is brown Frisbees, driven into the sand with sixteen-penny nails.

"We always go down on a night that's real dark, and the wind has got to be out of the southeast and the tide coming in. As soon as we got there (back when old Stingray was alive, that is; Stingray was the name of that flounder dog), we would put old Stingray in the water and he was something to see, for he had legs thirty-seven inches long, a neck a foot long, and he could just naturally point them flounder. As soon as he hit the water he started working. He would go real slow to the outside of our line of decoys and ever so often he would put his head under the water easy like and then he'd bark, real fast. The reason he did this is because he would after a while drive all those flounder into a little circle about twelve feet across. When your flounder are what you call corraled that way, that is when your dog goes into his point. Head high out of the water and the right front leg stuck straight up in the air. Old Stingray was so strong we always hung a Coleman lantern on that leg.

"This is where me and old Doug come in. I get in the water right by old Stingray and Doug gets up on the sand. I start hollering and beating on a foot tub and Stingray sticks his head under the water and sets up a ferocious barking and howling. Those flounder just naturally head straight away from us and up on the sand, where old Doug has got himself a gig or a rake or a pitchfork and he will smooth be cleaning up on them flounder . . ."

Which I thought was a most interesting report indeed, for I hadn't any notion flounder were ever caught with a hunting dog that way. But now here is Arp Harper with the sad story of how Stingray died: "We had a rookie on a floundering expedition with us one night last spring and he run over our dog with Doug's old GMC pickup truck, while he was chasing some of them sideways-running crabs on the sand. I got me a small logging chain and I antiqued that rookie with it while Doug tried some mouth to mouth reviving on old Stingray. But a human being just can't do that on a dog because their lips is just too long and when you try to blow down their throat the air just naturally slips right out the sides of their mouth. However, the logging chain did work pretty well on the rook."

If you keep running around East Texas listening to tales out of the past, sooner or later you cut the trail of Uncle Abe Frisby. He was a justice of the peace at Trinity in the early part of this century, and has the distinction that he's the only JP in Texas who ever sentenced a citizen to the state penitentiary.

Story goes that he kept getting a certain party in his court on theft charges, and no amount of laying out fines in county jail seemed to discourage this party from stealing. Finally Uncle Abe pronounced him an habitual criminal and sentenced him to a term in state prison at Huntsville, twenty miles away. The fellow may well have deserved the sentence, but the trouble was that a justice of the peace is not empowered to hand out stretches in the pen.

You hear different versions of this tale. Uncle Abe was a sort of East Texas Judge Roy Bean, and a lot of yarns are told about him. The first time I heard the state pen story, I was told that the prisoner actually went behind the walls at Huntsville and served time. At Trinity I tried to locate Vard Cannon, after I heard he is considered the authority on Uncle Abe Frisby stories. Couldn't find him, though, so I asked Vernon Marie Fitzgerald Schuder at Riverside. She is a collector of tales too. She said no, Uncle Abe's prisoner did get out of the county on the way to Huntsville, but a county official up in Groveton heard about the sentence and sent a deputy to rescue him before he got put behind the Walls.

Uncle Abe was a great practical joker. As far as I know the penitentiary sentence was not one of his jokes. If it was, I doubt the prisoner saw much humor in it. But then victims of practical jokes seldom feel entertained or rewarded. There was the visiting preacher they tell about in Trinity County. He stayed with Uncle

Abe and Mrs. Frisby. Before he rode away, Uncle Abe hid some of his wife's silverware, and also some of her underwear, in the preacher's saddlebags. Then when the preacher had ridden a mile or two, Uncle Abe sent the law after him to arrest him for stealing.

Uncle Abe didn't always escape retaliation. One time he was out on a fishing trip with a bunch of his buddies and it was Uncle Abe's turn to make coffee. Everybody was sitting around talking about the flavor of the judge's coffee, when one fellow looked in the pot and found a couple of horse apples floating in it. His fishing pals held Uncle Abe down, removed all his clothes, and went home, leaving the justice of the peace out on the river buck naked. They did tell Mrs. Frisby, who took some clothes out there and found her husband. I expect he was glad to see her.

Another popular Uncle Abe story is about the time he went to Dallas to visit his daughter and grandson. He took the little boy for a streetcar ride across town. They got off and went around and bought some candy and soda pop, and when it came time to go home Uncle Abe was distressed to find only a dime left in his pocket. Which wasn't enough to buy a streetcar ride back across town for the both of them.

Anyhow, Uncle Abe took his dime, went in a store, and bought a tin cup. He borrowed a piece of paper and wrote a sign, "I am blind." He pinned the sign on his shirt and got his grandson to lead him up and down the sidewalk until he collected enough money in the cup for the streetcar ride home. At least that's how the story goes as I heard it. I would think that fifty years ago a dime would be plenty for streetcar fare, but let's not be picky and ruin the tale. I'd like to have met Uncle Abe, even if half of what I'd heard about him isn't true.

The most famous Texan who ever lived was Sam Houston. I think Lyndon Johnson would have to rank second. If you made me pick somebody for third, I would say Clyde Barrow, and Bonnie Parker fourth. Behind Bonnie I would list a string of professional football and baseball players, twelve or fourteen of them. Then would come people like Sam Rayburn and John Nance Garner, who would rank among the top five in most other states. But in Texas their fame is far outranked by that of the outlaws and the athletes.

Any system of ranking people according to how well they are known or remembered is of course subject to challenge. So I think my system is as good as any. I judge 'em by how often I hear their names mentioned as I go around the state. Sam Houston leads the crowd by a mile. He still has the clout to make a tree famous just because somebody suspects he once sat under it. Lyndon Johnson is strong but fading. I wouldn't be surprised if Clyde Barrow passed him up in another fifteen years. Johnson just didn't get around the state and leave tracks the way Houston and Barrow did.

Even before that movie was made about Bonnie and Clyde, I was forever impressed by how often I'd hear Barrow's name. At river ferries, country stores, hunting camps, rural crossroads, I've come to expect somebody to tell me, "Clyde Barrow and Bonnie Parker passed this way, in nineteen and thirty-three." You won't hear that said about any other Texans, except Sam Houston and maybe one of the football players, like Sammy Baugh. Bonnie Parker is fourth on my list because her name is spoken, almost every time, in the same breath with Clyde's. Jane Long, the Mother of Texas, is a pure unknown compared to Bonnie Parker.

You wouldn't ever guess what I saw the other afternoon in a house at Broaddus, little town up near Lufkin and San Augustine. I saw a remnant of Bonnie Parker's drawers, framed and hanging on a living room wall. It's in the weekend house of Evon and Dale Tisdale of Lufkin. Of course a story goes with the piece of Bonnie's drawers. The Tisdales told it to me.

In the spring of 1934, when Clyde and Bonnie were still helling around the countryside, I. M. Tisdale was running a general merchandise store at Broaddus. This was Dale Tisdale's father. He was around seventy then, and tapering down his career as a merchant. Store was thinly stocked. One afternoon a woman came in and asked for step-ins. (I will save the youngsters the trouble of looking up that term. My American Heritage Dictionary announces that step-ins are panties with wide legs. As opposed, I think you could say, to pull-ons, which had elastic in the legs and couldn't be just casually stepped into. Or out of, either.) Tisdale didn't have step-ins stocked, and told the woman so. She pointed to some pink ladies' underwear in a display case and asked, "What's that?"

"Those are bloomers," Tisdale said.

"You got a pair of scissors?" the woman asked. So while Bonnie Parker stood in Tisdale's General Merchandise and held those bloomers, I. M. Tisdale used his scissors to convert them into step-ins, according to Bonnie's instructions.

Tisdale followed her when she went out, close enough that he recognized Clyde Barrow waiting in a car, his machine-gun showing through the window. When Clyde drove away, Tisdale took the leg pieces he'd cut, put them in an envelope, marked it "Bonnie Parker's," and stowed it in his safe. His son still has the envelope and one of the bloomer legs, framed, with a note his father wrote the summer of 1934: "I cut these bloomers for Bonnie Parker, Clyde's wife, in the spring of '34, a short time before she and Clyde were killed in Louisiana by officers." (I don't think Clyde and Bonnie ever married, but never mind.)

It's stuff like that, that gets Bonnie the fourth spot on my list of famous Texans. I'd bet a two-dollar bill she's the only Texas woman who ever had the legs of her drawers locked in a safe or framed and hung on a living room wall. What happened to the drawers leg that Dale Tisdale doesn't have? He isn't certain, but he suspects his father sold it. He does remember this, that back there in the deeps of the depression when thirty-five cents would buy a square meal, a traveling salesman offered Tisdale twenty-five dollars for one leg of Bonnie Parker's bloomers.

A lot of Nacogdoches people still like to tell the story of how Groucho Marx once tossed insults at a local audience from the stage of the Opera House on Main Street, and how an East Texas mule exerted his influence on the show-business career of the Marx Brothers.

When I was up that way recently, I went to see Aaron Cox, Nacogdoches banker, who has a great interest in things that happened in his town's past. He walked with me to the corner of Main and Church Street, where the Opera House building is. Of course it's been remodeled. There's a furniture store in it now. The upstairs— where the Marx Brothers thing happened—is used for storage. Around in back you can see some of the original brick of the building. It was built in 1888. It's owned now by Robert N. Cason, who has an office just behind it. Cox and I went to see him a minute. He brought out photos of the Opera House as it looked when new. The theater was upstairs. The lower floor housed stores from the beginning.

Cason has a newspaper clipping that says the Marx Brothers' Nacogdoches performance was in 1916. Cason said he's always thought it was earlier. But in his fine and funny book, *Life with Groucho*, Arthur Marx wrote that the Marx Brothers scored their first big comedy success in New York show business in 1919. So 1916 for the Nacogdoches happening seems about right to me.

In the act that came to the Opera House were Groucho and his brothers Harpo and Gummo and a girl named Janie O'Riley. They were not comedians but singers, and evidently not too hot. Because during a matinee performance their entire audience jumped up and left the Opera House to see a runaway mule going through town.

This made Groucho and his brothers furious. When the audience drifted back into the seats, the Marx Brothers began insulting them. The performers quit singing and began calling Nacogdoches citizens damyankees and other names a good deal worse. Groucho himself composed little rhymes, ad lib, and spit them at the customers. Simple stuff like "Nacogdoches is full of roaches." (In that book, Arthur Marx said it's just as well most of those Nacogdoches insults can't be remembered.) Anyhow, the audience thought the insults were funny. They howled, applauded for more. And went home happy and entertained.

After that afternoon in Nacogdoches, the Marx Brothers never again appeared as serious singers. They immediately adopted the crazy, ad libbing style of comedy that took them on to great success, and the beginning of it was the stage of the Opera House. Before Nacogdoches, the Marx Brothers were struggling unknowns. Their next date was at Denison, where they worked up a school-room comedy act because the audience included a lot of teachers in town for a convention. Groucho borrowed a frock coat to play the part of a schoolmaster. He also wore the fake mustache. Both these remain his trademarks. After Nacogdoches, the Marx Brothers were plenty popular comedians and played a wide circle of Texas theater dates before heading back north to become known all over the world.

It's just like I keep trying to tell 'em around the office. You can't hardly overestimate the influence of a Texas mule.

Uncle Billy Crockett used to tell the story of how he got Aunt Mary Wilson to keep her chickens penned up without making her mad at him. Something that came to me lately in the mail has caused me to remember the tale.

When Uncle Billy was forty-five, he was still a bachelor and living alone on a little place in Palo Pinto County. Aunt Mary Wilson lived just across the road. She was called Aunt Mary Wilson by the family even after she married the second time and her name was no longer Wilson.

About a year before the happening of the chicken story, her

husband Fletcher was breaking ground behind a red mule and a streak of lightning came down and sent him to glory. Killed him and the mule both, and ruined a Georgia stock plow not three years old. So at the age of thirty-eight, I believe it was, Aunt Mary Wilson became a real pretty widow woman. That attracted Uncle Billy's notice, him living just across the road, so close and all.

After a proper waiting time, which was something on the order of a year, Uncle Billy got to sparking around over there at Aunt Mary Wilson's. She kept a dozen big old fat Rhode Island Red hens, and sold eggs. She milked a couple of Jersey cows, and churned every day, and sold butter. That's how she got by. Uncle Billy would stop on his way home and get eggs, and generally he'd stay a lot longer than it took to buy a dozen eggs. Or a pound of butter, either.

Uncle Billy was what we called working off the place. He wasn't much on farming. He came from cattle people and stayed ahorseback all his life. He'd buy a few steers when he had grass on his place, but mainly he worked for other folks. At the time I am speaking of, he was looking after some cows for the Ledbetters over on Palo Pinto Creek. He'd ride off before day and come back in the evening, a lot like a man going to work in an office or store.

You wouldn't catch Uncle Billy keeping chickens or milking cows. But he loved a garden. In the spring he'd work up a garden and grow the prettiest roasting ears, and tomatoes, and cucumbers, and squash, and peas. And most of it he'd give away. The women would brag on how pretty it all was, and that was important.

Well, the spring after Fletcher Wilson got struck by lightning that time, Aunt Mary Wilson got to turning her old hens loose so they could rustle during the day. And they'd go singing across the road and get in Uncle Billy's fresh-planted garden and scratch it up. He'd come home from the pasture over on the creek and his corn he'd planted would be dug up and gobbled down by those old red biddies of Aunt Mary Wilson's. They'd scratch his tomato plants out, and his squash seed, and it was sure aggravating. But he wasn't real keen on complaining about those hens. He had a notion or two about Aunt Mary Wilson and wanted to stay on her good side. He replanted that garden four or five times, trying to keep from making that woman mad at him.

The last time he came in and found the garden scratched up again, he had this idea that I started out to tell you about. He took half a dozen nice big kernels of corn, and punched holes in them with a coarse needle. Through the hole he stuck good stout thread, and tied on standard shipping tags. He spent two hours sitting by a coal oil lantern that night, writing messages on those shipping tags. Next morning before he went to the pasture, he flung those corn kernels in the garden. Here came Aunt Mary Wilson's hens. They gobbled down the corn that Uncle Billy had sowed. When they went home, six of them had shipping tags hanging from their beaks. With little messages like, "I have scratched in Billy Crockett's garden." And, "I am a bad hen. Keep me home."

Uncle Billy replanted his garden. No hens came to scratch it up. And he was married in the fall, after the chicken story happened in the spring. He was together with his wife thirty years. We never called her anything but Aunt Mary Wilson.

On cold nights in the country, we would sit around the fireplace after supper, and pop popcorn, and sing songs, and this was the kind of night Uncle Billy Crockett would tell about the gunfight. It is not the classic American West type of gunfight story, and in fact it was not so much of a story at all. But we loved it because it added an expression to the family's language.

At the time I am talking about, some of our clan had moved out of the country into towns. Towns of 1,500 and 2,000 folks, with brick schools, and county jails, and picture shows. So they had got acquainted with fast-draw men in cowboy shows, such as Buck Jones and Tim McCoy. They would return to the country and ask Uncle Billy if he ever saw a gunfight. Because Uncle Billy went way, way back, and he had seen a great deal.

"The closest we got to a real gunfight in this country," he would begin, "was between Jessie McBride and Floyd Judson, when I was a boy . . ." You understand I have to reconstruct the story the best I can, because I don't recall it exactly, and I don't even remember the right names. I have just put in names that seem to fit. "The McBrides had killed hogs," Uncle Billy would go on, "and they ran short of salt. So Jessie McBride sent that youngest boy of his, Tolly, to the Judson place to get salt. Sent him horseback."

"Wasn't anything the matter with Tolly McBride except he was awful young, and he wasn't a very thoughtful boy. He trotted up to the Judson house and hello'd and said his pa had sent him to borrow forty bushels of salt. Floyd Judson said to him, 'Tolly, don't you reckon your pa meant forty pounds?' And Tolly said, 'No, he said forty bushels. Guess I better get forty bushels.' Floyd went ahead and gave him salt, not so much that he couldn't carry it behind his saddle, and Tolly rode on back home.

"Well, there was a good deal of laughing about that among the Judsons, about Tolly McBride riding five miles horseback to get forty bushels of salt, which would have been enough to salt the Clear Fork of the Brazos. And Jessie McBride finally got mad about Floyd and the other Judson boys telling the story, and making fun of the boy, and he threatened to shoot Floyd about it. So that's how the gunfight came up. They kept trading insults, and finally they made it up to meet at ten o'clock Saturday morning and shoot it out at Burnt Stump, which was a place people knew about on the creek, and had picnics there and all.

"Not many folks thought the fight would ever come off, because the McBrides and the Judsons were similar, in ways. They were quick about bristling up but fast about cooling down when they saw serious trouble coming. All the same, a pretty good crowd came to Burnt Stump. I was there myself, with a big cottonwood picked out to get behind.

"Some were surprised that Jessie and Floyd put in an appearance, but they did, and with shotguns. Not pistols, like your cowboys in moving picture shows. We weren't much on short arms. In this country sometimes you'd see a Colt's revolver in a dresser drawer, or a Winchester on the wall, but mostly these were shotgun people. Jessie and Floyd squared it off I guess about a hundred steps apart, and they'd glare at each other, and spit, and pace around, and check their guns, and look up at the road, and then the sheriff came. He didn't even get off his horse. He announced there wasn't going to be any gunfight and we could all go home. And that was about all there was to the fight."

Uncle Billy would wait then until somebody asked the question, "How did the sheriff find out about the gunfight?"

"He told Papa," Uncle Billy would answer, "that two people came to his house, one right behind the other, early that morning before day, and told him there was going to be a gunfight at Burnt Stump that ought to be stopped. One of them was Floyd Judson. And the other was Jessie McBride."

But what the family loved best about the story was the salt. To this day, when we're confronted with an impossible or ludicrous circumstance, we say it's like going horseback after forty bushels of salt.

Uncle Billy Crockett used to tell great panther stories. When my bunch was coming up in the country, all the good storytellers leaned toward panthers. I suppose that was because a panther was the final word in a thing to be afraid of. I've wondered in trying to reconstruct Uncle Billy's tales why he didn't tell stories about bears, or wolves. He never did. If he reached back to get a prime story, it would be about a panther every time.

He would have surely known wolves. Maybe not so much bears. Bears were mostly back east of us in the timber, I guess. But wolves, yes, because consider the years that produced his stories. He was talking mainly of his young manhood, when he was between twenty and thirty and was working for those big cattle people. His favorite story settings would be draws and ravines and box canyons and dry creek beds, riding alone, staying out days at a stretch without seeing another rider. That had to be around 1880, 1890. Sure there were wolves.

But for the purpose of stories, a wolf wasn't anything to a panther. It wasn't even as good as a snake. Uncle Billy was the devil on snake tales, too. Anything poisonous that way was good. Or even ordinary stinging propositions such as red ants and yellow-jackets and your common bumblebee. If you laughed when he named bumblebees, he would tell you again how he was blinded for twenty-four hours by a squadron of those evil-tempered insects. His old pony spooked. Because of a snake, he expected, but he never did see it because he was in flight. Pony pitched him into some catclaws and he must have landed with his nose in a bumblebee hole. Here they came out, little streaks of lightning in single file. Zump zump zump zump zump zump. Right between the eyes, the way they like to get you. Within half an hour he couldn't see. Eyes swelled tight shut. Sat there all night, blind as a mole. Don't tell *him* about bumblebees.

But mostly it was panthers. The only things that ranked anywhere in the neighborhood of panthers were mystery lights and apparitions.Things that challenged belief and defied explanation. Like the midnight gravedigger. Uncle Billy saw the gravedigger when he was riding along the turnrow of Milton Talbert's south field. Milton had corn there that year. Cutting through, along that turnrow, saved nearly a mile on the way home. He was coming from a play party at midnight.

"All of a sudden I saw this light off there to the west a little way, in that timber the other side of the fence." I am trying to remember his words, but of course I won't get them all just exactly the way he said them. "It wasn't your common light. It wasn't a campfire and it sure wasn't any coal oil lantern and it wasn't a carbide, either. It was too white, with a green touch.

"I climbed through the fence and saw a ghost digging a grave. I say a ghost. I don't know what else to say it was. It was wispy and glowing. It seemed to have a head and arms and a body. Not much on the question of legs. I called it digging a grave because of the way it moved its arms, like it was spading, and pitching out the dirt, and going deeper, and deeper, and finely it disappeared in the hole."

Then one of the men would snort and ask Uncle Billy what was in the jug that was passed around at that play party. Uncle Billy would guarantee no jug was passed. "I went back to the place the next morning and couldn't find any sign, except a kind of burnt place on the grass."

The panther stories all had a common thread. Which was that a panther liked to follow a man who was horseback. One would lope along behind, and if the rider slowed the panther would slow. If the rider stopped the panther would stop. Somewhere in the stories the panther would squall. And it would sound like a woman screaming.

Uncle Billy had been followed by "many a panther." He had felt the trembles in his belly when they squalled. He could copy a panther squall himself, and the sound would give you a thrill in the neck. He knew panther ways. How they almost never attacked human beings. But when one did, Uncle Billy knew about it, and was not far off when it happened. He could give you places, names, times. The depth of scratches, and how long they took to heal.

The men who sat on the porch would say it was strange, how Uncle Billy always had his panther experiences alone, never when anybody was with him. Those of us who sat in the shadows and held our breath during the stories, we couldn't see how it would make any difference whether anybody was with Uncle Billy or not.

The time of day I loved the most on the farm was after supper in summer, when we would all go out and be together on the front porch, to talk and to wait for dark and bedtime. The men would smoke and cough and deliver opinions. The women, tired-faced, still with their aprons on, would nod and agree, mostly, with what the men said. The younguns would play sheep board down, or one of those other running-hiding-chasing games. Or we'd catch lightning bugs in fruit jars. Or lie on the hard-packed clay of the yard at dusk and watch the bullbats dive, and hear the curious hum they make. Or we'd listen for owls.

On the porch somebody would say, "Maude? Whyn't you git Uncle Billy to tell his story about Gilbert sleepin' with the snake?"

There would be quiet snorts and chuckles and Maude would say, "I'm not sure he feels like talkin' that much. He ate that purple onion at dinner and he's been holdin' his stomach all afternoon."

"Well, ask him. Might make him feel better, to talk some."

After Uncle Billy got so he couldn't hear normal noises, they'd talk about him that way as if he was off somewhere else. When he was right there on the porch, in his rocking chair the women would bring out so he could sit with everybody.

"Uncle Billy?" Maude would get down close, and speak loud and distinct, right into his little old pink ear. "Uncle Billy!? They want you to tell about Gilbert and the snake that time!"

Maude would retreat from his ear and swing around to face him square, to see if he was receiving. He would blink, and make his white mustache go up and down. He'd say to Maude then, all weak and trembly, "A snake?"

"Yes! A big old *rattler*, remember? You and Gilbert were pickin' cotton on the Slaughter place? And you spent the night in the field? And slept in the turnrow? And Gilbert wrapped up in a wagon sheet, and that big old snake crawled up in there with him? *You* remember that. Used to tell it all the time."

She'd swing round again to check reception, and you could see she was getting through. Uncle Billy would be leaning forward a little, and making his mustache jump, trying to get something said. Finally he'd get it out, all high and croaky. "That was Gilbert."

Maude would brighten then. "It sure was, Uncle Billy! It was sure Gilbert, all right. Now, do you want to tell about the snake?" There'd be no response, right away, and Maude would turn to the others and say, "I don't think he's gonna be able to tell it."

Then one of the men would strike a kitchen match, pop it into flame off the metal suspender button on his overalls, and he'd light a Bull Durham cigarette and his face would show eerie and orange in the dying light. "Well," he'd say, "he dang sure *used* to could tell it." And another: "You can cut a watermelon on that. Used to throw them play parties? At the Huckabays and the Wheelers. And Walker Taylor's bunch used to have 'em. Wouldn't a *one* of them party people go home without they'd heard Uncle Billy tell that snake story." Then another: "Old Tyler Duggan, he used to say he'd give a wooden leg to have Uncle Billy tellin' that story on one of them Victrola records."

In the gaps between the comments you'd begin to hear little noises coming out of Uncle Billy, and he'd be over there trying to tell the story again. "We was just big old boys. Gilbert and me

. . ." He talked so dim and scratchy. "Pickin' for Old Man Jim Copeland at Chalk Bluff . . ." He'd bog down a minute, and stop, and try to get himself collected to go on.

Somebody would say, "He's telling it Chalk Bluff, at Copeland's. That snake thing didn't happen at Chalk Bluff, it was on the Slaughter place."

"Well, he's just mixed up." One of the women. "He gets mixed up. Law, yesterday you know who he thought I was? Aunt Rose Dean. It was plum ghosty. I walked in there to the east room, where Maude sits him in the sun a while after his bath? He looked me right between the eyes and he said, 'Rose Dean, honey, I hadn't seen you in so *long.*' Made me want to go off and cry. Aunt Rose Dean's been gone how long—twenty years? Law."

So they'd talk, not having patience enough to wait on Uncle Billy to get his story going. But he'd sit over there and try. ". . . we taken the notion to sleep there in the field, and not walk them six miles to the house . . . We was pickin' for a dime a hundred and furnish your sack . . . Was it Copeland's? . . ."

But his audience wouldn't wait. Maude would fuss at them some. "Now y'all wanted to hear him. Now be quiet and let him tell it." He couldn't keep it in gear, though. He'd get off on trying to decide whether it was a wagon sheet or a cotton sack that Gilbert slept in, there in the turnrow, and the folks on the porch would talk about how long Aunt Rose Dean had been gone. "Twenty years my foot. It's anyway twenty-five because at Aunt Rose Dean's funeral I was expectin' with Willis Junior (they could always date events from pregnancies that way) and he'll be twenty-six on the fourteenth day of next September." They would do that, while Uncle Billy struggled to get his story out, and no-body would be listening except maybe Maude.

One time they got into a discussion about how old he was. Nobody knew for sure how old Uncle Billy was. Records weren't well kept when he began. But I remember somebody saying he used to talk about helping to build the barn when he was a boy. So he was older than the barn. To me that was something, that a living person could be older than that barn. I didn't imagine humans could have knowledge of a grander structure. I supposed it had been there always, towering above windmills and tall trees and Egyptian pyramids. I didn't doubt it was the first thing Noah and his gang saw, sticking out of the water when the Flood was draining off. And Uncle Billy, older than the barn. They'd all be talking there on the porch, and Uncle Billy would be toiling still over his snake story. He'd be along toward the end, I guess, where Gilbert had discovered what had crawled into the cotton sack with him to sleep.

One night I saw the end of the snake story. Didn't *hear* it, now. I never did *hear* the end. Suddenly Uncle Billy's face contorted. His little old body began to shake. His arm, which had been gesturing before him, trembled all out of control. Was he having some awful rigor? And would he die of it, right there on the porch among his people? No, what he was doing, he was laughing. Uncle Billy Crockett, older than the barn, laughing, laughing about his own story that nobody heard. Because by then they'd have forgotten all about him. They'd be off onto other matters, saying things like, "Is that lightnin' yonder in the northeast? Wouldn't you know. And me with hay on the ground."

16

"I was at peace, chiseling bricks."

Not long ago I was among a little bunch of people sitting in a reception room outside a suite of offices, waiting to see a gent who's a plenty successful businessman. He came out to meet us, the way a lot of them do now. He shook hands all around, and sat down—you could tell he meant to perch with us for just a couple seconds before getting back to his lair—sat down on a little old piece of mod furniture that was trying to pass for a chair, and it tipped backward with him. He went flat on his keester. Now that's a stern test of a man's poise. Here he is one second full of cool and confidence, greeting the public, and suddenly he's sprawled on the carpet in his own reception room, before an audience.

I thought he recovered beautifully. I wish I could do a thing like that as well. He quickly rose to a sitting position but didn't scramble on up. He sat there a second or so, hands on knees, and grinned. Then he said to the receptionist, "Let's get rid of this thing. I don't mind it throwing me, but I sure don't want it spilling one of my customers." Then he got up and continued visiting and I swear he didn't even get the least bit red in the face. I admire that. He's the kind of citizen who could go to dinner at a U.S. senator's house and tip a glass of red wine onto the table cloth and it wouldn't much bother him. Or if it did, he wouldn't let it show.

I've admired poise in the face of embarrassment ever since I first recognized it, which I think was in about the second grade when a little old skinny kid whose name I can't remember tore a hole in the seat of his pants. In that generation of younguns, a hole in the seat of the britches was an awful blow. It carried a double dose of humiliation—not just that a private part of your body was exposed, although that was bad enough. It also reflected your family's financial position, meant you had to wear old and thin pants, and sometimes you just sat the seat out of them.

Your classmates would be considerate enough to sing out, "Needles, thread, thimbles, stitches, I see a hole in Billy Bob's britches." It took a pretty strong spirit inside an eight-year-old boy from a poor family to stand up under taunts like that. This little kid I am thinking about did it, though. Stood up proud and straight and walked to the blackboard and wrote spelling words with that hole in his britches looking at the class and he didn't even flinch. That was unbelievable to me. At that time a hole in the seat of my pants would have sent me home holding a speller across my behind.

In later times, the traditional test of composure under fire was provided, to boys, by the open fly. I don't know what it was for girls, but I'm sure it was something equally horrible. You'd be standing up in front of a class trying to give your current event or your book report, and you'd notice all the girls looking out the window and the boys sniggering into their grimy fists, and suddenly you knew, that your pants were unbuttoned.

So you'd stand there under torture and try to think of the choices open to you. You could turn around and fix yourself, which probably was the best course. But I'm talking about times before zippers. You couldn't just zip up, you had maybe six buttons to worry with, and in a nervous condition you were apt to have fumbly fingers and take more time than you could bear to get things secured. Or you could tough it out, and try to be defiant like the little boy with the hole in the seat of his pants, or cool and smiling like the business executive sprawled on the carpet. What most of us did was just stand and suffer.

There's this little bunch of middle-aged guys I get together with sometimes. We sit loose, and cut up old scores, and make short trips into the past, to the years when we were a lot younger, and freer, and not as well fed. At these gatherings we may speak of almost anything, without reason or excuse or advance notice. Like the other night we talked about fist fights we have seen, and about getting scared out of our hide by tough guys we thought were going to whip us.

Men talk quite a bit, when they get away from their women, about fighting. I think the reason is that when a man goes forth into public, there is always the chance he'll be obliged to fight before he gets home. Either that or walk away from a fight, and I have never managed to figure out which is worse. I doubt very many guys really worry about this possibility, at least not as long as they stay among bright lights where people generally behave in a civilized manner. But that remote possibility is always there, and it is one load a man carries that a woman does not.

At the gathering, one of the questions that came up was this: Of all the troublesome guys you meet in public, which general type do you consider to be the most dangerous? You might imagine a common answer was, "The biggest one in the bunch, of course." Not so. We agreed almost unanimously that the guy who scares us the most is the small and wiry one, with sharp elbows and lean arms and cold hard eyes. I wonder if you can see the type. I can spot one across a room, and feel that he'd hurt you if he had just a hint of a reason.

It's common to make jokes about getting scared by a big mean man the size of a small barn. But if you gave me a choice, I would ten times rather have trouble with the big man than the small one with the hard eyes. I tell you why. Even among brawlers there is honor, and pride. A huge man isn't likely to feed his pride by knocking my teeth out when he stands six inches taller and outweighs me by a hundred pounds, so he is more apt to brush me aside and forget the trouble. He may, in fact, have practiced self-restraint all his life, in the knowledge that he could kill a man with his great strength.

The small wiry guy hasn't got any such governor. Being smaller and lighter than the average fellow, and having entered the world wearing a bad disposition, he's got a chip on his shoulder about like a hub cap. No man is too big for him, and few are too small. And he is a whole lot more likely to know how to fight than the big man is. Sure he is, because he got whipped a lot when he was a kid in school and finally went to somebody who knew how to box and learned a few things. Even just the basics of boxing can enable a small man to lay a bigger one absolutely waste, if the big man knows nothing at all about self-defense.

I don't mind admitting I often avoid the slender, quick-handed, chip-shouldered fellows, especially in places where any drinking is going on. They seem wired for automatic trouble just as soon as the second round is served. A man's expression, I know, is not always an easy thing to read. But I have looked pretty close at a few of these wiry brawlers when they're primed on a couple of beers, and they have disturbing faces. I find in their eyes a sort of anxious darkness, of the same kind you see when looking into gun barrels.

Monday morning one of my fellow workers came waltzing in with about half a grin on his face and a little light in his eye, and so of course I asked him what had happened. I knew something was bound to have happened because ordinarily he doesn't come in grinning and gleaming that way, not on Monday morning.

He said he was feeling good because he'd been mad at his neighbor for about six months and finally they'd called off the feud and shook hands and it was a big relief, not being mad. Made him feel good, Monday morning or not. He didn't tell me what the fuss was about, but I understand the feeling. Made me think of the year I spent being mad at Jimmy the Storekeeper. Did I ever tell you about that?

Jimmy had this little store, sort of a mom-and-pop operation, with a couple of sons and a daughter to sack potatoes and punch the cash register, and they made a nice bunch, all working together that way. I liked to go in there and spend my money because everybody would have something to say, and those youngsters were good workers and knew how to meet people and how to say thank you. Then too, like a lot of old-fashioned businesses, the store had become a sort of social center. Jimmy had a small space toward the back he kept clear, and he put some saggy old cane-bottomed chairs around, and the customers would get back there and jaw and tell stories and it was all right.

Well, one day Jimmy and I got crossways with each other over some little old something didn't amount to a dime's worth of liver. I was feeling punk, and I expect Jimmy was too, and we got to arguing about the price of an item I was buying, and first thing you know we were serious and mad. I told him I kind of liked to be treated with courtesy when I spent my money. He said if I didn't like the way I was being treated I could go somewhere else. I said I might do that. He said go ahead, that he could get along without my business. I said he was sure gonna have a chance to see. He said that was fine with him, and I went out.

For almost a year I didn't go back. I wasn't mad anywhere near that long, though. In fact I was mad less than a week. But the first four days, I was *really* mad. I mean the anger just spewed out of me, flaming and smoking, and I got a grand satisfaction from it. I was able to see during those first four days that Jimmy had made himself one big mistake, and he would be sorry. Almost every hour I thought of something else he would be sorry about, losing my business that way. Think of this, I would say. He just may find out he has lost more than one guy's trade. Because there were witnesses to that little scene, pal, witnesses. Likelihood was that they wouldn't want to keep trading with Jimmy after they'd heard him talking that way to a longtime customer. So staying mad for four days wasn't any strain or inconvenience.

The fifth day, though, the bloom began to fade from my wrath. After that I had to invest energy and thought into keeping the furnace hot. I would re-enact the scene, for example, between Jimmy and me and have myself making remarks far more cutting and poisonous than I really had. That would renew the tempest within me. But overnight it would grow calm, and I'd need to work harder at it each day.

I became discouraged. I would drive by the store about five-thirty when the stories were best, and Jimmy's parking lot would be full of cars. Hurt my feelings. You mean they were going ahead without me, the same as ever?

I tried other places, but the crowd was different and the stories bland. At that time I was fishing a lot, and Jimmy's was always my last stop on the way fishing. I'd get ice there, and similar necessities, and we'd say funny things to each other, and it was part of my recreation, stopping at that store. I didn't enjoy going fishing as much after Jimmy and I had the falling out.

So it was a hard year, I tell you. Listen, trying to stay mad at a friend for a whole year is *work*. I finally quit. I couldn't carry the burden. One afternoon I went back to the store and stuck out my hand and told Jimmy I was tired, that I didn't want to be mad any longer. He said he was tired too, and welcome back. After that we never mentioned the matter again.

A sister of mine who lives in Fort Worth flew down to Houston on Christmas Eve with a fruitcake and several gifts in her luggage. One of the presents was a new yo-yo, a sort of joke gift she meant for me. She had a hard time passing the security check at the airport. They sent her purse and carry-on luggage through the test chute several times, and bingo, the warning light kept coming on. Finally they had to open up her bag and ferret out the problem. And it was that yo-yo. It's mostly plastic but it's got a metal shaft.

That tickles me a little, to know that all the marvels of technology and logistics necessary to getting a great airliner off the ground can be frustrated by a new yo-yo in the handbag of a trim little Fort Worth widow. It's the best yo-yo I ever owned.

The reason it was brought to me, this sister used to sit and count long ago when I was trying to set the world's yo-yo record. At least that is what I thought. I had a good many curious notions about the world at that time, which was in 1929, I guess, or 1930. That must have been when the yo-yo craze was working up steam. And young citizens the nation over were standing around playing with wooden spools on a string.

In the beginning a yo-yo could be bought for a quarter or maybe even less. (My new one cost $1.29. I knew you were going to ask.) All the early yo-yo did was roll down the string, and back up again. You would stand for an hour yo-yoing up and down, up and down. And counting the times. At last that got dreary, and some of the sharper operators created variations. They would make the yo-yo loop the wrist, or they would throw it up instead of down, or flick it out to the side from time to time as they walked along.

Then homemade yo-yos began to appear. Some were oversized and hand-painted with floral designs or funny faces. The long-string yo-yo made a brief flash on the scene. This was a yo-yo with a string much longer than standard. Maybe six feet. So it could not be thrown straight down unless the operator had altitude. For instance, he might stand on the top step of a high-porched house.

I remember an exciting day in Fort Worth. Two high school

boys had made a yo-yo about two feet in diameter, and undertook to operate it at the school on Saturday morning. That thing was loaded with goodness knows how many feet of string. Sash cord, I think. They got up on a fire escape landing at the third-floor level of the school. A pretty nice crowd gathered to watch the experiment. Which failed. That giant yo-yo was a winner at going down, but it never would climb back up. Some basic law of physics, installed ages ago by the maker of the universe, probably doomed that experiment before it was hatched. But that's all right. It needed to be tried.

I haven't been able to find out exactly when it came, but some time in the thirties a breakthrough in yo-yoing was made. It had to do with the way the string was attached to the shaft. Instead of just knotting or noosing it, some guy had the idea to separate the strands of the string and, in effect, insert the shaft between them. This gave him a loose connection down there, so that when the yo-yo was flung down, the shaft would slip and spin and just hang there, spinning. Then, before it lost momentum, the operator could give a certain little tug on his string and the yo-yo would climb back up.

I expect it was a pretty nice little thrill for the person who made that discovery. Because there is a huge satisfaction in operating a yo-yo in this way. You get the feeling that you are challenging physical laws, and winning. It's an ego booster, that you can make the yo-yo stay at the end of the string and spin, or bring it back up as you choose. So long as you don't let it run out of steam and die before you call it back.

This split-string method of tying gave a new dimension to yo-yoing. It made all manner of fancy yo-yo stunts possible. Round the world. Walk the tight rope. Climb the ladder. Dozens of them. And so yo-yoing has never died. Even today you will find widows in places like Fort Worth buying $1.29 yo-yos for younger brothers fifty-four years of age.

It's like I've been trying to tell you for ten years now, everything is being controlled by these condemned computers. Business, government, your own personal affairs, nothing escapes the affliction of computeritis. A few days ago I got a letter from a department-store computer about a bill that I do not owe it. Nevertheless, it wants me to pay. I have written back and tried to tell it that the bill does not exist and therefore is impossible for me to pay. I have little hope the matter will ever be resolved.

Let me quote directly the first paragraph of what the computer wrote. (Notice that this machine, as many letters as it writes now, has not learned how to punctuate around the conjunction "however," and has also stuck a hyphen in a curious place in the phrase "up to date." Don't you agree that if computers are to handle correspondence they ought to be taught precise English?)

"Your payment of $13.74 is appreciated, however, it does not bring your account up-to date, and $0.00 is still past due and must be paid." In the remainder of the letter, the computer lectures me about my bill-paying habits. It makes clear that I should pay it $0.00 immediately, if I want to maintain a good credit standing "with us."

That "with us." I understand well enough what that means. That means it and all the other computers that are running the store. It does not mean the store at all, in my view. I do not believe there is a living creature at that store who knows that the computer has sent me a dun for $0.00 and demanded that I pay immediately. Because I know that store, from way back when real people wrote its letters. I studied the pictures in its mail-order catalogue before I could read. Listen, in 1929 when I was eight years old I received a hand-written letter from this store, about an air gun I had ordered for $2.19. "Dear Mr. Hale," the letter began. *Mister!* The first time in this life I was called mister. I took the letter to school, and showed it around. The people at that store, far away, *cared* about me.

But now I write to computers. And this one is scolding me, giving me its little sermon about keeping my nose clean. Saying it wants me to have "the full benefit of a satisfactory account, but this is not possible unless you pay as you agreed." Of course I did not agree to pay a bill for $0.00, but that is a detail the computer doesn't care about.

I hear you talking: "Well, big deal, it's a mistake, your being dunned for zero dollars. Just forget it. No harm done." My experience with computers tells me I am not sure no harm has been done. I suspect that deep in the entrails of that machine, forever and ever, will remain a record of the fact that I am a welsher, and won't pay my bills.

Let us say that fifteen years from now I want to buy another air gun. By then air guns will be high as smoke, and I will need to pay it out by the month, under contract. So all the computers will meet, and pool their circuitry, and scan the application, and the chaircomputer will say, "Well, shall we enter into the contract, and let him have his air gun? He seems to have kept his nose clean all these years." But one old rusty computer in the back will light up, and whir hoarsely: "No, wait. In the spring of 1979 this guy was sent a dun for an outstanding balance of $0.00, and he has never paid it. It is still on the books." And all the computers will shake their antennas sadly, and turn me down, and I will not get my air gun.

When this letter came, I knew it would be trouble. I sat down and made out my check for $0.00, figuring I would need to do that to satisfy the computers. But I was afraid to mail it. There are computers at the bank, too, and when *they* saw that check for $0.00, they would kick it out and refuse to pay it. Because bank computers are more sensitive about dollar amounts than department-store computers. Bank computers would know something was wrong with that check and send it back to the store marked "Insufficient Funds." Then I would go on record at the store as a giver of bad checks.

What I've decided to do, right now, is wait until I hear from the computer again. If I get a second dun, and it insists I still owe the $0.00, I intend to go wherever that computer is, walk in empty-handed, pay cash, and demand a receipt.

When I was on vacation I dragged the vacuum cleaner out on the driveway, and cleaned under the seats of the car, and threw away the winter's accumulation of trash, and in the glove compartment I was pleased to find half a roll of quarters. That lifts the spirit, to find half a roll of quarters I didn't know I had, because it amounts to five dollars. I can now remember sticking those coins into that pistol pocket so I wouldn't lose them. In addition to the quarters I found my fish knife, in the neat slender leather scabbard. It was under my tool box in the trunk. I bought that knife more than a year ago, and it is a perfect sweetheart, so sharp it will cut anything except the federal budget. But it had gotten down in there out of sight, and I had forgotten I had it. All my life I have been wealthier than I thought, owning things I didn't know were in my possession. Don't you suppose this may be true of us all?

I remember a day back in the fifties when my friend Ed Ashbaugh was running cattle up on the Navasota River, and I stopped by his place one afternoon to visit. He was out at his pens, leaning against a fence post, and grinning, and feeling really fine. He was looking at a good fat mother cow he had penned up, and he told me why he was feeling so good. More than a year before, that cow had wandered off down into the river bottom and disappeared. Ed had ridden up and down the river a dozen times looking for her, and no sign. Finally he had to figure she was a goner. Stolen, he guessed, because we did have a good bit of cattle rustling going on in this state then, and do yet.

Well, I never have met a man in the cattle business, no matter how big, who didn't go into mourning when he lost a really good mother cow. I've heard 'em pretty near deliver sermons about what a good mother cow means. An old sister that'll have a calf every year, and she's thrifty, as they like to say. She'll be a hustler, find enough to keep herself in good shape without a lot of that expensive feed. I've known ranchers I think would write poems, if they could, odes and elegies to good mother cows. So you see why old Ed was grinning. That morning he'd walked out on the front porch, and there was his cow that had disappeared so long ago. She was grazing around there just like she'd never been gone.

Ed hadn't seen her in more than a year. She was nice and fat and healthy, and the best thing was, grazing along beside her was a pretty heifer calf about eight months old. No, Ed told me, maybe that *wasn't* the best thing. The best thing might be that the cow, from the look of her, was fixing to have still another calf. And the way he had it figured was, she had swum the river, and been all that time over there in his neighbor's pasture, and like as not the daddy of the calf she was carrying was his neighbor's high-bred bull, which was way yonder a better bull than his own.

Ed made a little talk about it all. Said it was the best trick he'd ever learned, about making money in the cattle business—to own a good cow you don't even know you own, so you don't see her for a year, and you can't feed her, or doctor her, or spend a nickel on her, and then here she comes walking up with a healthy calf by her side, and carrying another one by a high-bred bull. Ed said it made him feel so good he was thinking about dressing up and going to a dance somewhere.

I can remember my father making a similar kind of speech about something like a suit of clothes. He'd dig around in the back of his closet and maybe he'd bring out a suit he hadn't worn in a year, and he'd just about forgotten he owned it. He'd decide it looked as good as it ever did, and he'd have it cleaned, and go strutting forth in that old suit, and it was like he owned a brand new one, back in the times when buying a suit, for him, would have been as serious a proposition as Ed Ashbaugh buying a new cow. But that was his special thing, to dress in a spiffy style, and have his pants pressed and his collar starched and his necktie knotted just right. Me, I never could get that worked up about clothes, or cows either. But I could always get really interested in cash. Five dollars' worth of quarters is about the best thing I ever found in a glove compartment.

The last time I rode in a small airplane, the fellow doing the driving let me steer a while, and make a couple of shallow turns. I was pleased and somewhat surprised that the airplane did not zoom out of control the second my feet hit the rudder pedals.

I have not been able to trust flying machines since 1943. In that year I attained for the first time in my life an altitude higher than the monkey board on a windmill. I did it by getting in a Piper Cub, and tried to guide it around according to the instructions of a teacher in the front seat. My feeling about that craft was that the controls were hooked up backward.

A few months later I washed out of pilot training. The reason was, the Army Air Corps noticed that when I wanted an airplane to turn right, I would push on the left rudder pedal. The Air Corps considered this a bad habit.

I picked it up in the 1930s from driving apple-crate cars. An apple-crate car was a wooden, makeshift vehicle that boys used to build. They were similar to the Soap Box Derby cars we used to see on the newsreel at the picture show. Except these were pretty crude. Most weren't made out of apple crates at all. They were made up of just your basic parts—two axles, four wheels, and a frame.

You sat on the sturdy plank, usually two inches thick, that connected the front wheels with the back. To steer, you put your feet forward on the two-by-four that was attached to the front axle with nails driven in to half their length, then hammered over and around the shaft. You got at the top of a hill and let gravity provide the energy. Steering was plenty important, because of holes you had to miss, and mesquite saplings, and boulders, and clumps of thorny brush. The front axle and wheels were attached loosely to the frame by a bolt, which made steering possible. If you came to a rock you needed to go around, and wanted to turn left, you pushed on the right side of the axle with your right foot. If you wanted to turn right, you pushed on the left side.

So that was the rule of steering: Push left to go right. Push right to go left. For approximately three years in my early times I drove those homemade cars that way, and the principle of steering became branded in me mighty deep. It had to be, or else I would have ended up astraddle an oak stump about two-thirds the way down a hill.

One summer we even rode strip-down buggies on hills and steered them that same way. You could find an old buggy and take the seats and the shaft off and strip it down to the basics. And lie back behind the front wheels and steer with the feet, and oh, that was a ride. It would scare the pants, shirt, and shoes off you.

My cousin George once built a fancy apple-crater with rope steering. Instead of guiding with the feet, he pulled on ropes attached to the front axle. This allowed him to sit on a seat in the haughty manner that pleased him, with his legs folded beneath himself like some kind of an Eastern potentate. It wouldn't work, I could see it. You want to turn left, pull on the left rope, the same as guiding a horse. But by then I had been through all those years of foot steering and in tense situations I would return to it every time. When a stump got in my path, my reason deserted me and I would resort to the foot steering that I was raised on and pull at the wrong rope and hit whatever it was I was trying to miss. And splinters would fly, and pieces of kindling, and wheels, and cotter pins, and tennis shoes.

Years later they tried to teach me about airplanes, about how to steer one, how when you wanted to turn left you pushed on the left rudder. I agreed with that in theory, and even accepted it in practice for short periods when things went smooth. All I had to do was keep reminding myself that the controls were hooked up wrong. But let an emergency arise, and I would stomp the right rudder every time and expect the plane to go left. It never would. So far as I know, all airplanes are wired to work backward that way, and in my judgment are dangerous to fool around with.

It's always been remarkable to me that people and machines can operate on such rigid schedules that require them to do certain things at a set time, and they do it, and keep doing it over and over for years. Like the bus that leaves every morning for Dallas at 6:57. We make jokes about buses and planes being late, but don't they generally run almost on time? Considering that any one of a hundred things could happen to put them off schedule, it seems to me they do mighty well at sticking to their set times.

There's something in the nature of humans that creates satisfaction when they perform the same act at the same time every day. We're told that it's healthy to break the rhythm, to burst out of the set procedure. Yet most of us seem to do best when we stick to routine. A couple of times in my life I have had a job in an office building, and an hour of the morning that I had to report, and a time that I was allowed to quit and leave, and I was even in car pools. Now car pools, that's where you find out how important routine is to some people.

For I suppose a year I was in a car pool with four other guys, so that each of us drove one day a week. On four days of the week, we could play it a little loose, and stay cool if one of us was running eight or ten minutes late. But the fifth day was Oscar's turn at the wheel, and when he drove, that car pool ran like a forty-dollar watch. Oscar's turn was my least favorite day of the week because he picked me up first, and that meant I had to get up earlier and be ready at 6:45, because that's exactly when he pulled up in front of the house, and I don't mean 6:44 or 6:46.

What he liked to see was you walk out the front door when he turned the corner, so you'd be standing at the curb when he stopped and you could swing in and his wheels wouldn't be still more than a second before he was off again for the next pickup. You lost points with Oscar if he had to honk and wait for you to emerge. And if you were still in the bathroom when he arrived, and he had to get out and ring your bell, he seemed almost insulted, as if he didn't much care to be associating with an old slugabed who wasn't finished shaving at a quarter to seven.

I never did see the necessity for operating a car pool on that tough a schedule. But I do know the feeling of satisfaction that can come from performing routine activity. A thing, for instance, like making a path. Even dogs and cows and other creatures obviously like to produce paths, and I don't think it's just because paths make easier walking. I think they get satisfaction out of doing it, and maybe fun.

Dingbat, the resident yard dog at our house, has a distinct path she uses when passing from the front yard to the back. She won't deviate an inch from that neat trough her feet have pressed in the St. Augustine. Yet there is no practical need for a path. It doesn't lead through anything, as a trail points the way through a forest. It simply goes along in the grass. But that old sister is proud of that path, you can tell. It's her mark, her sign that she is living in this world, and functioning in a way that she believes is proper and right. I think she is saying, "This is my trail, that I have made. It says that I passed this way, and that I'll pass again."

Did you ever carry papers? Walk a paper route? They used to

do it that way. Not on a bicycle. You put your paper bags on your shoulders and you walked, and folded the papers as you went, and flung 'em onto front yards and porches. One year in my old home town I "carried a paper route," as we said, and made some personal trails along the way, and I took a secret pleasure in them. I never imagined they would be mentioned in print, and maybe they aren't worth a mention, at that. But I remember them, and what they meant to me.

The best one led across a huge vacant lot. An entire vacant block, really. The hospital is on that block now. I left a paper at the creamery and then cut across the vacant lot to the Methodist parsonage. The first time I cut across there it was muddy and the next day I could see my footprints, and I got to following them, just exactly. After a few days I had the johnson grass and the goatheads sort of knocked down, and it was the beginning of a trail.

I didn't *need* a trail across there, anymore than old Dingbat needs one on the lawn. But I liked producing that path because it was all mine, that I made as I went along doing something that needed doing, something that would make a difference to a good many people. Then what pleased me even more, after a few weeks when the trail got plain, others began using it. Kids coming from school. People walking to town, because in those days people did walk to town. The trail got pretty wide, and beat down in the middle so even a goathead wouldn't grow on it. The trail stayed in use several years, and I always looked on it as my personal path that I established, although I had better sense than to mention it.

There were other satisfactions in paper-route work. You could have a contest with yourself, for instance, on the matter of doing a routine job in a prescribed time. Which sounds dull, but I am talking about things like learning a certain house where you could look in a window as you passed and see the kitchen clock. And knowing, that if you were going to finish the route by 6:00, you had to be passing the kitchen-clock house at 4:45. Gauging your progress that way, and speeding up if you were behind schedule, and then feeling as if you'd won some kind of game if you threw the last paper and it thunked on the porch and the six-o'clock whistle blew, way back in town at the laundry. I don't know, maybe that's sort of kin to the satisfaction my old friend Oscar got out of running that car pool like a military mission.

It was late afternoon on an almost perfect fall day, and we had driven out in the country to see the new house he's building. He said he needed to go out there and check, to be certain a few things were being done right. But the main reason was, he wanted to show the place to a friend. That's fine. I liked looking at it.

He's one of my rich ones. I've got a few friends now who are really wealthy. Guys I started out with back in the forties, and they didn't have a shirt without a hole in it any more than I did, and now they are rich. I enjoy them so much. Oh, sure, I've got friends who are just pretty well off, and I've got some who aren't any better situated than I am, and I've got some who're almost flat out poor, and they are good to have too. But the rich ones are interesting to me in an exceptional way, I suppose because their lives are so different from my own. I mean I already know about the *other* ways to live. I know about being broke, or just getting by. I've been to that town and I know everybody who lives there. I never have been rich, though, and so I am naturally curious about how it feels.

He stopped at the bottom of the hill, at the foot of the long wooded slope that leads up to the building site. He likes to park there and check how the house has grown since the day before. "I picked this spot for a house thirty years ago," he said, "and bought this piece of property for $60 an acre. Now, fronting on this highway, no telling what it would bring." Not that it matters, since you can bet a stack of blues he wouldn't sell it for half that mint in Denver.

The house is just now being framed up, and you can't really tell what it'll be like. Except that it's going to be so big. A mansion. With a pool and a horse barn and tennis courts and about a fifty-acre front lawn that'll give steady work to an entire family of yard-keepers. What that place will cost, materials and labor being the way they are, I expect you would warp a pencil writing it down.

He drove up the slope and stopped in front of the house with the car pointed back toward town. Two or three miles, I guess, into town. He'll be able to look out the front window and see the water tower and the church steeples and the courthouse and the one tall commercial building in town. He owns it. Built it.

"You know," he said quietly, "in the last twenty years I've made a lot of money. Really a lot." I appreciate that, having that said to me. I take it as a compliment, because it's not something a rich man can say except to a friend he knows will understand the need to say it.

It'll sound cornball, but the truth is I am proud of this guy, and how he has done. I admire the way he has handled his success. Listen, he has been a one-man United Fund to that place where he lives. He has Given. Somebody is always ready to say, about a wealthy man, that he could have given twice as much. Maybe so, but figuring on a percentage basis, if you and I and the others had given as much, we would have put the welfare program out of business. My friend in the long black car doesn't really get much personal credit, in that town, for the good that he does with his money. Because of the popular notion that "he married it."

What he did, thirty years ago, was marry the daughter and the only child of the man who at that time had the reputation, at least, of having all the money in town. So if you asked a citizen standing on the street corner, very likely you would be told that all my friend is doing, he's just spending his daddy-in-law's money. When the fact is, as any banker in town will tell you if you ask, the fact is that the father-in-law's business was in trouble when he got married. And what saved it was the energy and drive and skill of the guy who married his daughter.

I bet you could go to my friend's town right now and sit in the cafe, and you wouldn't get through one cup of coffee before you'd hear somebody commenting on that big house he's building with all that money he married.

At a nursing home I've visited a few times, due to having a friend who lives there, a few of the residents are very, very old, and all worn out, and have already left us and are living in another time. Some of them travel way, way back, and act and speak as if they are a great deal younger, and sometimes as if they are small children.

One day I went by there to leave off a little bunch of flowers that Christina, my friend Mel's wife, had gathered for this person we know at the home. In the lobby I was stopped by a tiny little bent-over woman with the thinnest hair and fingers. I could see the dark blood vessels beneath the skin on the backs of her hands. She took hold of my sleeve and stopped me and asked, "Are those flowers for me?"

I explained they were for a woman who was back in her room, and couldn't move about very much. But the explanation was not a success. The little person held onto my sleeve and shuffled along with me when I tried to go on. She wrinkled her mouth, all pouty and little-girlish, and scolded me. "Why didn't you bring those flowers to me?"

Then I was rescued by a woman who works there, or maybe she is a volunteer. Anyway, she told me, "I think if you'll just give her one small flower out of the bouquet, it would make her happy." So I did that, and the little person took the one flower and went away smiling, and I felt stupid at not having thought of the solution myself. I wonder if bouquets in such places would cause more smiles if they were divided up, and handed out one flower at a time to everybody that wants one.

Very old people can seem mysterious to me, and even a little ghosty, and I can get uncomfortable around them. But one thing for certain is that all of us ought to try to understand them, because eventually both you and I are likely to become one of them.

There is one woman in that place who spends a great deal of her time calling out. She calls Mary. I have never seen her, but I have heard her, calling in the old style that country people called to make themselves heard from the house to the barn, or from one room to another when waking someone who needed to get up. She pronounces the name "May-ree."

"May-ree! May-ree!" Over and over, calling. Then occasionally the more insistent tone on the first syllable of the name. "*May*-ree!"

Hearing that reminded me of the old woman in the hospital out in my old home town. She was across the hall from my father when he had a stroke. I sat with him a few nights after he had improved but was still somewhat confused, at times, about what had happened to him. The old woman would call, and call, in such a melancholy, long-ago way, and it sure sounded haunting in the dim hall of that hospital in the middle of the night.

I can't remember the name she called, but it had two syllables—Milton, or something like that—and she would do the syllables much the same way the woman did that Mary name in the nursing home. "Mil-ton! *Mil*-ton! Mil-*ton?* Oh Milton!"

Sometimes my father would answer her. I would sit there studying him, trying to decide whether he was with me at the moment in the hospital, or whether he had roamed off into some early compartment of his life. And he would surprise me by rising up when the old woman called and answering, asking her what she wanted.

For a few minutes then he would be so clear on where he was, and what had happened, and we would have a long discussion about who Milton might have been, and why the old woman was calling him. Then he might surprise me by saying, "Well, I got a letter off to Walter today." And I would know that he had left again and gone on back, toward where the old woman was, because Walter was his older brother who had been dead several years.

Old and mind-weary people that way can seem so sad, and yet interesting, too, and there are lessons to be learned from them. One thing I learned, at least, is that at the nursing home where my friend lives, when I walk through the lobby with a bouquet, I ought to distribute a few flowers.

The two people I used to refer to as my offspring and my dependents are now twenty-five and twenty-seven and are off going about their own business. I don't see them often. When I do, they always surprise the pants off me by telling me things, by talking to me so frank and open. I have to say that one of the greatest shocks I've had as a parent came when my children began talking to me.

Oh, we always said a lot of words to one another, but I see now that mostly we were just circling the bush, not being straightforward. One of the problems was, back in those times I was pretty knuckle-headed. I knew so little about what was going in the skulls of those two, and yet I imagined I knew everything. Hoo boy.

Listen, I spent years trying to keep that pair from finding out things that they already knew. It was a lot of trouble to do that, but I kept up the effort as a form of protection. They're young, I said, and tender, and formative, so don't let them know this yet, or hear that, or see another thing. When the likelihood was that they'd already found out, and heard, and seen what I thought they hadn't. Why, I kept it up so long I was trying to protect them from things they were being taught at school. I am amazed to find that out now. I don't see how I could have been so blind.

But even a greater surprise was to learn, as I have in only recent times, that in so many ways they were also protective of me. What I mean, if they found out a shocking thing, they so often didn't tell me about it. The reason was, they knew it would upset me. Their position was, "I know about it, but I won't tell him, because he doesn't want me knowing such things, and if he finds out I know it will make him feel bad." What a revelation it is now, to sit with them and hear them talk to me about matters we didn't even mention to each other the year before last. (Oh, all right then, ten years ago, I guess. The time gets away from me.)

But about their not telling me things, I am now impressed by the wisdom, in some cases, of their not telling. Only recently, for example, I found out about a monstrous injustice suffered by one of them, and I was not told about it. The victim suffered in silence, until finally the hurt of it was worn away by time. It makes me angry even now, finding out about it so many years after it happened. So if I had known about it at the time I would have entered into a rage, and probably charged out and retaliated and committed a really bad act that couldn't have been undone.

Then sometimes they didn't tell me things as a protection for themselves, to escape getting a dozen lashes with an imitation leather belt. They seem to get a kick now out of confessing what they got away with, knowing the statute of limitations has run out. Since they survived all those doings, I am just as glad that I didn't know they were happening. But I am not saying a parent ought not to know. I think he should know, and I think the most successful parents do.

When my kids were growing up, I secretly looked on myself as a cool parent, pretty well in control. I considered that I was a benign dictator, calmly exerting my will on the children, never raging about and shouting. I felt that sometimes they were afraid of me, and that was good. My daughter visited not long ago and told me this: That the only time she and her brother were ever afraid of me was when I was asleep. They always avoided waking me, because I would rise abruptly to a sitting position, as if yanked up by a giant spring, and yell *Hoop!*, or some such, and it just scared the whey out of them.

Then she remembered this, about my not having temper spells: That one day I got mad at them and jerked away a water gun they were playing with and stomped that weapon into forty plastic pieces. I remember doing that now, and it felt good. She insists that was my most impressive performance as a disciplinarian. She was proud of it, and told about it the next day at school.

All my life I have listened to women complain about housework, and how hard it is. I have lately found out that such work is quite easy. I've been doing housework for myself now for several weeks, and I don't see that there is much to it. I spend very little time on keeping house. Why do homemakers say it's so hard? What I think is, they are mostly inventing make-work jobs. Things that don't even need doing.

Consider the matter of making beds. It's not necessary. I have proved that it isn't. I have slept about six weeks in a bed in this very room where I sit right now, and I have not made up the bed once. Not a single bad thing has happened as a result. Imagine all the energy, the steps, the reaches, the grunts, the groans, the complaints that are wasted across America by homemakers making up beds. And it doesn't need to be done.

Let us consider floors. Floors in houses are an industry in this country. We have corporations making great fortunes off the care of floors. Floors don't really need care, or at least very little of it. I do not sweep here. I have no broom. If a broom is on these premises I have not been introduced to it and don't want to be. What do I need with brooms?

There's a noisy vacuum cleaner that I have used once. I got it out to suck up the dirt off the carpet after I tipped over the pot plant that time. But I find no reward in using that machine. Its racket offends my environment, and it's cranky, too particular to suit my circumstance. It doesn't ingest paper clips and loose change without making a fuss. And it rejects the waste paper and plastic spoons and ballpoint pens generally found on floors. Let it stay in its closet.

Looking outdoors to my right, I can see a neighbor woman half a block away while she washes her windows. I can't see her right this second, because she is not on windows. I expect she is inside cleaning something else that's not dirty. But when she does wash windows I can see her, and she washes them once a week. I submit that is nothing but a bad habit, and I have the evidence to support my position. I have it in my own window here. This window has not been washed in six weeks, *and yet it is the very window through which I watch that neighbor half a block distant.* You're not going to get that kind of visibility through a dirty window.

Oh, sure, there is washing to be done. Clothes, yes. But there are machines for such chores. I have one here. I simply dump everything in, hit the switch, and walk away. When I return the machine has cleaned my clothes. This is hard work? Two weeks ago I ran out of soap and I stopped using it. And I have proved that soap wasn't necessary to begin with. I can't see a shade of difference in my undershirts now than when I was washing them with all those soapsuds.

Women launder items that don't require laundering. It's the same old make-work story. Bath towels for instance. Now think with me a minute about a bath towel. You take a bath. You get clean. You step out. You dry yourself with a new bath towel. Look what we have. We have a clean towel drying a clean hide. No dirt is involved. When you get dry, the towel is damp but it's not soiled. Mildred, honey, it doesn't need washing. It only needs drying. I can't see that a bath towel would ever need laundering if the user knows how to take a proper bath.

We come now to cooking. This is where you get the most complaints from women. Cook cook cook. Three times a day. Day in. Day out. What nonsense. For less than fifty dollars you can buy enough frozen dinners to cover your evening meal for a month. I have done it. The work involved is putting the dinner in the oven, and taking it out in half an hour. And there is no dish to wash. About 90 percent of dishwashing is unnecessary, too. I have proof of this but no space to present it right now.

I realize some homemakers are dedicated to health-type foods, especially where they have children and husbands and the like. Well, the grocery stores are jammed with bargains on health foods. Bananas at 39 cents a pound. I wish you would find me a more healthful food than bananas. In six weeks I have consumed thirty-two pounds of bananas at a total cost of only $12.48. I am bulging with nutrition.

And, as you can see, I am finding out important things about how easy housework is.

On a recent vacation, for an entire week I spent several hours a day sitting in the dirt, cleaning old bricks. I liked doing that. I found it to be relaxing, as good a way as any to spend vacation time. Cleaning that brick impressed upon me the value to the spirit of doing manual work that is considered menial.

These bricks were used almost thirty years ago in the construction of a low wall, which was decorative more than functional. Now the wall has been torn out. But the bricks are of special value because they match those on the house, and they are needed in a little add-on building project. They are Roman bricks, and no bricks like them are being made and so far as I know, none exactly like them are anywhere on the market.

So that is why I spent all those hours in the dirt, chipping old mortar away from those bricks with a hammer and chisel. When I managed to chisel out a whole brick without breaking it, that was like creating a brick with my own hands because each one is irreplaceable. But the best thing about the job was that it required pure-dee concentration. You cannot think about something else and chip mortar off old bricks at the same time. As sure as you do you'll make a wrong lick and break a brick. So, for all those long dusty hours, the most important question in my life was—will I be able to chisel the mortar away from this next brick without breaking it?

If I let my head stray off onto another question even for a minute, the result was a busted brick. Therefore, I didn't think about any of the perils or pestilences that bedevil us in this life. I didn't think about money problems, and I didn't think about crime, or about traffic, or about health. I didn't think about the environment being poisoned, or about the greed and ignorance that make the world such an unperfect place. And I didn't think about the hundred ways a paragraph in the paper can get messed up, so that it comes out saying something I don't want it to say. All I thought about was chiseling bricks. And I liked that. I was at peace, chiseling bricks.

There is plenty of reward in that work. Once in a while I would hit a lucky lick with that hammer and chisel, and the mortar would fall away and out would come a flawless brick. Not a chip in it anywhere. Not a spot of mortar left on it.

There is also a penalty for such labor. Penalty for carelessness, for poor judgment, for lack of control. For instance, I would get going really well, my hand and my hammer and my chisel so beautifully coordinated that every blow was producing exquisite results. And I would be overwhelmed by my own confidence. I would work faster, and faster, and hit harder, and harder, and I would say, "Hey, look at that, why, I am the grand champion brick chiseler of the blinking universe. I could make a *living* at this. There must be a huge demand for such talent. It would beat the newspaper business by four miles." Then—click! A busted brick, and I would descend from that throne of overconfidence and return to my seat in the dirt.

I think it would be a good thing if all of us could spend more time doing work that has little similarity to what we do for our daily bread. Let the bookkeepers go and spend two months working at jobs that have nothing to do with columns or figures. Let the doctors go and chop firewood in the forest. The pipefitters could be temporary police officers. The stenographers could become window washers, and so forth.

In my short career as a brick chiseler, I cleaned 300 bricks. They are lying out there now in neat rows, waiting for the bricklayer who will come and build them into the house. Cleaning those bricks may be the most lasting and valuable work I will ever do in this life. A hundred years from now they could be still in that wall, doing their work, when nobody is left alive that ever read a sentence I wrote in the paper or anywhere else.